C000065264

EVERTON

Player by Player

EVERTON

Player by Player

Ivan Ponting

Hamlyn

ACKNOWLEDGEMENTS

The author would like to thank the following: Pat, Rosie and Joe Ponting, Bob Bickerton, David Johnson, Andy Cowie and all at Colorsport, Steve Hale, Steve Small, Adam Ward, Trevor Davies, Julian Brown, Adrian Killen, Barry Hugman, Les Gold, the Barretts of Crosby, Bobby Collins, John Hurst, Andy King, Brian Labone, Derek Temple, Ronnie Goodlass, Dave Hickson, Syd McGuinness, the Marks family of Ince Blundell, Wayne Slater, Graham Hart, Mike Beddow, Chris and Jo Forster, Terry Mealey, Trevor Hartley, Colin Hunt.

The author is also grateful for permission to reproduce photographs.
The vast majority are from Colorsport, who never cease to amaze with their ability to come up with a picture of just about anybody who has ever kicked a ball. Further contributions from Steve Hale, Associated Sports Photography /Stuart Franklin /Nigel French /George Herringshaw, Terry Mealey, Steve Hale, The South Wales Evening Post and the Liverpool Daily Post And Echo.

Efforts have been made to trace copyright holders of all photographs used in this book. We apologise for any omissions, which are unintentional, and would be pleased to include appropriate acknowledgement in any subsequent edition.

Pictured on the front cover are: Duncan Ferguson (left), Andy Gray (centre), Neville Southall (top right), Alan Ball (centre right), Peter Reid (bottom right).

First published in 1992 by
GUINNESS PUBLISHING
33 London Road, Enfield
Middlesex, EN2 6DJ

Text copyright © 1998 by Ivan Ponting

Illustrations copyright © 1998 as credited

A catalogue record for this book is available
from the British Library

All rights reserved. No part of this publication may be reproduced or transmitted in any form or by any means, electrical or mechanical, including photocopy, recording or any information storage retrieval system without permission in writing from the publisher.

Printed and bound by

Graphycem, Spain

INTRODUCTION

I was in my father's cowshed when first I heard the name . . . Everton. As a little boy, isolated in the depths of Somerset, my Saturday afternoons were often spent ferrying buckets of milk from cow to churn while acquiring the rudiments of a football education by listening to Sports Report on a fuzzy, but trusty, old radio. I had fallen in love with the game already, instinctively; not just for the joy of playing, the exhilaration of scoring a goal (all too rare, in my case), or the brisk edge of competition relished by most healthy youngsters. There was something else, indefinable at the time, but looking back it appears as a heady mixture of romance and mystery.

It was encapsulated in the names. To an unworldly seven-year-old, the mere mention of the great clubs provoked visions of inaccessible places and magical events. I had already heard of Manchester United, my best friend supported Spurs and my dad would talk of Arsenal; then one day, somewhere between the rear end of dear old Fillpail (Dad was nothing if not original in naming his animals) and the cool room that served as our dairy, there was Everton. The wireless voice - it might have belonged to Eamonn Andrews - announced that the club I would subsequently learn so much about had beaten Bolton, or Preston, or Burnley, I can't remember just who. Everton: it was a good, satisfying name; but where did they play, what were their colours, who scored their goals? Duly, I discovered all I wanted to know about the men who wore the Royal Blue, and now I have set it down in this book.

Since those far-off days, I have watched the Toffeemen on countless occasions, and my observations from trips to Goodison and elsewhere have gone far in forming my opinions. I have been blessed, also, with the help of a number of former Everton players, who have been gracious with their time and knowledge. A number of supporters, too, have assisted tremendously with their reminiscences. For *Everton Player by Player*, I collected a picture of every man to turn out for the Toffees in the Football League, FA Cup, League Cup (in all its manifestations) and European competition since 1958/59, the season in which Johnny Carey took over as manager and my interest in the club took root. Alongside each photograph, in almost every case, appears my personal assessment of the player; where he has played so few games as to render this treatment inappropriate, only his career statistics are included. All records, including service with other clubs, are complete to May 16, 1998.

My intention was to capture, in words, the essence of each player, and I have kept the emphasis on footballing rather than off-the-field matters. Various first-class statistical works exist already, so I have limited myself to basic numerical information - games played (with substitute appearances in brackets), goals scored, previous clubs, caps won etc. - which are needed to place each man in context. Everton appearance and scoring figures refer to all matches (a breakdown for each competition appears at the end of the book) but under the heading of 'Other Clubs', the games and goals are in the League only. The dates in large type refer to the seasons in which each player appeared in the Blues' first team, not when he joined or left the club. Under 'Honours' I have included only those won with Everton, except in the case of caps, the figures for which cover complete careers to date. All transfer fees are those reported in the press.

After a brief tribute to Everton's early years, when Dean, Sagar and company held sway, there follow my portraits of the men who have brought delight, and sometimes despair, to the Goodison faithful over the past 40 years. Some of the names read like a litany of footballing excellence: Hickson, Young, Labone, Ball, Kendall, Latchford, Reid, Southall, Gray, Ferguson . . . and there are some 200 more, all of whom have played their part in the story. Of course, the script has taken a sorry twist recently, yet while the travails of 1997/98 caused prolonged anguish to some of the proudest supporters in the land, there was blessed relief at season's end and the FA Youth Cup triumph offered genuine hope for the future. In itself, escape from relegation is hardly a cause for exultation, but it can signal the start of better days. May that apply to Everton . . . and soon.

Ivan Ponting,
Chewton Mendip,
August 1998

CONTENTS

THE ROYAL BLUE TRADITION

FA CUP WINNERS 1933

Back row *(left to right):*
HARRY COOKE (trainer)

CLIFF BRITTON (30/1-38/9, wing-half, 240 games, 3 goals; manager 48-56).

WARNEY CRESSWELL (26/7-35/6, full-back, 306 games, 1 goal).

TED SAGAR (29/30-52/3, goalkeeper, 495 games, 0 goals).

BILLY COOK (32/3-38/9, right-back, 249 games, 6 goals).

TOMMY WHITE (27/8-36/7, centre-half/ centre-forward, 202 games, 66 goals).

JOCK THOMSON (29/30-38/9, wing-half, 294 games, 5 goals).

Front row:

ALBERT GELDARD (32/3-37/8, winger, 179 games, 37 goals).

JIMMY DUNN (28/9-34/5, inside-forward, 154 games, 49 goals).

BILL 'DIXIE' DEAN (24/5-37/8, centre-forward, 431 games, 377 goals).

TOMMY JOHNSON (29/30-33/4, inside-forward, 159 games, 64 goals).

JIMMY STEIN (28/9-34/5, winger, 215 games, 65 goals).

TED CRITCHLEY (26/7-33/4, winger, 229 games, 42 goals).

Throughout the century and more since Everton became founder members of the Football League, they have never been far from the limelight. Nine League titles, four FA Cup triumphs and one European trophy have been spread across the decades, and this book deals in detail with the players who wore the Royal Blue from the late fifties onwards. However, the scene must be set, and pictured on these two pages are some of the best-remembered Evertonians of the preceding years. Most revered of the lot, of course, is that extraordinary goal-scorer, Bill Dean - how he despised the nickname of 'Dixie' - who reigned supreme in the twenties and thirties. Other names, too, live on in countless Merseyside memories, the likes of that great and loyal goalkeeper, Ted Sagar; the genial, inspirational wing-half, Joe Mercer; the prolific centre-forward, Tommy Lawton; the list goes on. They laid firm foundations for the later years and for the men whose stories form the main part of this book.

BILL 'DIXIE' DEAN

Ted Sagar, one of the most accomplished goalkeepers Everton ever had, is chaired off at Goodison Park as his illustrious career comes to a close in 1953.

TOMMY LAWTON

TOMMY EGLINGTON

TOMMY G. JONES

CYRIL LELLO

STAN BENTHAM (35/6-48/9, inside-forward, 125 games, 17 goals).

TED BUCKLE (49/50-54/5, winger, 107 games, 33 goals).

DON DONOVAN (51/2-57/8, wing-half/full back, 187 games, 2 goals).

TOMMY EGLINGTON (46/7-56/7, winger, 428 games, 82 goals).

PETER FARRELL (46/7-56/7, wing-half, 453 games, 17 goals).

JACKIE GRANT (46/7-54/5, wing-half, 133 games, 11 goals).

NORMAN GREENHALGH (37/8-48/9, full-back, 115 games, 1 goal).

TOMMY G JONES (36/7-49/50, centre-half, 175 games, 5 goals).

TOMMY LAWTON (36/7-38/9, centre-forward, 95 games, 70 goals).

CYRIL LELLO (47/8-56/7, wing-half, 254 games, 9 goals).

JACK LINDSAY (50/1-53/4, full-back, 115 games, 2 goals).

TONY McNAMARA (51/2-57/8, winger, 113 games, 22 goals).

JOE MERCER (32/3-46/7, wing-half, 184 games, 2 goals).

J.W.PARKER

NORMAN GREENHALGH

STAN BENTHAM

JOE MERCER

JACK LINDSAY

TONY McNAMARA

JACKIE GRANT

DON DONOVAN

TED BUCKLE

PETER FARRELL

ERIC MOORE

GEORGE SAUNDERS

ALEX STEVENSON

EDDIE WAINWRIGHT

ERIC MOORE (49/50-56/7, full-back, 184 games, 0 goals).

JOHN WILLIE PARKER (50/1-55/6, inside-forward, 176 games, 89 goals).

GEORGE SAUNDERS (46/7-51/2, full-back, 140 games, 0 goals).

ALEX STEVENSON (33/4-48/9, inside-forward, 271 games, 90 goals).

EDDIE WAINWRIGHT (46/7-55/6, forward, 228 games, 76 goals).

DAVE HICKSON

Half a lifetime after the prime of Dave Hickson, his name leaps vividly from the pages of Everton history. An archetypal warrior centre-forward of the fifties, the flaxen-maned swashbuckler captured the imagination and affection of Goodison fans in a manner granted to only a select band of players down the years. His rumbustious, unfailingly couragageous style, his spectacular heading ability and a series of spirited scrapes with referees and defenders created a charismatic cocktail sorely needed in one of the club's more lacklustre eras.

It should be added that although Dave was known widely as soccer's stormy petrel, his characteristic honesty shone through the controversy like a redeeming light, and, in fact, he didn't rely solely on the raw-meat-and-razor-blades approach. Though undeniably in his element when engaged in aerial combat or pounding in pursuit of a long through-pass, he was also adept at subtle flicks to his sidemen, and was under-rated as an all-round performer.

Dave first attracted the attention of Blues boss Cliff Britton as a free-scoring teenager with non-League Ellesmere Port, but after crossing the Mersey to join the Goodison cause in May 1948 his progress was interrupted by National Service. However a crucial phase in the Hickson development had already taken place. While playing for Cheshire Army Cadets he had been under the aegis of the great Bill Dean, Everton's former goal king, and acquired priceless first-hand expertise from the incomparable 'Dixie' that was to stand him in good stead.

After two years in khaki, Dave found himself returning to a team in the doldrums. Everton had slumped to the Second Division and the dynamic 21-year-old was called to the colours at Leeds in September 1951 - replacing a certain Harry Catterick - to help effect a revival. Soon he claimed a regular berth, linking fruitfully with the more cultured John Willie Parker, and earning himself an eternal place in Toffeemen folklore during the stirring run to the 1953 FA Cup semi-final. First, in the fifth-round home encounter with Manchester United, he endeared himself to the success-starved supporters by scoring the winner after leaving the field to receive five stitches in a gashed eyebrow, later confirming his gladiatorial stature by reopening the wound with a header against the post; at the end of 90 minutes his face was a bloody mask, and he received a rapturous ovation. Then, Dave notched the only goal of the quarter-final at Villa Park with a scorching drive from just inside the penalty box after starting the move near the half-way line.

Confirmation of his predatory talents came with his 25 League strikes during the 1953/54 promotion campaign, but after just one term in the top flight manager Britton, impressed by the youthful promise of Jimmy Harris, sold Dave to Aston Villa for £17,500. However, he never settled in the Midlands, nor at Huddersfield, his next port of call, and in August 1957 the Goodison faithful were delighted to welcome home their old hero for a bargain £7,500. His zest and aggression were intact and even though his strike rate was lower than during his first spell, there was a public outcry when he was allowed to cross Stanley Park to Anfield in November 1959. Indeed, the £10,500 deal caused the sort of furore which would have followed the transfer of latter-day idols such as Dalglish or Rush in the opposite direction.

Later Dave - ironically a quiet fellow away from the action - completed his Merseyside hat-trick with a stint for Tranmere, but there has never been any doubt about where his heart lies. He is an Everton man from the tip of his blond head to the toecaps of his shooting boots which, at the age of 60-plus, he was still wearing with distinction in charity matches during the early nineties.

BORN: Ellesmere Port, Cheshire, 30.10.29. GAMES: 243. GOALS: 111.
OTHER CLUBS: Aston Villa 55/6 (12, 1); Huddersfield Town 55/6-56/7 (54, 28);
Liverpool 59/60-60/1 (60, 37); Cambridge City (non-League); Bury 61/2 (8, 0);
Tranmere Rovers 62/3-63/4 (45, 21); Ballymena United, Northern Ireland.

1951/52-1955/56 & 1957/58-1959/60

TOMMY JONES

In every sense, Tommy Jones was a man to look up to. As a player he was tall and commanding, the fortress at the heart of the Everton defence throughout the fifties; as a character, he exuded dignity and decency. Once, having spotted a small boy who looked lost after wandering off the tram on match day, he took the lad's hand and led him to the gates of Goodison. To this day that young fan, now a Liverpool-based sports photographer, recalls the incident with shining eyes.

Yet those self-same chivalrous qualities offer a clue, perhaps, to Tommy's failure to progress beyond the ranks of consistent First Division centre-halves to international status. Although he was a doughty tackler and a powerful aerial combatant - he invariably excelled in clashes with Nat Lofthouse, the formidably physical though equally fair Bolton Wanderers and England centre-forward - he lacked the streak of ruthlessness that runs through most top-level defenders. Quite simply, the idea of Tommy stooping to foul methods was utterly inconceivable.

Initially a full-back, Thomas Edwin Jones was converted to the role of pivot when the Blues needed a long-term replacement for his namesake, the great and gifted Thomas Gwynfor Jones, in 1950/51. Though more basic in style than his illustrious predecessor, he reigned supreme for the rest of the decade, along the way earning a reputation as a cool converter of penalties and becoming skipper on Peter Farrell's departure in 1957.

Eventually, however, the slowness on the turn which had always been slightly in evidence grew more marked - Arsenal's David Herd netted four times and gave him a fearful chasing at Goodison in 1958 - and he was replaced by the young Brian Labone. Even then Tommy was not finished, reverting to left-back before a shattered kneecap forced him to retire. When he left to coach in Italy in the early sixties, Everton bade farewell to a loyal servant and one of nature's gentlemen.

BORN: Liverpool, 11.4.30. GAMES: 411. GOALS: 14.

1950/51 - 1961/62

WALLY FIELDING

Wally Fielding was a schemer of flair and inventiveness who shone like a beacon through the grey shroud of mediocrity that descended on Goodison Park after the Second World War. In fact, so highly regarded were his precision of passing, reading of the game and ability to swerve past defenders with the merest shimmy of his stocky frame that the ball-playing Londoner was dubbed 'Merseyside's answer to Len Shackleton', a glowing tribute in an era when Sunderland's sumptuously gifted inside-forward was revered by almost everyone but the England selectors.

Yet Wally might never have played for the Blues, certainly not if Charlton Athletic had their way. As a youthful amateur he had turned out for the Valiants and when he left the Army in 1945 they believed they held the right to his continued services. But Goodison boss Theo Kelly pipped them for the Fielding signature, and he made the Toffeemen's number-ten shirt his own for the next dozen seasons.

Everton thus acquired not only a strategist who became the starting point of countless attacks - his perfectly weighted passes inside the full-back to flying flankman Tommy Eglington became a devastating trademark - but also a canny campaigner quite capable of looking after himself in the face of the most ferocious tackles, and an occasional marksman who carried a powerful and accurate shot. If Wally had a fault it was lack of pace, but few contemporary pundits would disagree that he was unlucky never to win a full England cap.

'Nobby', as he was invariably known, was a chirpy character and a positive influence on the Goodison youngsters who loved to ape his mannerism of clutching his rolled-down shirt-sleeves as he ran. By the time he left for Southport in 1959 he was nearing 40, yet still bubbling with enthusiasm; those young stars of the future had lost both a friend and an inspiration.

BORN: Edmonton, London, 26.11.19. GAMES: 410. GOALS: 54.
OTHER CLUBS: Southport 58/9 (20, 1).

1945/46 - 1958/59

BOBBY COLLINS

Bobby Collins was as potent a mixture of skill and fire as ever crossed the Scottish border. Indeed, many would contend that Everton never had a better all-round inside-forward than the effervescent, tank-like imp, who was dubbed the 'Pocket Napoleon' but who differed from most generals in that he was invariably found where the battle raged fiercest.

The 5ft 4in Glaswegian exerted influence out of all proportion to his physical stature. Bobby's supreme talent was to make teams play, dictating the pattern of games with his crisp, incisive passes. He loved the ball and he demanded it, using it to pick out colleagues in dangerous positions with astonishing accuracy; when possession was lost he took it as a personal insult and he fought to win it back, hurling his compact frame into tackles with a demonic aggression that made giants shudder. He was quick, too, his control was impeccable, and he carried a searing shot that produced a goal tally to shame many an out-and-out striker. The pity was that such a complete footballer was allowed to slip away from Everton in March 1962 when, as subsequent heroic deeds for Leeds United proved, he had much more to offer.

In fact, Bobby might have settled on Merseyside some 11 years before the managerless Blues paid Celtic £23,500 for his services in September 1958. As a baby-faced teenager he had been a Goodison triallist and been offered a contract, but had opted instead for the more familiar surroundings of his home town. During his final seasons at Celtic Park, the Scottish international scored heavily, and was initially employed as a front-man with his new club. Quickly, however, he expressed his need - with characteristic force - for more constant involvement, and adopted a deeper-lying role. As captain under newly-appointed team boss Johnny Carey, Bobby became the motivator-in-chief and creative mainspring of a moderate side, and for two seasons was arguably the premier factor in retaining the Toffeemen's top-flight status. As well as setting up untold opportunities for fellow forwards, he top-scored with 14 goals in 1959/60 and went three better the following term.

Ironically it was the advent of the successful Catterick era that paved the way for his exit. Two unyielding characters, manager and player could not always agree, and when Dennis Stevens was bought to wear the number-eight shirt, it was scarcely surprising when Bobby scorned Harry's invitation to contest the right-wing berth with Billy Bingham. In fairness to the Everton boss, although the Collins exuberance was undiminished, his birth certificate showed that he was 31 and it was not unreasonable to plan a new side around younger men.

Significantly, two of soccer's shrewdest judges begged to differ with the Catterick verdict - Don Revie, who paid £30,000 to make him the centrepiece of the great Leeds revival, and Bill Shankly, who put in a belated bid on the day his tiny countryman pledged himself to Elland Road. In fact, the Anfield sage tried a second time, six months later, but by then Revie was drooling over the inspirational qualities of the man he described as 'my teacher on the pitch'. How emphatically did Bobby, his pride stung, prove that he was far from finished! He served the Yorkshiremen for five years, won a Scotland recall and became Footballer of the Year in 1965, later battling back after shattering a thigh bone and lending his craft to Oldham Athletic at the age of 42.

Come the early nineties, the 60-year-old Bobby was still competing vigorously at amateur level. He told this writer, with a rueful grin, of a recent encounter in which he had resorted to mild fisticuffs with an opponent little more than half his age. Such undying passion, at a stage in life when the majority of his peers are content with a leisurely round of golf, speaks volumes for the commitment of one of football's most remarkable personalities.

BORN: Glasgow, 16.2.31. GAMES: 147. GOALS: 48.
HONOURS: 31 Scotland caps (50-65). OTHER CLUBS: Celtic 49/50-58/9 (220, 81); Leeds United 61/2-66/7 (149, 24); Bury 66/7-68/9 (75, 5); Morton 69/70-70/1 (54, 2); Ringwood City, Australia; Oldham Athletic 72/3 (7, 0). MANAGER: Huddersfield Town (74); Hull City (77-78); Barnsley (84-85).

1958/59 - 1961/62

JIMMY O'NEILL

In the early fifties, Goodison Park offered an especially demanding starting point for a young goalkeeper's career. Ted Sagar, one of the greatest names in Everton history, was approaching retirement and the hunt was on for a replacement. There was no shortage of talented candidates - the likes of Harry Leyland, George Burnett and Albert Dunlop were all pushing for recognition - but the man who picked up the gauntlet and retained it for much of the decade was Jimmy O'Neill.

Inevitably, the tall, almost willowy Dubliner could never match the revered Sagar for sheer class, yet he matured into an accomplished custodian who performed ably during a frustrating period of under-achievement for the Blues. An acrobatic shot-stopper, he was adept at embracing crosses in his long, almost spidery arms, and at his best was a breathtaking entertainer, though there were occasions when his confidence appeared to desert him. Ironically, one of his most memorable displays came in a home thrashing by Arsenal in September 1958, when he was blameless for all six Gunners goals and single-handedly saved his side from further humiliation.

Jimmy, the son of a professional golfer, was recruited from amateur football in his home-town of Dublin. He was given his senior baptism during the relegation term of 1950/51, then became firmly established during three years in the Second Division wilderness before playing a prominent part in the 1953/54 promotion campaign. Back in the top flight, he held sway for two more seasons before being supplanted by Dunlop, thereafter serving as a deputy. The left-footed Eire international was rescued from reserve football by Stoke City, who paid £5,000 for his services in July 1969, and he was an ever-present as the Stanley Matthews-inspired Potters regained their place among the elite in 1962/63. Subsequent stints in the League's lower reaches completed a creditable career.

BORN: Dublin, 13.10.31. GAMES: 213. GOALS: 0.
HONOURS: 17 Republic of Ireland caps (52-59).
OTHER CLUBS: Stoke City 60/1-63/4 (130, 0);
Darlington 63/4-64/5 (32, 0); Port Vale 64/5-65/6 (42, 0).

1950/51 - 1959/60

JIMMY TANSEY

With his bandy-legged gait and rather deliberate style, left-back Jimmy Tansey presented an at times irresistible target for frustrated Goodison Park fans as Everton struggled throughout the late fifties. Yet behind the occasional baiting was genuine respect for a whole-hearted and thoughtful competitor, who missed only six League games in three campaigns before the arrival of John Bramwell cost him his place in 1958. In fact, Jimmy - a renowned dressing-room humorist - revelled in comic cut-and-thrust with hyper-critical denizens of the now-defunct Paddock terrace, once miming a machine-gun attack on his tormentors, a spontaneous act greeted with vociferous delight.

Jimmy - who tackled firmly enough but was especially adept at positional play, jockeying his opponents away from the danger area - had seemed unlikely to make the grade until he was converted from wing-half to full-back at junior level in 1952. There followed several terms spent mainly in the reserves before he claimed a regular senior berth in 1955/56. One of Jimmy's finest hours was at Old Trafford in October 1956, when he subdued lively winger Johnny Berry as the lowly Blues inflicted a shock 5-2 defeat on their table-topping hosts.

By 1960, however, he was suffering reduced pace following injuries, and one of the nicest men in football departed to Crewe.

BORN: Liverpool, 29.1.29. GAMES: 142. GOALS: 0.
OTHER CLUBS: Crewe Alexandra 60/1 (9, 0)

1952/53 - 1959/60

JOHN BRAMWELL

A wicked line in wisecracks and an 'educated' left foot were the two main assets John Bramwell took with him when he made the quantum leap from non-League Wigan Athletic to First Division Everton in April 1958. His wit stood him in good stead - even the resident Scouse comedians had to admit second best when the jokes started to fly - and his accurate passing won widespread praise, but the tall, strong left-back failed to carve out a long-term niche at Goodison Park.

On arrival, the former Bolton amateur was handed an early and extended opportunity, replacing Jimmy Tansey in September 1958 and retaining the number-three shirt until the end of the season. John proved himself a steady performer, though he lacked pace and was occasionally guilty of hasty commitment in tackles, which left him stranded. Once at Blackpool he threw himself into an enthusiastic challenge on Stanley Matthews, only for the great man to dance away with the ball, leaving John to cannon into abrasive team-mate Bobby Collins. Not recommended!

After a second campaign of intermittent appearances, during which he contested the left-back berth with displaced centre-half Tommy Jones, John moved to Luton Town in a deal that took Billy Bingham to Everton, and went on to show the most accomplished form of his career.

BORN: Ashton-in-Makerfield, Lancashire, 1.3.37.
GAMES: 56. GOALS: 0.
OTHER CLUBS: Luton Town 60/1-64/5 (187, 1).

1958/59 - 1959/60

KENNY REA

Kenny Rea was a studious, constructive wing-half with an abundance of skill whose slight stature left him ill-equipped for the physical demands of life in the Everton engine room. The wavy-haired Merseysider, who joined the club in 1952, made his senior debut at Wolverhampton in September 1956 as a replacement for the veteran Cyril Lello, but never became fully established.

Though a gifted passer who offered subtle service to his forwards, he rarely asserted himself in the tackle and was a ponderous runner, doubtless being handicapped by the injuries that dogged him throughout his professional career. Nicknamed 'Groins' by irreverent colleagues, he played in a custom-made harness which could hardly have been conducive to fluent movement.

Kenny's most encouraging season was 1957/58, when he made 29 senior appearances, mostly on the right, and linked promisingly with successive inside-forwards Derek Temple and Eddie Thomas. During lengthy spells out of the senior side, he was ever-willing to help the club's youngsters, who benefited from his astute tactical approach. However, by 1959 it was clear that Kenny had no future at the top level, and he joined non-League Runcorn.

BORN: Liverpool, 17.2.35.
GAMES: 51. GOALS: 0.

1956/57 - 1958/59

ALAN SANDERS

Alan Sanders was a flamboyant right-back with the stature of a body-builder who radiated confidence; unfortunately, although he was blessed with a fair degree of ball skill for such a strapping man, he was a rather cumbersome mover who found it difficult to recover his ground if given the slip by a fleet-footed opponent. The Sanders game was also blighted by a tendency to dwell unwisely on the ball, which occasionally resulted in dire defensive consequences.

The jovial Lancastrian started his career with Manchester City, joining Everton on a free transfer in July 1956 after failing to make a senior appearance for the Maine Road club. He worked enthusiastically to break into the first-team ranks, which he did at Tottenham in November 1957, thereafter missing only two games for the rest of the season.

For a time it seemed that he might prove a worthy successor to long-serving Irishman Don Donovan, but as his flaws became more apparent, the gifted Alex Parker was signed and Alan was reduced to the role of deputy. With his height and strength he might have fared better as a centre-half, but with the young Brian Labone already laying immutable claim to that position there was no future for Alan at Goodison, and in November 1959 he was transferred to Swansea Town.

BORN: Salford, Lancashire, 31.1.34. GAMES: 63. GOALS: 0.
OTHER CLUBS: Swansea Town 59/60-62/3 (92, 0); Brighton and Hove Albion 62/3-65/6 (80, 0).

1957/58 - 1959/60

JOHN KING

Few players held dominion over Bobby Charlton, but John King, in his only two senior confrontations with the Manchester United star, never allowed his celebrated opponent the luxury of an unattended moment - and Everton won both matches. John was a fast and fearless wing-half, a man of infectious, driving enthusiasm for whom no task was too big. He would snap into the tackle against the most formidable of adversaries, and one enduring image is of the diminutive Merseysider clinging ferret-like to the back of West Bromwich Albion's hulking striker Derek Kevan in a League clash during the late fifties.

Unfortunately, all that dash and resilience was not complemented by the necessary ball skills to make John a top-class all-round performer. Having won possession, he tended to negate his good work through wayward distribution, a drawback which barred his way to a long-term career in the top grade. Accordingly, when the arrival of Jimmy Gabriel in 1960 effectively snuffed out his first-team hopes, he moved into the League's lower reaches, enjoying his most creditable spell at Tranmere. John was destined to return to Prenton Park for two managerial stints, and in 1991 led Rovers into the Second Division, their dizziest height since the war.

BORN: Liverpool, 15.4.38. GAMES: 49. GOALS: 1.
OTHER CLUBS: Bournemouth 60/1 (21, 1);
Tranmere Rovers 60/1-67/8 (241, 4);
Port Vale 68/9-70/1 (101, 0).
MANAGER: Tranmere Rovers (75-80 and 87-96).

1957/58 - 1959/60

EDDIE O'HARA

There were two sides to Eddie O'Hara. Off the pitch the Glaswegian left-winger was carefree and relaxed, a personable fellow who lived life to the full; but all too often, come three o'clock on a Saturday afternoon, his confidence seemed to drain away and be replaced by a diffidence that prevented him from realising his considerable potential.

Under-23 international Eddie, who shared in a Scottish FA Cup triumph with Alex Parker at Falkirk in 1957 before signing for Everton with the full-back a year later, was no speedster, though his characteristic loping stride could carry him past defenders with deceptive ease. Combative in the air for a small man, he also possessed a fierce shot, but often seemed reluctant to use it; indeed he found the net only twice for the Blues after averaging a goal every four games in his final term with Falkirk.

After vying for a place with Bobby Laverick and Graham Williams for nearly two seasons, Eddie joined Rotherham United in February 1960, later going on to a more successful spell with Barnsley.

BORN: Glasgow, 28.10.35. GAMES: 31. GOALS: 2.
OTHER CLUBS: Falkirk 55/6-57/8 (95, 18);
Rotherham United 59/60-60/1 (20, 3); Morton 61/2;
Barnsley 62/3-64/5 (127, 37).

1958/59 - 1959/60

ALBERT DUNLOP

Albert Dunlop was a bit of a rascal, a colourful character whose memory will always be recalled fondly by the men who played alongside him. And he was a pretty good goalkeeper, too. Indeed he became a respected First Division regular, disappointing only those optimists who had believed that the stocky Merseysider - whose predilection for small-time wheeler-dealing earned him the affectionate nickname of 'The Bandit' - was capable of scaling even loftier peaks. Those same observers were surprised that Albert's senior debut was delayed for seven years after he signed for the Blues, but when it came, at Old Trafford in 1956, it was worth the wait. That day the stocky custodian was in superb form as the mighty Busby Babes were humbled 5-2, and he was not to be seriously challenged for the green jersey until Gordon West arrived in 1962.

Albert cut a contrasting figure to his predecessor, Jimmy O'Neill, standing several inches shorter than the Irishman, a deficiency which at times left him fallible on crosses, and there was also a question-mark over his concentration. Against that was his athleticism on his line, his bravery at forwards' feet and the capacity to dispense and receive knocks with equal facility. The vociferous Albert was also renowned for pointing out team-mates' mistakes - real or imaginary - almost every time he was beaten. As one ex-colleague put it: 'At times he seemed to complain in mid-dive!' Certainly, there was ample scope for moaning at Tottenham in October 1958 when he let in ten, though the blame for just two - including one when he shouted 'Leave it' to his defence as Bobby Smith was in the act of scoring - could be laid at his door.

As a final flourish, Albert deputised splendidly for the injured West during the 1963 title run-in, before joining Wrexham. Sadly, after his retirement he was involved in brushes with the law, and in 1989 he died. The name of Albert Dunlop, however, will live on at Goodison; he was not the type of man that people forget.

BORN: Liverpool, 21.4.32. GAMES: 231. GOALS: 0.
OTHER CLUBS: Wrexham 63/4-64/5 (15, 0). DIED: 1989.

1956/57 - 1962/63

ALAN SHACKLETON

If ever a man took on a difficult job at a tense period in his club's history, then it was Alan Shackleton when he inherited the leadership of the Everton attack from Dave Hickson in the autumn of 1959. The team was struggling and the supporters were in turmoil over the Goodison idol's transfer to the arch enemy, Liverpool. With only a few Blues appearances behind him, the raw recruit from Leeds United stepped into the cauldron for the home encounter with Leicester City - the first game since Dave's move - to be faced with a scathingly critical terrace jury wielding banners proclaiming the merits of his predecessor.

That day the tall, rangy Lancastrian emerged with honour, scoring once and hitting the woodwork twice in a 6-1 victory. But the chorus of disapproval directed at Everton was only mollified temporarily and Alan became an innocent victim, leaving the club in 1960. Yet by no means had be proved an abject failure, netting ten times including a hat-trick at home to Birmingham City. He had an instinct for taking up promising positions near goal, and was especially dangerous when running on to long passes from Bobby Collins. But with the likes of Jimmy Harris and Frank Wignall in contention for a place, he was unable to make his mark, and accepted a move to non-League Nelson.

BORN: Padiham, Lancashire, 3.2.34. GAMES: 27. GOALS: 10. OTHER CLUBS: Burnley 56/7-58/9 (31, 18); Leeds United 58/9-59/60 (30, 16); Nelson (non-League); Oldham Athletic 61/2 (10, 7).

1959/60

EDDIE THOMAS

By no stretch of the imagination did Eddie Thomas resemble a professional athlete. Slight of build and pallid of complexion, he looked like so much cannon fodder for the average husky defender. But ask any of his First Division contemporaries from the late fifties and they will speak with respect of an incisive inside-forward armed with a whiplash shot, a deft scorer whose record for a poor side was enviable.

Eddie, a born trier and a lovely, modest man, relied on speed over short distances and perfect timing when striking the ball, but also boasted considerable all-round skill. Blues fans witnessed a typical example of the Thomas craft against Arsenal at Goodison in October 1957, when he seized possession in a crowded penalty box and weaved past two challenges before beating 'keeper Jack Kelsey with an angled drive.

A product of Everton's youth system, Eddie was given his debut by team coach Ian Buchan in March 1957 and was the club's top League marksman with 15 goals in 26 appearances during the following campaign. He continued to net regularly but was allowed to join Blackburn Rovers in February 1960 as part of the deal that took Roy Vernon to Goodison. The highlight of his subsequent career was a prolific spell with Derby County.

BORN: Newton-le-Willows, Lancashire, 23.10.33. GAMES: 93. GOALS: 41. OTHER CLUBS: Blackburn Rovers 59/60-61/2 (37, 9); Swansea Town 62/3-64/5 (68, 21); Derby County 64/5-67/8 (105, 43); Leyton Orient 67/8 (11, 2).

1956/57 - 1959/60

GRAHAM WILLIAMS

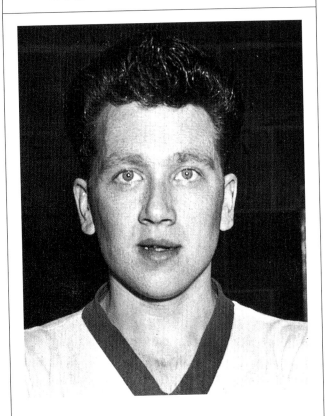

Graham Williams was a jaunty little flankman who sped up and down Everton's left touchline exuding a sense of urgency, his sturdy legs revolving like the pistons of some frenzied 'Puffing Billy' that was running late but was determined to make up for lost time. Unfortunately for the skilful Welshman, he surfaced during a period of continuous flux at Goodison, and never did full justice to his undoubted talent.

After making his debut at home to Sunderland in March 1956, Graham was granted his first substantial run of games a year later, netting three times in nine outings and raising hopes of an effective long-term future. Though capable of juggling tricks, he opted more often to knock the ball past his full-back and tear after it before aiming a cross for his centre-forward's head or attempting a long-distance strike himself, finding the net from outside the box on several occasions.

Frequently, however, his headstrong style ran him into blind alleys, and with a plethora of wingers in competition for his place, he was allowed to join Swansea Town in February 1959. At the Vetch Graham reached his peak, winning a handful of caps before a broken leg in 1962 halted his international impetus. Nevertheless, his League career continued until the end of the decade.

BORN: Wrexham, 31.12.36. GAMES: 33. GOALS: 6.
HONOURS: 5 Wales caps (61).
OTHER CLUBS: Bradford City 55/6 (9, 2);
Swansea Town 58/9-61/2 (89, 20); Wrexham 64/5 (24, 6);
Tranmere Rovers 66/7-67/8 (73, 12); Port Vale 68/9 (23, 1).

1955/56 - 1958/59

BOBBY LAVERICK

One of a procession of left-wingers to arrive at Goodison Park around the turn of the decade, Bobby Laverick never evinced the burning desire to succeed that is crucial to any professional footballer.

Tall for a flankman, yet rather lightweight, the blond north-easterner made a promising start after signing from Chelsea and displacing Eddie O'Hara in February 1959. He scored on his debut, a 3-3 draw at home to West Bromwich Albion, and went on to finish the season with five strikes in 11 outings, but his form fell away rapidly during the following campaign.

A former England youth international, Bobby was quick, could control the ball at speed and could shoot with crispness and accuracy, as he demonstrated with a neat curler against Arsenal at Goodison in October 1959. He also linked cleverly, at times, with inside-forward Bobby Collins and clearly possessed considerable potential.

But when he found himself in and out of a team in the doldrums, the application necessary to establish himself was not apparent, and he was allowed to join Brighton in the summer of 1960. At the Goldstone Ground, Bobby enjoyed his most productive spell, before bowing out of the League following a brief stay with Coventry.

BORN: Trimdon, County Durham, 11.6.38.
GAMES: 23. GOALS: 6.
OTHER CLUBS: Chelsea 56/7-57/8 (7, 0); Brighton and Hove Albion 60/1-61/2 (63, 20); Coventry City 62/3 (4, 0).

1958/59 - 1959/60

TOMMY RING

Tommy Ring spent only a short time with Everton, but the impression he made was deep and lasting. From the first moments of his debut against Nottingham Forest in January 1960, it was evident to all connoisseurs of quality football – and there has never been a shortage of those at Goodison – that a performer of pure quality was parading his wares.

The Scottish international left-winger, then approaching 30, had been signed cheaply from Clyde in an attempt to add much-needed inspiration to a side that was hovering dangerously near the relegation zone. Some said he was past his prime – and they were probably right – but the pale Glaswegian with the dark, slicked-back hair still had plenty to offer.

It was not just that Tommy waltzed past defenders as if they were rooted to the spot, it was the stylish way he did it. He would sway one way, dipping a shoulder as if betraying his intentions, and then he was gone in the opposite direction; opponents knew what he was going to do but were powerless to stop him. Though not quick over long distances, his change of pace was so devastating that few full-backs recovered in time to prevent one of his tantalising centres, either floated or curled, that had the purists purring at the accuracy of his left foot. Not that he lacked skill in his right – as anyone who saw his 25-yard chipped goal at home to West Ham in September 1960 would testify – but, demoralisingly, as he shone that day his Everton career had only a week to run.

In the next game, at Stamford Bridge, Tommy broke his leg in an accidental collision with Chelsea goalkeeper Reg Matthews. The break mended, eventually, but the ageing Scot never returned to top-flight duty, instead leaving to make a handful of appearances for Barnsley before retiring. Many respected judges maintain that the Blues were thus deprived of their most gifted wingman since the war; and to this day, there are still those at Goodison who sigh wistfully at the mere mention of Tommy Ring.

BORN: Glasgow, 8.8.30. GAMES: 27. GOALS: 6.
HONOURS: 12 Scotland caps (53-57).
OTHER CLUBS:
Clyde 50/1-59/60; Barnsley 61/2-62/3 (21, 1).
DIED: October 1997.

1959/60 - 1960/61

JIMMY FELL

Jimmy Fell was a clever, dependable outside-left who had looked like an outstanding prospect with his first club, Grimsby Town, but never quite lived up to that early billing during subsequent travels. Everton boss Johnny Carey was grappling with a long-term injury list that included wingers Tommy Ring and Micky Lill when he signed the easy-going East-countryman from the Mariners in March 1961. Accordingly, Jimmy was pitched straight into top-flight action, and did well enough to retain his place - give or take the occasional fleeting absence - until the following January.

The Fell method was to lurk on the touchline, where he sought to outwit defenders by guile rather than pace, habitually feinting to cut inside before going the other way. Heavily biased towards his left foot, Jimmy was a consistently accurate crosser who also possessed a powerful shot. His most productive return was a smartly-taken brace in the 6-0 hammering of Nottingham Forest at Goodison Park in October 1961, though more valuable was a point-saver at Blackpool the following month.

In the spring of 1962, having lost his place to the more dynamic Derek Temple, Jimmy joined Newcastle United. His year on Merseyside had been worthy, but uninspired.

BORN: Cleethorpes, Lincolnshire, 4.1.36.
GAMES: 28. GOALS: 5.
OTHER CLUBS: Grimsby Town 56/7-60/1 (166, 35);
Newcastle United 61/2-62/3 (49, 16);
Walsall 63/4 (21, 4); Lincoln
City 63/4-65/6 (63, 10).

1960/61 - 1961/62

MICKY LILL

In the opening weeks of 1960/61, right-winger Micky Lill played football to match his personality - bright, direct and with an endearing spirit of adventure. He struck seven goals in as many games, displaying speed and skill in copious quantities, and manager Johnny Carey must have been blessing the day, in February that year, that he had persuaded Wolves to part with the extrovert entertainer for £25,000.

With Tommy Ring showing superb form on the left, Everton fans were anticipating a season of dazzling flank-play; alas, by the end of October their optimism was cruelly dashed. First, Tommy suffered a broken leg; then his versatile partner switched to the left, where he played one game before a cartilage injury sidelined him for the rest of that campaign. It was the first disturbing hint that the Blues' new flyer was built for dash rather than durability.

By the next term Micky - who failed at his local club, West Ham, before becoming a prolific scorer at Molineux - was back in contention. But with Billy Bingham by then ensconced in the number-seven shirt, and with the Lill knee still causing pain, the former impetus was gone. Come 1962, Micky accepted a £12,500 transfer to Plymouth, later moving along the coast to Portsmouth before emigrating to South Africa.

BORN: Romford, Essex, 3.8.36. GAMES: 34. GOALS: 12.
OTHER CLUBS: Wolverhampton Wanderers 57/8-59/60
(30, 15); Plymouth Argyle 62/3 (21, 7);
Portsmouth 62/3-64/5 (39, 5).

1959/60 - 1961/62

JIMMY HARRIS

Jimmy Harris scorched across the First Division firmament in 1955/56, a shooting star apparently heaven-sent to rescue Everton from the black hole of mediocrity. Yet somehow, although the searingly fast centre-forward went on to enjoy a creditable career, he never scaled the dizziest heights that had seemed to beckon during his debut campaign.

The curly-haired front-runner, born around the corner from Tranmere's Prenton Park, came to the Blues' notice on the say-so of his aunt, who reckoned that his 60 junior goals in a season must qualify her prolific nephew for a trial. Jimmy progressed rapidly and in August 1955, with Everton struggling, was called up unexpectedly to replace Dave Hickson.

Blessed with a capacity for hard work to match his pace, slick control and lethal finishing power with his right foot, the dashing youngster panicked defences and set the Goodison terraces humming. By April he had netted 21 League and FA Cup goals, and was rewarded with an England under-23 cap. But in 1956/57 injuries and loss of form limited his appearances, and some critics reckoned the lightly-built marksman lacked the necessary physical presence. Ironically, however, the return of Hickson from his transfer travels revived the Harris fortunes. Jimmy moved to the right wing - occasionally turning out at inside-right - and the goal touch returned, notably at White Hart Lane in October 1958 when he notched a splendid hat-trick. Understandably, he wasn't too impressed with the efforts of his team-mates that day: Spurs won 10-4!

Soon he was picked for the Football League and in early 1960 - after Dave had departed once more - Jimmy resumed his central position, but he didn't shine and in November Alex Young arrived to take his place. A month later, Jimmy joined Birmingham City for £20,000, helping them to reach the Inter Cities Fairs Cup Final and to win the League Cup. Fine achievements, but those who recalled his quicksilver youth could not suppress a nagging feeling of disappointment.

BORN: Birkenhead, 18.8.33.
GAMES: 207. GOALS: 72.
OTHER CLUBS: Birmingham City 60/1-63/4 (93, 37);
Oldham Athletic 64/5-65/6 (29, 9).

1955/56 - 1960/61

MICK MEAGAN

As a man and a footballer, Mick Meagan was the salt of the earth. But such a description, an appropriate tribute to the undemonstrative Irishman's traits of loyalty, honesty and dedication, should in no way be construed as a polite way of saying 'worthy, but dull'. In fact, Bobby Collins, that most shrewd and forthright of soccer judges, rates Mick as the best exponent of one-two passes he has ever seen, and the classy utility man's former colleagues queue up to praise both his delightful first touch on the ball and his calmness in playing his way out of tight corners. All Mick lacked was pace, a drawback that consigned him to stand-in status for much of his Goodison tenure, though he would have walked (literally!) into most other top-flight sides.

'Chick', as he was known at the club, joined the Blues in 1952 as an 18-year-old inside-forward, finding his most effective role as a wing-half after moving back to deputise for an injured team-mate in a reserve game. Such was the competition for places that he did not make his senior breakthrough until 1957/58, when he played 38 matches at left-half. Thereafter, the excellence of Brian Harris and Jimmy Gabriel limited Mick's opportunities, though his appearance total never fell below double figures in any one season. Typically, the versatile Eire international never complained when out of favour, and reaped his reward in 1962/63 when he won a Championship medal as a full-back, at first replacing the injured Alex Parker on the right, and then ousting George Thomson from the left-flank berth on merit.

Mick was 30 when he left for Huddersfield in the summer of 1964, valued at £15,000 in the deal that took Ray Wilson to Goodison. He thrived in Yorkshire, becoming skipper both at Leeds Road and in a subsequent spell at Halifax. After bowing out of the League, he returned to his homeland, leaving behind a spotless reputation and a host of friends who would miss his warm, if sometimes barely intelligible, Irish brogue.

BORN: Dublin, 29.5.34. GAMES: 176. GOALS: 1.
HONOURS: League Championship 62/3. 17 Republic of Ireland caps (61-70). OTHER CLUBS: Huddersfield Town 64/5-67/8 (121, 1); Halifax Town 68/9 (23, 0); Drogheda, Republic of Ireland.

1957/58 - 1963/64

FRANK WIGNALL

A strike rate of better than one goal every two games, achieved in intermittent outings over four seasons, was not enough to win Frank Wignall a regular place in the Everton attack. It was a frustrating situation for the young Lancastrian, a boyhood Bolton fan who had once dreamed of succeeding Nat Lofthouse as the Trotters' spearhead.

Frank, who scored on his 1959 debut against Burnley, was fashioned in the burly mould of his hero. Brave, strong in the air and blessed with a ferocious shot in either foot, he covered ground more quickly than might be expected from his rather ponderous gait, and though his control was not delicate, he was adept at keeping possession by shielding the ball.

His most productive term was 1960/61, when he netted 15 times in 19 League and Cup matches, but even such an impressive tally was not enough for Frank to emerge from the formidable shadow cast by Alex Young and Roy Vernon. After making only one appearance in the title-winning campaign of 1962/63, he opted for a fresh start, joining Nottingham Forest for £20,000 and soon was showing the form that won him a brace of England caps. In 1967 it was rumoured that the Blues wanted to re-sign him, but he went to Wolves instead. Everton and Frank Wignall, it seemed, were just not meant for each other.

BORN: Chorley, Lancashire, 21.8.39. GAMES: 38. GOALS: 22. HONOURS: 2 England caps (64).
OTHER CLUBS: Nottingham Forest 63/4-67/8 (156, 47); Wolverhampton Wanderers 67/8-68/9 (32, 15); Derby County 68/9-71/2 (45, 15); Mansfield Town 71/2-72/3 (56, 15).

1959/60 - 1962/63

COLIN GREEN

Eighteen-year-old full-back Colin Green could hardly have faced a more daunting adversary on his senior debut for Everton in September 1960. Shuffling down the wing to meet him was none other than the peerless Stanley Matthews, but come the end of an eventful afternoon at Bloomfield Road, it was the enthusiastic Welsh rookie rather than Blackpool's evergreen maestro who took the honours. The Toffeemen ran out 4-1 winners and the great Stan had been unable to unsettle his callow opponent.

Despite his encouraging debut, Colin was not destined for glory at Goodison. Though quick, strong and a tight marker, he was apt to commit himself to tackles when it might have been wiser to hold back, and his distribution was erratic. With the likes of George Thomson and Mick Meagan ahead of him in the pecking order for the number-three shirt, the under-23 international accepted a £12,000 move to Birmingham in December 1962, and reaped the rapid dividend of a League Cup winner's medal.

Colin, who could also play on the right, matured as a footballer at St Andrews and the full caps he won during his Midlands sojourn were richly deserved. After suffering a succession of injuries, he ended his playing days at non-League Tamworth, before going into the garage business.

BORN: Wrexham, 10.2.42. GAMES: 18. GOALS: 1. HONOURS: 15 Wales caps (65-69).
OTHER CLUBS: Birmingham City 62/3-70/1 (185, 1); Wrexham on loan 70/1 (3, 0).

1960/61 - 1961/62

BRIAN HARRIS

Rarely has an Everton footballer been as comprehensively underrated as Brian Harris; indeed, when his Goodison career is evaluated, words like 'staunch' and 'trusty' tend to be trotted out with a glibness which does scant justice to an all-round performer of enviable talent. Consider Brian's record: he alone played First Division football during the Cliff Britton era and survived to win major honours under Harry Catterick; during his dozen campaigns in the senior squad he occupied every position except that of goalkeeper; and he maintained a degree of consistency that few of the Blues' more feted individuals came close to emulating.

Brian was also a natural comedian who rendered priceless service to team morale with his wicked practical jokes, although he was commendably level-headed when it came to footballing matters. Even the unhappy experience of being axed for expensive import Tony Kay in December 1962, midway through a Championship-winning season, did not destroy the Harris equilibrium. Where many other players would have responded angrily with an immediate transfer request, Brian elected to stay and fight for his place. Admittedly, the circumstances of his restoration to the number-six shirt in 1964 - the bribes scandal which resulted in Kay's imprisonment - were bizarre, but the fact remains that manager Catterick rated the resilient Merseysider highly enough to give him three more terms at the top level.

Brian was an ebullient, determined winger when he arrived at Goodison from non-League Port Sunlight in January 1954, and it was on the right flank that he made his senior debut, 20 months later at Burnley. As a forward, he contributed some lively performances and a smattering of goals, but it was after his conversion to wing-half in 1958, during the early days of the Johnny Carey regime, that he began to develop his full potential. Right-footed, though destined to make most of his appearances on the left to accommodate Jimmy Gabriel, Brian was an accurate, quickfire passer who specialised in early balls that frequently caught opposing defenders unawares. This skill and vision was supplemented by a brisk tackle, aerial solidity and - although much of his time was spent as a defensive midfielder - a savage shot.

In this deep-lying role, interspersed with occasional stints at full-back, Brian played an integral part in Everton's transformation from fifties strugglers to one of the major powers in British soccer throughout the sixties. Perhaps his greatest personal triumph was at Wembley in 1966 when, two days short of his 31st birthday, he gave a supremely influential display to help the Blues overturn a two-goal Sheffield Wednesday lead on the way to lifting the FA Cup. On that dramatic afternoon, his combination of calm expertise and passion for the game shone through as he demonstrated the same unshakeable self-belief that had carried him through the Kay interlude.

It was a fitting finale to Brian's tenure as a Toffeeman, though his departure during the following autumn by no means signalled the end of his professional career. He went on to make more than 250 senior appearances for Cardiff and Newport, playing until he was 39 before flirting briefly with management. But Goodison saw the prime of Brian Harris, a period of honourable accomplishment which does not deserve to be damned by faint praise.

BORN: Bebington, Merseyside, 16.5.35.
GAMES: 358. GOALS: 29.
HONOURS: League Championship 62/3; FA Cup 65/6.
OTHER CLUBS: Cardiff City 66/7-70/1 (149, 0);
Newport County 71/2-73/4 (85, 0).
MANAGER: Newport County 74.

1955/56 - 1966/67

ALEX YOUNG

Few footballers, at any club in any era, have been idolised to the extent of Alex Young by the blue half of Merseyside during the sixties. A centre-forward of matchless grace and subtlety, he was practically deified by the fans. Their devotion to 'The Golden Vision' - an inspired and everlasting nickname which was also the title of a TV play about Evertonians in general and the artistic Scot in particular - was even more intense, somehow, than the straightforward hero-worship accorded to the new wave of heroes headed by George Best. Not even other highly regarded figures in the Goodison camp were proof against this near-hysterical adoration: when Harry Catterick had the temerity to drop Alex for an untried Joe Royle in January 1966, he was shoved and threatened by outraged supporters, and Brian Labone, no less, was once booed by his home crowd because he had injured Alex in training.

But why all the fuss? And just how good a player was the man whose comparatively paltry total of eight international caps was viewed by his English admirers as an eternal affront? Well, Alex Young simply oozed charisma, his halo of blond curls and elegant, almost ethereal style of movement fuelling the theory that after a match he would simply float home to Olympus. A deep-lying, elusive leader of the line, he stroked the ball rather than kicked it, his touch infinitely sure as he glided past opponents with the merest shimmy of his hips. Some claimed he was over-elaborate, but that was unfair; in fact, he was a perfectionist who abhorred making a pointless pass, and such was his awareness that he seemed able to dispatch the ball accurately without looking up.

Though not a powerhouse number-nine in the Toffeemen's tradition of Dean, Lawton and Hickson, Alex was majestic in the air, his timing so exquisite that he seemed to hover, a talent never better illustrated than by his near-post header past Bill Brown in the crucial single-goal victory over Spurs at Goodison in April 1963 during the title run-in. His detractors reckoned he shied from the heat of battle, but although not an overtly physical player, he was able to look after himself, as might be expected of a man who had worked in a mine and served in the Army.

A more telling criticism was that he tended to be inconsistent - breathtaking one moment, exasperating and seemingly casual the next. Indeed, this perplexed Alex himself, for he could never explain such fluctuations in form, though he acknowledged them readily. More understandably, one of his most disappointing periods was immediately after arriving on Merseyside in November 1960 to the accompaniment of scoffing from Scottish pundits who reckoned that the £40,000 signing from Hearts was seriously over-priced. However, after throwing off a niggling knee injury, Alex went on to prove his worth conclusively, though there might have been a degree of truth in the contention that while he was a jewel in a successful side, he could have been a luxury in a struggling one.

His peak, perhaps, was during the 1962/63 Championship campaign, when he contributed 22 goals and laid on many more for striking partner Roy Vernon, despite suffering from appalling blisters on his feet which were to bedevil him throughout his career. Nevertheless, he remained a joy to watch even after he slowed down - though he was always more ghost than greyhound - towards the end of the decade.

Alex departed the scene of his triumphs in 1968, putting in a fleeting stint in charge of Glentoran before ending his playing days at Stockport. But it is at Goodison that his memory will be forever revered; as long as the name of Everton survives, men and women will speak with awe of 'The Golden Vision'.

BORN: Loanhead, Midlothian, 3.2.37. GAMES: 268 (3). GOALS: 87.
HONOURS: League Championship 62/3; FA Cup 65/6. 8 Scotland caps (60-66).
OTHER CLUBS: Glentoran, Northern Ireland; Stockport County 68/9 (23, 5).
MANAGER: Glentoran, Northern Ireland (68).

1960/61 - 1967/68

BILLY BINGHAM

If the peak of Billy Bingham's career was behind him when he joined Everton in October 1960, his early performances in a blue shirt offered no hint of imminent decline. Though in his 30th year, the Northern Ireland star - one of the most entertaining wingmen in Britain throughout his fifties prime with Sunderland and Luton - was still supremely fit, and his penetrating style on the right flank became a key ingredient in the 1962/63 Championship side.

Yet if it hadn't been for an accident, Billy would never have joined the Toffeemen. Manager Johnny Carey, bereft of an experienced top-class winger after Tommy Ring broke his leg, persuaded Luton to part with their main attraction in exchange for John Bramwell, Alec Ashworth and £15,000. Immediately striking up a beguiling partnership with inside-right Bobby Collins, Billy began to show the form that had helped his country to the World Cup quarter-finals in 1958. Quick, direct and always capable of the unexpected - though a distinctive habit of patting the ball from foot to foot often offered a clue that an explosive burst was imminent - the Ulsterman was capable of 'skinning' any full-back on his day, and could cross the ball with precision. In addition, he was brave and possessed a pugnacious streak behind his charm and ebullience.

For a winger, Billy was unusually combative in the air, as he showed with a courageous diving header at Molineux in October 1962, although more of his goals came from long distance. When shooting, he tended to favour his right foot, and on the rare occasions he hit the target with his left, he would endure merciless ribbing from his team-mates.

Eventually Billy lost his place to new signing Alex Scott half-way through the title campaign, going on to serve Port Vale before embarking on the management path that would one day lead him back to Goodison.

BORN: Belfast, 5.8.31. GAMES: 98. GOALS: 26.
HONOURS: League Championship 62/3. 56 Northern Ireland caps (51-63).
OTHER CLUBS: Glentoran, Northern Ireland; Sunderland 50/1-57/8 (206, 45); Luton Town 58/9-60/1 (87, 27);
Port Vale 63/4-64/5 (40, 6). MANAGER: Southport (65-68); Linfield, Northern Ireland (68);
Plymouth Argyle and Northern Ireland (68-70); Greece (70-73); Everton (73-77);
PAOK, Salonika, Greece (77); Mansfield Town (78-79); Northern Ireland (80-94).

1960/61 - 1962/63

ALEX PARKER

Alex Parker is the man who elevated the sliding tackle into an art form. Though it would be inaccurate to describe the classy but heavily-built right-back as sluggish, he was no greyhound either, a circumstance which he rendered irrelevant by the impeccable timing of his challenges. So often, just as a dashing winger thought he had eluded the stretching Scottish international, the ball would be whisked away to safety at the last moment. Invariably Alex chose his ground with care, seeking to win possession near the touchline to avoid the risk of conceding penalties, but so precise was his method that, even inside the box, the hazard was a marginal one.

Not that he was a one-trick wonder. The Parker game positively oozed quality, his cultured distribution being of particular benefit to both Billy Bingham and Alex Scott, the flankmen who played in front of him during 1962/63, when Everton topped the First Division.

Signed with Eddie O'Hara from Falkirk in the summer of 1958 - a year after they helped the Bairns win the Scottish FA Cup - Alex was prevented by National Service from making an early Blues debut, his duties for the Royal Scots Fusiliers taking him to Cyprus until November. It wasn't long before he made up for lost time, though, displaying consistently immaculate form, and always seeming to excel in potentially harrowing encounters with Spurs' Welsh flyer, Cliff Jones.

It was something of a mystery that, after his move, Alex was picked just once more for his country, and there was no shortage of pundits on Merseyside who blamed the fact on his 'Anglo' status. However, there was warm consolation in the vast popularity he won with Everton supporters, who rarely fail to recognise and appreciate a thoroughbred footballer.

Come the mid sixties, the ageing Alex lost his place to the promising Tommy Wright and moved to neighbouring Southport, whom he later managed before becoming a publican.

BORN: Irvine, Ayrshire, 2.8.35. GAMES: 219. GOALS: 5.
HONOURS: League Championship 62/3. 15 Scotland caps (55-58).
OTHER CLUBS: Falkirk; Southport 65/6-67/8 (76, 0);
Ballymena United, Northern Ireland.
MANAGER: Ballymena United (68-70); Southport (70).

1958/59 - 1964/65

ALEC ASHWORTH

PETER HARBURN

JACK BENTLEY

ALEC ASHWORTH   1957/58 - 1959/60

Inside-forward. BORN: Southport, Lancashire, 1.10.39.
GAMES: 12. GOALS: 3. OTHER CLUBS: Luton Town 60/1-61/2 (63, 20);
Northampton Town 62/3 (30, 25); Preston North End 63/4-65/6 (43, 14).

BRIAN GODFREY   1959/60

Inside-forward. BORN: Flint, 1.5.40. GAMES: 1. GOALS: 0.
HONOURS: 3 Wales caps (64-65). OTHER CLUBS: Scunthorpe United
60/1-63/4 (87, 24); Preston North End 63/4-67/8 (122, 52);
Aston Villa 67/8-70/1 (143, 22); Bristol Rovers 71/2-72/3 (81, 16);
Newport County 73/4-75/6 (118, 14). MANAGER: Exeter City (79-83).

BRYAN GRIFFITHS   1958/59

Full-back. BORN: Liverpool, 21.11.38. GAMES: 2. GOALS: 0.
OTHER CLUBS: Southport 60/1-62/3 (117, 1).

PETER HARBURN   1958/59

Centre-forward. BORN: Shoreditch, London, 18.6.31.
GAMES: 4. GOALS: 1. OTHER CLUBS: Brighton and Hove Albion
54/5-57/8 (126, 64); Scunthorpe United 58/9-59/60 (20, 8);
Workington Town 59/60-60/1 (67, 23).

ALAN TYRER   1959/60 - 1961/62

Forward. BORN: Liverpool, 8.12.42. GAMES: 10. GOALS: 2.
OTHER CLUBS: Mansfield Town 63/4-64/5 (41, 5);
Arsenal *(League Cup appearances only)*; Bury 67/8 (2, 0);
Workington Town 68/9-75/6 (243, 18).

JACK BENTLEY   1960/61

Outside-right. BORN: Liverpool, 17.2.42. GAMES: 1. GOALS: 0.
OTHER CLUBS: Stockport County 61/2-62/3 (49, 5).

PETER KAVANAGH   1960/61

Outside-left. BORN: Romford, Essex, 3.11.38. GAMES: 6. GOALS: 0.

BRIAN GODFREY

BRYAN GRIFFITHS

ALAN TYRER

PETER KAVANAGH

MICK GANNON

KEITH WEBBER

GEORGE HESLOP

ROY PARNELL   1960/61 - 1963/64

Full-back. BORN: Birkenhead, 8.10.43. GAMES: 3. GOALS: 0. OTHER CLUBS: Tranmere Rovers 64/5-66/7 (105, 2); Bury 66/7-69/70 (97, 2).

MICK GANNON   1961/62

Defender. BORN: Liverpool, 2.2.43. GAMES: 3. GOALS: 0. OTHER CLUBS: Scunthorpe United 62/3-63/4 (15, 0); Crewe Alexandra 64/5-69/70 (210, 2).

KEITH WEBBER   1960/61 - 1961/62

Centre-forward. BORN: Cardiff, 5.1.43. GAMES: 6. GOALS: 1. OTHER CLUBS: Brighton and Hove Albion 62/3-64/5 (35, 14); Wrexham 64/5-65/6 (73, 33); Doncaster Rovers 66/7-68/9 (67, 18); Chester 69/70-70/1 (70, 14); Stockport County 71/2 (40, 7). Died 1983.

GEORGE SHARPLES   1960/61 - 1963/64

Wing-half. BORN: Ellesmere Port, Cheshire, 20.9.43. GAMES: 11. GOALS: 0. OTHER CLUBS: Blackburn Rovers 64/5-68/9 (103, 5); Southport 71/2 (25, 0).

GEORGE HESLOP   1962/63 - 1965/66

Centre-half. BORN: Wallsend, Tyneside, 1.7.40. GAMES: 11. GOALS: 0. OTHER CLUBS: Newcastle United 59/60-61/2 (27, 0); Manchester City 65/6-71/2 (162, 1); Bury 72/3 (37, 0).

JIMMY HILL   1963/64

Inside-forward. BORN: Carrickfergus, Northern Ireland, 31.10.35. GAMES: 7. GOALS: 1. HONOURS: 7 Northern Ireland caps (59-63). OTHER CLUBS: Linfield, Northern Ireland; Newcastle United 57/8 (11, 2); Norwich City 58/9-62/3 (161, 55); Port Vale 65/6-67/8 (63, 8).

ROY PARNELL

GEORGE SHARPLES

JIMMY HILL

JIMMY GABRIEL

When Harry Catterick's first, exhilarating Everton side were pouring forward, putting their opponents to the sword, Jimmy Gabriel was an efficient component in a smooth machine, clearly an accomplished First Division performer; but it was when the Blues had their backs to the wall that the indomitable right-half was seen in his full glory. Tackling like a runaway battering ram and rallying his team-mates with the fervour of some ancient Scottish warlord, he seemed to grow in stature, his effectiveness increasing in direct proportion to the heat of the battle raging around him.

Jimmy was recruited to the Goodison cause in March 1960, when Johnny Carey paid £30,000 for the blond 19-year-old whose exploits for Dundee had encouraged rashly optimistic comparisons with his majestic compatriot, Dave Mackay. The older man had crossed the border a year earlier to become an instant inspiration to Spurs, but, understandably, young Jimmy needed more time to settle. In only his third outing he was given a fearful run-around by West Bromwich Albion's Derek Kevan, who scored five times as Everton were thrashed at the Hawthorns. He reacted positively, volunteering for extra training to hone his fitness as he acclimatised to the more rigorous demands of the English game.

Soon the true Gabriel mettle was revealed, and most immediately obvious was the combativeness that became his trademark. Such a physical - and occasionally impetuous - competitor was bound to suffer knocks, but he took them without moaning, and there were times when he played on with wounds that demanded numerous stitches after the final whistle. In fact, he tended to be more upset if violence was visited on less forceful team-mates, for whom he appeared to act as 'minder'.

Yet it would be doing Jimmy a grave injustice to dwell solely on his aggression. While not an extravagantly gifted ball-player, he was comfortable in possession and passed accurately with his right foot, though he lacked a degree of vision that might have turned a very fine player into a great one. He was powerful in the air, creating a formidable barrier when standing shoulder to shoulder with stopper Brian Labone, and contributed several stirring performances as an emergency centre-forward. In the midfield, he melded splendidly with left-half Brian Harris, each man being capable of slotting in as an extra defender or moving forward to support the attack. Jimmy's ability to complement first Brian, and then his replacement Tony Kay, was a major factor in lifting the League title in 1962/63, and he was also a leading light in the 1966 FA Cup Final victory over Sheffield Wednesday. Indeed, pictures of his unconfined joy at the end of 90 minutes, all gap-toothed grin and sweat-soaked shirt, somehow evoke the atmosphere of that heart-stopping afternoon more vividly than a host of action replays.

Despite such success, however, Jimmy was not destined to see out his prime with Everton. In July 1967, with the newly-arrived Howard Kendall laying persuasive claim to his position, the 26-year-old Scottish international was sold to Southampton, where he contributed five years of yeoman service. After further travels, both playing and coaching, he returned to Goodison in the summer of 1990 to help manager Colin Harvey look after the first team, later taking over as caretaker boss at either end of Kendall's second reign. Subsequently Jimmy remained part of the coaching set-up and exerted a particularly valuable influence on the club's youngsters until he headed for the USA in 1997. Indubitably, though, it's as a fire-and-brimstone wing-half that the fans will forever remember Jimmy Gabriel; he never quite became another Dave Mackay - who could? - but he left an indelible mark on Everton history.

BORN: Dundee, 16.10.40. GAMES: 300 (1). GOALS: 36.
HONOURS: League Championship 62/3; FA Cup 65/6. 2 Scotland caps (60-63).
OTHER CLUBS: Dundee 58/9-59/60 Southampton 67/8-71/2 (191, 25);
Bournemouth 72/3-73/4 (53, 4); Swindon Town *on loan* 73/4 (6, 0); Brentford 73/4 (9, 0).
MANAGER: Everton (caretaker, 90, 93-94).

1959/60 - 1966/67

DENNIS STEVENS

Ask most outsiders to reel off the key influences on Everton's 1962/63 Championship triumph and the name of Dennis Stevens is unlikely to crop up. But try the same exercise with one of his team-mates in Harry Catterick's exciting side, or with any regular visitor to Goodison Park during that fulfilling campaign, and the workaholic inside-forward will not be short of honourable mentions.

Not that anyone would pretend that Dennis could turn a game on its head with a moment of magic. His forte, prosaic yet essential, was in ball-winning and maintaining a supply of possession for the artistic likes of Alex Young and Roy Vernon. Standing only 5ft 7in but immensely strong, he tended to impose a cumulative rather than instantaneous effect on a match, labouring relentlessly and perceptively in the common cause.

Dennis cost £35,000 when he was signed, in March 1962, from Bolton Wanderers, whom he had helped to win the FA Cup four years earlier. At Burnden Park he had been a potent attacking force, packing a stinging shot and in 1959/60 succeeding Nat Lofthouse as the Trotters' leading goal-scorer. But midfield duties were central to his brief with the Blues, and after surviving a hostile reception from a vociferous contingent of home supporters - they blamed him, wrongly and illogically, for the departure of terrace favourite Bobby Collins - Dennis won them round with a succession of sterling performances.

After being ever-present at inside-right for more than two seasons, he switched to wing-half in 1964/65 as the purchase of centre-forward Fred Pickering heralded a reshuffle. By then past 30, Dennis - a cousin of the great and much-lamented Duncan Edwards - was finding it difficult to retain his place, and in December 1965 joined Oldham for £20,000. An unassuming, pleasant fellow, he later became a gents' outfitter in Bolton, and could look back with pride on distinguished and honest contributions to every club he served.

BORN: Dudley, Worcestershire, 30.11.33.
GAMES: 142. GOALS: 22.
HONOURS: League Championship 62/3.
OTHER CLUBS: Bolton Wanderers 53/4-61/2 (273, 90);
Oldham Athletic 65/6-66/7 (32, 0);
Tranmere Rovers 66/7-67/8 (31, 3).

1961/62 - 1965/66

GEORGE THOMSON

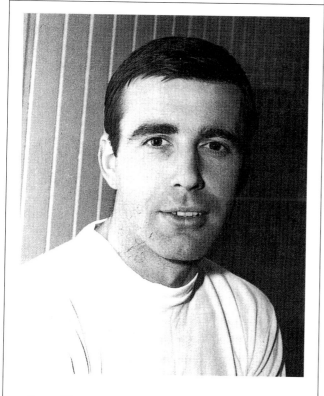

RAY VEALL

George Thomson was a stylish left-back who stroked the ball around like an inside-forward; unfortunately, he had an alarming tendency to practise these skills *inside* his own penalty area. It wouldn't have mattered if the swarthy Scot had been quick enough to get away with his tricky manoeuvres, but too often he was caught in possession, a habit hardly conducive to Harry Catterick's peace of mind or, consequently, to George's long-term future at Goodison.

He joined the Toffeemen in November 1960, valued at £15,000 in a package from Hearts that also included Alex Young, and brought with him an enviable reputation. At Tynecastle he had helped to lift two titles and two League Cups, won under-23 caps and been selected for the Scottish League, so the Everton boss was justifiably optimistic over prospects for a fruitful full-back partnership with Alex Parker.

Indeed, after a somewhat shaky debut at Highbury, George seemed to settle in, his sturdy tackling, high-quality passing and smooth control auguring well. Sadly, these attributes were to be outweighed by his over-elaboration and lack of pace, and after making enough appearances to win a 1962/63 title medal, the man team-mates dubbed '007' - for his film-star looks - lost his place to the reliable Mick Meagan and was sold to Brentford in the following November.

BORN: Edinburgh, 19.10.36. GAMES: 77. GOALS: 1.
HONOURS: League Championship 62/3. OTHER CLUBS: Heart of Midlothian; Brentford 63/4-67/8 (162, 5).

Outside-left Ray Veall made but a fleeting contribution to the Blues, but deserves inclusion in this section of the book because each of his 11 senior games was played during 1962/63, when the Championship pennant returned to Goodison for the first time in 24 years.

Ray, known as 'Pork Chop' in reference to his surname, was signed as a 19-year-old from Doncaster Rovers for £7,500 in September 1961. After being called up in an injury crisis for the opening two matches of the title campaign, he was offered a seven-week settled sequence in mid-season because of injuries to Johnny Morrissey and Derek Temple. Responding pluckily and showing admirable skill, Ray weighed in with some useful displays, notably at the City Ground in November where his sole Everton goal tipped the balance in a 4-3 victory over Nottingham Forest.

However, the diminutive flankman, who would have needed three more appearances to win a medal, was clearly not in the class of his rivals for the left-wing berth and slipped back into the reserves, where he spent the next two terms. Realising there was little future for him at the club, Ray accepted a move to Preston in May 1965, going on to a short stint with Huddersfield Town before leaving the League.

BORN: Skegness, Lincolnshire, 16.3.43.
GAMES: 11. GOALS: 1.
OTHER CLUBS: Doncaster Rovers 60/1-61/2 (19, 6);
Preston North End 65/6 (11, 0);
Huddersfield Town 65/6-66/7 (12, 1).

1960/61 - 1962/63

1962/63

TONY KAY

Never has football talent been squandered with more futility than by Tony Kay. The dynamic wing-half was banned from the game for life and jailed for four months in 1965 for his part in the soccer bribes scandal. It was a personal tragedy for a player who had recently broken into the England team, and a crushing, undeserved blow for Everton, for whom he had signed *after* committing his calamitous offence.

No one was more dismayed than Harry Catterick at the loss of such an inspirational performer. Not only could Tony tackle with pulverising power, he was also a perceptive passer and a superb motivator whose own swaggering self-confidence permeated to his colleagues. Though he was biased towards his left side, and was too small to dominate in the air, he imposed himself on most matches, and was the sort of character that opposing fans profess to loathe while secretly coveting him for their own team. Harry and Tony had first linked up at Sheffield Wednesday where the manager, recognising that he could build a team around the pugnacious redhead, had made him skipper, and within a year of taking him to Goodison in December 1962 for a fee of £55,000 - a record for a British half-back - he had handed him the Blues' captaincy.

By then, Tony - who had taken over from the unlucky Brian Harris - had already helped his new club to lift the title, and it seemed a fair bet that, Nobby Stiles notwithstanding, he might become Alf Ramsey's 'hard man' in time for the 1966 World Cup. It seemed that the Yorkshireman had everything to look forward to, but in April 1964 a Sunday newspaper dropped the bribes bombshell, and he never played League football again. Sympathise with Everton, who were innocent victims, but most of all, pity Tony Kay: he had thrown away a glittering career for a paltry £100 - his betting proceeds for helping to 'throw' a match - and, though he later returned to the amateur game when his ban was lifted, was condemned to a lifetime of bitter regret.

BORN: Sheffield, 13.5.37. GAMES: 57. GOALS: 4.
HONOURS: League Championship 62/3. 1 England cap (63).
OTHER CLUBS: Sheffield Wednesday 54/5-62/3 (179, 10).

1962/63 - 1963/64

ALEX SCOTT

There were few frills or variations to the game of right-winger Alex Scott; quite simply, he didn't need them. The dashing, curly-haired Scot believed in the direct approach, lacerating defences with sheer pace and then dispatching the ball, often when sprinting at full stretch, into the penalty box for the urgent attention of Messrs Young, Vernon and Temple. Most full-backs loathed a confrontation with the international flankman whose slight pudginess belied supreme athleticism. If they marked him closely, he was likely to knock the ball past them before disappearing into the distance; if they gave him space, it left them vulnerable to passes on their inside, on to which their tormentor would run with relish.

Alex - known as 'Chico' to the fans because his swarthy skin tanned easily to a Mexican hue, but dubbed 'The Head Waiter' by team-mates in reference to his habit of running with one arm held stiffly, as if carrying a tray - made his name with Rangers, helping the Ibrox club win every major domestic honour before joining Everton for £40,000 in February 1963. The transfer represented a considerable coup for Harry Catterick, who had been locked in a protracted duel with fellow Championship challengers Spurs for the player's signature, clinching the deal only after a hurried last-minute rendezvous as Alex considered an offer from White Hart Lane.

The Goodison boss's tenacity paid off handsomely and immediately. Replacing the gifted but ageing Billy Bingham, the newcomer provided a timely tonic as the Blues emerged from a patchy midwinter spell to take the title. Thereafter Alex was a model of consistency as a goal-maker - he was never a prolific scorer himself - dazzling frequently during the triumphant 1966 FA Cup campaign.

His peak was passing, however, and the following year he joined Hibernian for £15,000, later going into business with his brother Jim, the former Hibernian and Newcastle player.

BORN: Falkirk, Scotland, 22.11.36.
GAMES: 176. GOALS: 26.
HONOURS: League Championship 62/3; FA Cup 65/6; 16 Scotland caps (56-66).
OTHER CLUBS: Glasgow Rangers 54/5-62/3 (216, 68); Hibernian 67/8-68/9;
Falkirk 69/70-71/2 (23,1).

1962/63 - 1966/67

ROY VERNON

'There's Denis Law, there's Jimmy Greaves, and there's me . . .' So said Roy Vernon in the mid sixties when asked to name the most talented goal-scorers of his day, a response that owed nothing to false modesty, but plenty to a natural, devilish arrogance that characterised the tempestuous Welshman's colossal contribution to one of Everton's greatest sides.

Roy was a footballer of sublime talent: built like a Biro but as tough as rawhide, he was in his element in the penalty area, lurking like some dark assassin to deliver the deadly stiletto thrusts that were his trademark. He struck the ball with immense power, especially with his right foot, employing barely perceptible backlift and possessing the knack of keeping his shots low, a technique that was difficult to combat. Extremely quick in short, sharp bursts, and with darting skills to carry the ball past opponents, Roy had the quicksilver reflexes to perform precise one-two combinations under pressure, though there was no denying the touch of selfishness that is part of the make-up of all top marksmen. He would play a 'wall' pass with anyone, but usually it was a team-mate who was the wall!

Fiery and prone to rebellion, Roy nevertheless proved irresistible to Johnny Carey when Blackburn Rovers made him available in February 1960. The Blues boss had already encountered the Vernon temperament during his own spell at Ewood Park, but was ready to weigh the outstanding gifts of an established international against non-footballing considerations, and Roy - who had turned down the offer of a Goodison trial as a schoolboy - joined Everton for £27,000 plus Eddie Thomas. He set about his work with compelling efficiency, heading the club's goal chart in each of his four complete seasons on Merseyside, and skippering the side to the 1962/63 League title, which he clinched with a slick hat-trick against Fulham in the final game. Admittedly, there were periodic brushes with Carey's successor, Harry Catterick, who made Roy captain in the hope that the responsibility would mellow and mature him. A bold move, it could be called a partial success, although not before the errant Welshman had been sent home from a tour of the United States for breaking a curfew.

But minor indiscretions could never diminish the long-term stature of such a major figure. Roy Vernon deserves to be remembered in his waspish pomp, from which priceless fleeting images remain fresh in the mind: of his snaking past three challenges in five yards before netting at home to Arsenal in April 1961; of how he deceived two Wolves defenders with one deft touch before freeing Alex Young with a perfectly weighted 30-yard through-ball at Molineux in October 1962; and of any number of penalties, driven with ruthless power and accuracy beyond the reach of hapless custodians.

However, he continued to be less than enamoured with Harry's disciplinary regime, and when the chance of a £40,000 move to Stoke City arose in March 1965, all parties concerned were happy to complete the deal. Roy proclaimed at the time that he would 'do a Bobby Collins' for his new club - referring to Bobby's fabulous achievements after leaving for Leeds - and though that proved an unrealistic ambition, he spent five generally productive years in the Potteries.

Later he was reunited with former Blackburn team-mates Bryan Douglas and Ronnie Clayton in amateur football, an incongruous setting for one of Everton's finest post-war strikers but one which left his sardonic humour unimpaired. He was once chided by an over-enthusiastic non-League manager: 'The midfield can't find you, Roy, you're standing still.' To which he replied: 'If they can't find me when I'm standing still, how the hell do you expect them to find me if I'm running around?' Harry Catterick *might* have appreciated that.

BORN: Ffynnongroew, North Wales, 14.4.37. GAMES: 200. GOALS: 110.
HONOURS: League Championship 62/3. 32 Wales caps (57-67).
OTHER CLUBS: Blackburn Rovers 55/6-59/60 (131, 49); Stoke City 64/5-68/9 (87, 22);
Halifax Town *on loan* 69/70 (4, 0). DIED: 5.12.93.

1959/60 - 1964/65

DEREK TEMPLE

The celebrity of scoring the winning goal in the 1966 FA Cup Final will pursue Derek Temple until his dying day, and understandably so; it was a coolly clinical exhibition of finishing under well-nigh unbearable pressure. However, unlike Mike Trebilcock - with whom he shared centre stage on that highly-charged afternoon - the versatile Merseysider can point to long and accomplished service in the Goodison cause. Although rewarded with just the one major club honour, Derek was in contention for a first-team slot for 12 years, performing with distinction in all five forward positions and achieving a well-earned, if fleeting, full international breakthrough.

But before examining the Temple career in detail, a closer look at *that* goal is in order. It was ten minutes from time, the match poised at 2-2 after Trebilcock had wiped out a two-goal deficit; a long pass out of defence by Colin Harvey dropped beyond the centre circle, where Gerry Young seemed to have it covered; but the ball squirmed under the Sheffield Wednesday defender's boot and Derek pounced. Carrying the ball unchallenged for what seemed like an eternity, he advanced towards Ron Springett. There was time to panic, time to freeze, but the Blues' number-eleven did neither; on reaching the edge of the box, he arrowed a low, inch-perfect drive past the England 'keeper's right hand into the corner of the net to lift the cup and win everlasting personal fame.

Such moments of supreme elation are granted to few sportsmen, though in truth Derek had always been a a candidate for glory. As a free-scoring schoolboy he had been a target for both Liverpool and Everton, and after throwing in his lot with the Toffeemen, made a promising senior start at centre-forward in the spring of 1957. The following campaign he consolidated, moving to inside-forward and linking fruitfully with Dave Hickson - his double strike in a 3-3 home draw with Manchester United in Septmber 1957 was a highlight - but was then interrupted by two years of National Service.

On his return from duty in East Africa, where he had become used to playing at 7,000ft above sea level, Derek struggled to pick up the threads and there was talk of a transfer. But he built up his strength and fitness, new manager Harry Catterick switched him to the wing, and he found himself back in the limelight. In 1961/62 he netted ten times in 17 outings, and seemed set fair for a regular place during the following term, only to be sidelined by a cartilage operation and miss out on a title medal.

Thereafter, Derek came into his own: usually on the left wing, though sometimes moving to inside-left to accommodate Johnny Morrissey, he was rarely absent from the side over the next four seasons. A fast, fluent mover who seemed to have a low centre of gravity, he could sway past defenders and climaxed many a thrilling dash with a rasping shot. He was adept at timing his arrival in the penalty box to capitalise on long crosses from right-winger Alex Scott, one of his most spectacular strikes being a shoulder-high left-foot volley against Manchester City in an FA Cup quarter-final second replay at Molineux in April 1966.

Skilful with both feet, Derek could create opportunities out of nothing, and his merits were recognised by Alf Ramsey, who handed him his sole cap against West Germany in 1965. But there were times when the quietly-spoken local boy seemed to lack the confidence his ability warranted. Perhaps as a result, he was not always a favourite with the crowd, and after winning them around in the mid sixties, suffered further in 1967. That September he accepted a £35,000 transfer to Preston North End, thus ending a Goodison tenure of which he could be immensely proud

BORN: Liverpool, 13.11.38. GAMES: 272 (1). GOALS: 82.
HONOURS: FA Cup 65/6. 1 England cap (65).
OTHER CLUBS: Preston North End 67/8-69/70 (76, 14).

1956/57 - 1967/68

FRED PICKERING

Fred Pickering's Everton career divides neatly into two parts - the first prodigiously productive, the second overwhelmingly frustrating. In the two years after joining the Blues from Blackburn Rovers in March 1964, he netted 68 times in 107 outings for his new club and five times in three England appearances; thereafter he suffered a serious knee injury, was omitted controversially from an FA Cup Final, never won another cap, and was sold in August 1967 having played but eight games during the previous campaign.

It was an unfulfilling conclusion to what might have been a monumental Goodison tenure, yet but for an inspired gamble by Ewood Park boss Jack Marshall, the Pickering goal machine might never have roared into life at all. As the fifties drew to a close, Fred was a distinctly ordinary left-back with limited defensive aptitude and with prospects to match. Then Jack pitched him into the front line and, after 18 months of learning his new trade, a richly promising marksman emerged from the shell of the failed number-three.

So prolific did Fred become that when Harry Catterick's £85,000 bid was accepted there was outrage in Blackburn, where fans had been revelling in Rovers' unaccustomed position as springtime Championship contenders and in the prominent part the dashing local boy had played in their rise. On Merseyside, in contrast, there was unalloyed delight as he signalled his arrival with a hat-trick at home to Nottingham Forest and, two months later, notched another three in his first match for England.

At his rampaging best, Fred was an irresistible performer. Though neither outstanding in the air, nor over-physical for a man of his power, nor even particularly fast, he could disrupt the tightest of defences with his determined running and a savage right-foot shot that earned him the nickname of 'Boomer'. Boasting nimble footwork for one so burly - he could nutmeg an opponent as comprehensively as many a winger - he was especially dangerous when cutting in from the flank, a manoeuvre that yielded some of his most spectacular goals.

Though Fred had enjoyed his most bountiful term in 1964/65, when he scored 37 times in 51 League and Cup games, he remained in splendid form come the spring of 1966, underlining his effectiveness with a scorching volley in the FA Cup quarter-final defeat of Manchester City. But a cartilage problem was becoming increasingly painful, forcing him to miss the semi-final victory over Manchester United and perhaps contributing to several lacklustre displays in the League.

He declared himself fit for Wembley but Harry Catterick clearly harboured doubts about his principal striker's ability to last 90 minutes, and proceeded to drop the bombshell from which the two men's relationship was never to recover. Fred was axed for the final against Sheffield Wednesday, and he spent a mortifying afternoon sitting beside Harry on the bench as his replacement, Mike Trebilcock, scored twice to set up a memorable triumph. It was a debilitating blow to a player who had netted in every round on the way to the semis; his subsequent bitterness was perhaps as understandable as the manager's refusal to take a risk. After all, substitutes were not allowed at that time and an early breakdown might have cost Everton the match.

As it was, Fred's Goodison days were numbered. After starting the following season as first choice, he was injured, and - with young Joe Royle emerging - it was no surprise when he joined Birmingham for £50,000. But such an unsatisfactory departure, 15 months after his great disappointment, should never obscure Fred's achievements with the Toffeemen; he can point to a fabulous average of two goals every three games, and hold his head high.

BORN: Blackburn, Lancashire, 19.1.41. GAMES: 115. GOALS: 70.
HONOURS: 3 England caps (64).
OTHER CLUBS: Blackburn Rovers 59/60-63/4 (123, 59);
Birmingham City 67/8-68/9 (74, 27); Blackpool 69/70-70/1 (49, 24);
Blackburn Rovers 70/1 (11, 2).

1963/64 - 1966/67

RAY WILSON

In football, as in any walk of life, the highest professional compliments a man can receive are the respect and admiration of his peers. Accordingly, Ray Wilson must be regarded as the premier British full-back of his generation, and probably the finest since the war. Indeed, both team-mates and opponents during his sixties peak are adamant - and unanimous, in this writer's experience - that the Derbyshire miner's son was the nearest to perfection they have ever seen in a number-three shirt.

Ray's catalogue of attributes was comprehensive. Light, compact and wiry, he was devastatingly quick in short bursts, could either tackle crisply or jockey his winger into blind alleys as the situation demanded, and was blessed with positional flair that hinted strongly at a sixth sense. His left-footed distribution was precise, imaginative and calm, he never passed to team-mates in dangerous positions - so many defenders dispense hot potatoes under pressure - and his powers of concentration were worthy of Geoffrey Boycott with his score on 99.

Surprisingly for one who achieved so much, Ray did not sample life with a top club until his 30th year. After joining Huddersfield as a goal-scoring inside-forward, then making little progress when switched to wing-half, he was converted to full-back by the shrewd Andy Beattie, nurtured in the role by Bill Shankly, and won a third of his England caps while serving the Yorkshiremen. Understandably, the Town didn't want to lose their most accomplished defender - especially after bidding farewell to their greatest attacker, Denis Law - and Ray's various attempts to leave were blocked. However, Harry Catterick - who had once tried to sign Ray for Sheffield Wednesday - was a persistent fellow, and he finally got his man in July 1964, in exchange for Mick Meagan and £35,000.

After struggling successfully to adapt to the Blues' more rigorous fitness demands, the Goodison newcomer suffered a swift setback, being sidelined for 15 weeks by a hip injury received against Nottingham Forest in his first home match. Happily, it proved to be a minor blip: on his recovery, Ray was soon showing the style and efficiency on which he had built his name, and his game reached new heights under the stimulus of regular top-flight competition.

Of course, his golden year was 1966. After throwing off a niggling back problem to help Everton win the FA Cup, he was to savour an even more momentous Wembley triumph two months later, as Alf Ramsey's England lifted the world crown. That day Ray demonstrated both his class and his character as he refused to be ruffled by an uncharacteristic error, a weak header that had let in the West Germans for the opening goal, and was duly rewarded with footballing immortality.

Seemingly unaffected by the passing of time - except perhaps that he spent more time on the treatment table than in his youth - Ray maintained his supreme standards for two more seasons until twisting a knee during preparation for 1968/69. Thereafter, his pace was gone and in the following July so was he, to Oldham, where he stayed for a term before joining Bradford City as player-coach. At Valley Parade, Ray took over as caretaker boss for a spell and was offered the manager's chair on a permanent basis, but passed it up to become an undertaker.

Thus did one of British soccer's most distinguished practitioners depart the game, leaving behind an unassailable reputation and having set an example that remains as the ultimate standard to which any young full-back can aspire.

BORN: Shirebrook, Derbyshire, 17.12.34. GAMES: 150 (3). GOALS: 0.
HONOURS: FA Cup 65/6. 63 England caps (60-68).
OTHER CLUBS: Huddersfield Town 55/6-63/4 (266, 6);
Oldham Athletic 69/70 (25, 0); Bradford City 70/1 (2, 0).

1964/65 - 1968/69

JIMMY HUSBAND

Jimmy Husband was a dashing but unpredictable entertainer. When the force was with him, he could turn a game on its head with his mesmerising body swerve, devastating change of pace and wicked finish; but the following week he might drift anonymously, unable to make an impact, and then the brilliance of which he was capable seemed like a frustrating illusion.

Having joined the Blues as an inside-forward, Jimmy found his most effective role wide on the right. He specialised in diagonal runs across the face of defences, dragging opponents out of position with his teasing skill. So often the mercurial Geordie appeared to stumble, luring his full-back into a rash tackle, before nicking the ball away at the last moment and heading full-tilt for goal. Another asset was astonishing speed of recovery when floored, bouncing to his feet like some indestructible jack-in-the-box to resume the assault.

Jimmy, a relaxed character who enjoyed his football, made his debut as a 17-year-old at Fulham in April 1965, gradually becoming established over the next three years and winning under-23 international recognition. He was at his sharpest in successive FA Cup quarter-finals, giving the Blues a two-goal lead - which they lost - against Nottingham Forest in 1967, and inspiring victory over Leicester City with another brace in 1968. That campaign was not to end happily for Jimmy, however, as he fluffed a free header at Wembley - he was never at ease in the air - a miss which condemned Everton to extra time against a largely outplayed West Bromwich Albion, who then proceeded to lift the trophy.

In 1968/69 he made amends with his most prolific season, linking lethally with Joe Royle and scoring 20 goals in all senior games, and the following term played a creditable part in winning the Championship. Thereafter his form was affected by injuries, he slipped to the fringe of the team, and in November 1973 opted for a fresh start at Luton.

BORN: Newcastle, 15.10.47. GAMES: 189 (8). GOALS: 55.
HONOURS: League Championship 69/70. OTHER CLUBS:
Luton Town 73/4-77/8 (143, 44); Memphis Rogues, USA.

1964/65 - 1973/74

MIKE TREBILCOCK

If Everton fans at Wembley in May 1966 had been told that Mike Trebilcock had been sent down from above, they would have believed it. Indeed few footballing interventions have been more divine than the diminutive Cornishman's in the FA Cup Final against Sheffield Wednesday.

Mike was an unsung reserve, a recent £20,000 signing from Plymouth, when he replaced the injured Fred Pickering for the semi-final against Manchester United. He was expected to lose his place for the big day, but he didn't, and it was his goals - both firmly-struck, first-time drives from inside the penalty box - that hauled the Blues back from a 2-0 deficit and paved the way for ultimate victory.

And that, in terms of his top-level career, was just about that. After a few subsequent appearances in which he drifted on the edge of the action - at the end of his final match, on a muddy pitch at Leeds, he was the only man with clean shorts - Mike joined Portsmouth for £35,000 before emigrating to Australia.

He was not without talent, being quick and a crisp striker of the ball, but lacked First Division class. However, no one can ever erase the glory of Mike Trebilcock's golden day, and former Goodison team-mates agree that the fairy-tale could not have happened to a more genuine lad.

BORN: Gunnislake, Cornwall, 29.11.44. GAMES: 14.
GOALS: 5. HONOURS: FA Cup 65/6.
OTHER CLUBS: Plymouth Argyle 62/3-65/6 (71, 27);
Portsmouth 67/8-71/2 (109, 33);
Torquay United 72/3 (24, 10).

1965/66 - 1967/68

ERNIE HUNT

Ernie Hunt was a perky, carefree character who, during his six-month sojourn with the Blues, made a greater impact as a dressing-room raconteur than as a goal-scoring inside-forward. Yet the chunky entertainer, dubbed 'Farmer' for his West Country accent and bow-legged gait, had all the natural ability to become a lasting Everton star.

Indeed, when Harry Catterick paid Wolves £80,000 for Ernie in September 1967, it was regarded as a shrewd purchase. The brave, skilful 24-year-old had built a splendid reputation with Swindon, his home-town club, enhancing it further during two years as a striker-cum-midfielder at Molineux. Though he lacked pace, he was a reliable finisher, crisp passer and specialist bender of free-kicks - later he was to enjoy brief notoriety for an enterprising but soon-to-be-outlawed 'donkey-flick' routine with Willie Carr at Coventry.

However, at Goodison - where perhaps he did not revel in the manager's martinet approach - Ernie did not settle, making merely a handful of appearances before being sold, at a £10,000 loss, to the Sky Blues. At Highfield Road, he performed enterprisingly for six years, and Everton remained the one club for whom he played during his prime and did not succeed; a case, maybe, of making the right move at the wrong time.

BORN: Swindon, Wiltshire, 17.3.43.
GAMES: 14 (2). GOALS: 3.
OTHER CLUBS: Swindon Town 59/60-65/6 (214, 82);
Wolverhampton Wanderers 65/6-67/8 (74, 32); Coventry City 67/8-73/4 (144, 45); Doncaster Rovers *on loan* 72/3 (9, 1);
Bristol City 73/4-74/5 (12, 2).

1967/68

ALAN BALL

In the spring of 1971, Harry Catterick was asked to put a value on the head of Alan Ball, the top English footballer of the day. The Goodison boss pondered deeply, recalled that the domestic record stood at £200,000, then announced that he would expect offers in the region of £1 million. So would he really part with his premier asset, the Blues' inspiration on the way to Championship glory in 1969/70, even for such a fantastic sum? 'I'd consider it, and then I'd say no' came the reply that produced a warm, reassuring glow in the breasts of Everton supporters everywhere. Imagine, then, their utter consternation when Alan departed to Arsenal for £220,000 just nine months later. Admittedly, the Merseysiders had slumped mysteriously since the title triumph, but the explanation that both club and player would benefit from a new direction seemed more than a little thin.

In retrospect, however, there is one consolation for fans who felt let down by the move: they did, at least, see the best of Alan Ball. Though he served the Gunners with characteristic passion, much of his Highbury sojourn was spent in a declining side, and while a spell with Southampton in his thirties was admirable, autumn at The Dell could hardly compare to high summer at Goodison.

Alan joined Everton in August 1966, immediately after his scintillating contribution to England's World Cup victory. The £110,000 deal went through to the chagrin of Don Revie, who wanted desperately to sign Blackpool's star attraction for Leeds but was unable to persuade his board to pay what was then the highest fee to pass between British clubs. The scale of the Elland Road blunder was soon glaringly apparent as the 5ft 6in Lancastrian with the high-pitched voice and carrot-coloured thatch became the catalyst in the Toffeemen's steady transformation from merely a good side in 1966 to the exhilarating, stylish champions of four years later.

Alan's game was a heady mixture of delicate skill and rampant fire, unquestionable bravery and overwhelming self-confidence. He was a study in perpetual motion to all corners of the pitch, now displaying his uncannily precise first touch in a dazzling interchange of short passes, next demonstrating his vision with a sublime raking pass, then popping up to finish the move with a cheeky attempt on goal. In his early days at Everton, Alan combined constant midfield creativity with a strike rate that many a front-runner would have been proud of, netting 56 times in three terms. Subsequently, when the well of goals ran almost dry, he became frustrated and confrontations with colleagues ensued. Indeed, the emotional side of the Ball persona was to be a major factor throughout his career; a born motivator but no diplomat, he lifted some individuals while upsetting others, also falling foul of referees at times, and in 1970 Catterick made him captain in the partially gratified hope that responsibility would curb his temperamental excesses.

Occasional storms, however, were a small price to pay for so much that was glorious. From his arrival, Alan was beloved of the Goodison faithful - how they revelled in his goals that inflicted 1966/67 League and FA Cup defeats on Liverpool - and they will cherish forever their memories of the noisy little man in white boots whose tiny steps led opponents such a merry dance. There was barely an aspect of the game at which he didn't excel, his performances were remarkably consistent and his fervour was such that defeat could move him to tears. Former colleagues talk of Alan Ball as one of Everton's finest players of all time, and who could argue? Physically there wasn't much of him; in terms of talent, commitment and value to the team he was a veritable colossus.

BORN: Farnworth, Lancashire, 12.5.45. GAMES: 249. GOALS: 78.
HONOURS: League Championship 69/70. 72 England caps (65-75).
OTHER CLUBS: Blackpool 62/3-65/6 (116, 41); Arsenal 71/2-76/7 (177, 45);
Southampton 76/7-79/80 (132, 9); Vancouver Whitecaps, Canada; Blackpool 80/1 (30, 5);
Southampton 80/1-82/3 (63, 2); Hong Kong; Bristol Rovers 82/3 (17, 2).
MANAGER: Blackpool (80-81); Portsmouth (84-89); Stoke City (89-91); Exeter
City (91-94); Southampton (94-95); Manchester City (95-96); Portsmouth (98-).

1966/67 - 1971/72

ANDY RANKIN

Harry Catterick made remarkably few blunders as Everton boss, but one of them, surely, was his failure to install Andy Rankin as Gordon West's medium-term successor in the early seventies. Perhaps Andy's problem was that he had been second-string 'keeper for too long - his first taste of senior football had been in 1963/64 - and that familiarity had fostered a chronic lack of recognition. Ironically, it had been Harry who in 1961 had persuaded Andy not to leave the game to join the police force, thus providing the impetus for the callow custodian to emerge as a high-class alternative when Gordon lost form in November 1963. But despite displaying remarkable agility as a shot-stopper, reassuring dexterity in taking crosses and unquestionable courage, Andy could never make the position his own.

In retrospect, it might have been wiser had the quiet Merseysider - such a contrast to the voluble West - moved on earlier. But anyone who had watched him at his best - as at Anfield in 1964 when he performed near-miracles as his team-mates ran up a 4-0 win - would have sworn that the England under-23 international must one day earn the premier spot.

However, it wasn't to be. After a rare indifferent showing in a 1967 FA Cup quarter-final against Nottingham Forest, Andy was consigned even more emphatically to the wilderness, not reappearing at senior level until 1970/71. That term he made 37 appearances, and was the hero of a European Cup victory over Borussia Moenchengladbach, making the crucial save in a penalty shoot-out. But the resilient Gordon was to bounce back again, and this time the faithful deputy made his exit, a £20,000 fee taking him to Watford, whom he served admirably for a decade.

Considering such longevity, and the comparative fallibility of subsequent Goodison 'keepers Dai Davies and David Lawson, Andy could be excused if he cursed his luck. His career deserved a more exalted epitaph than 'the best reserve goalkeeper in Division One.'

BORN: Liverpool, 11.5.44. GAMES: 103 (1). GOALS: 0.
OTHER CLUBS: Watford 71/2-79/80 (299, 0);
Huddersfield Town 79/80-81/2 (71, 0).

1963/64 - 1970/71

SANDY BROWN

The name of Sandy Brown is synonymous with enthusiastic toil, vigorous but occasionally ill-timed tackles, and one of the most spectacular own-goals ever seen on Merseyside; in fact, while each of those references is relevant in portraying his Everton career, they fall far short of evaluating the full contribution of the Scottish utility man. Indeed, it should be stressed that Sandy, signed for £38,000 from Partick Thistle in September 1963, made more than 250 appearances for a successful club - and no one does that on effort alone.

Admittedly, his most obvious assets were athleticism and physical hardness - he was once dismissed in a stormy clash with Leeds during which the referee took both teams off the field to cool down - but he worked to hone his skills and sometimes displayed a surprisingly delicate touch. Sandy's reading of the game was criticised often, and justly, but it improved, as Harry Catterick recognised by deploying him in front of the back four in certain matches, notably against West Ham when he was detailed to intercept passes intended for Hurst and Peters.

Perhaps most effective as an overlapping full-back, he was also a doughty emergency attacker - witness his Goodison strike in a European tie against Real Zaragoza in 1966/67, and the nodded goal that clinched a home win over Liverpool that same term. However, it was another derby-day header that earned him notoriety, an acrobatic dive at a Peter Thompson cross that sent the ball crashing into his own net in December 1969. Actually it was but a minor blemish in a season that was to end with Sandy - real name Alex - pocketing a title medal, a reward that made up for missing the 1966 FA Cup Final after playing four times on the way to Wembley.

Off the pitch, he was a popular character who accepted with good grace the frequent joshing of team-mates amused by his broad accent, and there was genuine regret when he left to join Shrewsbury in May 1971.

BORN: Grangemouth, Scotland, 24.3.39. GAMES: 208 (43). GOALS: 11.
HONOURS: League Championship 69/70.
OTHER CLUBS: Partick Thistle; Shrewsbury Town 71/2 (21, 0);
Southport 72/3 (19, 0).

1963/64 - 1970/71

HOWARD KENDALL

Few pleasures in life delighted Harry Catterick more than stealing a march on Liverpool, so what sweet satisfaction must have engulfed the Everton manager's soul when he whisked one of Britain's most promising wing-halves from under the nose of Bill Shankly.
For weeks in the spring of 1967 the press had been adamant that Howard Kendall was on the verge of leaving Preston North End for Anfield; it was merely a matter of time before the Reds got their man. But, demonstrating the same single-minded opportunism that had pipped Tottenham Hotspur for the services of Alex Scott four years earlier, Harry pounced to sign the stylish 21-year-old Tynesider for £80,000. The Catterick coup capped a hellish few days for Shanks, who the previous Saturday had watched his side knocked out of the FA Cup - at Goodison Park!

Howard was pitched straight into top-flight action two days later for the home encounter with Southampton, and endured a traumatic 90 minutes, missing an open goal and looking out of his depth. But there was no doubting the ability of the former England Youth captain who, in one of his first games for the Deepdale club, had become the youngest man to appear in an FA Cup Final. Indeed, the Kendall quality quickly became apparent as he took his place alongside Alan Ball and Colin Harvey in one of the classiest midfield trios modern football has known.

Working tirelessly down the right, the calm, self-possessed newcomer complemented the livewire duo perfectly. As a creator, Howard was blessed with the vision and touch to make long, meticulous first-time passes that made the game flow, yet unlike many skilful schemers he was an expert at winning possession, too. Sometimes he would make challenges in which colleagues feared he must break his leg, but such was the timing and precision of his tackle that he invariably came way intact, and with the ball at his feet. Sturdy enough to deputise in the back four, where he had spent his final days at Preston, he was not ideal for the role because of a slight weakness in the air, though his inspired reading of the game and flair for organisation might have made him an ideal sweeper.

Finding the net was not one of Howard's premier responsibilities, though he chipped in with his share of crucial goals, such as the Merseyside derby winner at Goodison in February 1968 (more salt for the Shankly wound) and a European Cup equaliser in an away clash with Borussia Moenchengladbach in October 1970. Perhaps his most spectacular strike, however, came in the 1968 FA Cup quarter-final at Leicester, when he capped a brilliant personal display by smacking home a waist-high volley following a slick interchange of passes initiated by himself.

Howard's most memorable achievement as a player - he was woefully unlucky never to win full England recognition, and is widely regarded as his country's most accomplished uncapped performer - was his key contribution to the title triumph of 1969/70, though his manful striving as skipper of a team that lost its way so unexpectedly over the next three seasons should not be under-estimated. Those efforts notwithstanding, he was allowed to join Birmingham City in February 1974 as part of the deal in which Everton secured Bob Latchford, though he was destined to play a still more momentous part in the Goodison story.

In August 1981 Howard was recalled to the Blues banner as manager, retaining his playing registration and boosting an inexperienced midfield in a handful of outings before retiring to dugout and desk. What followed was truly momentous, but the glory of Kendall the boss must not be allowed to overshadow completely the attainments of Kendall the footballer. He was one of Everton's finest.

BORN: Ryton, Tyneside, 22.5.46. GAMES: 272 (2). GOALS: 29.
HONOURS: League Championship 69/70.
OTHER CLUBS: Preston North End 62/3-66/7 (104, 13); Birmingham City 73/4-76/7 (115, 16); Stoke City 77/8-78/9 (82, 9); Blackburn Rovers 79/80-80/1 (79, 6).
MANAGER: Blackburn Rovers (79-81); Everton (81-87); Athletic Bilbao, Spain (87-90); Manchester City (90); Everton (90-93); Notts County (95); Sheffield United (95-97); Everton (97-).

1966/67 - 1973/74 & 1981/82

JOHNNY MORRISSEY

Johnny Morrissey turned an ancient tradition on its head. Football folklore bulges with tales of faint-hearted flankmen who spared no effort in escaping the attentions of, shall we say, the more physical members of the full-back fraternity. However, Johnny was that rarest of birds, a winger around whom the most abrasive of defenders was wise to tread a circuitous and respectful path. In short, the pugnacious, muscular little Merseysider - his calves wouldn't have looked out of place on a young rhino - was as ready to give knocks as take them. A telling testimony to the Morrissey mean streak is that he was always the first man to be picked for five-a-side matches in training; after all, his team-mates knew him better than anyone.

Not that Johnny lacked finesse. His ball control, with either foot, was impeccable and his intelligent assessment of attacking situations was a potent weapon in the Everton armoury. Perhaps at his most effective when taking possession in deep positions - he was invariably to be found near the touchline, providing a constant option for colleagues looking to make a pass - Johnny was explosively quick in short bursts. Sometimes he jinked inside to make space for a rasping shot, but was most productive when he tricked his way to the byline before delivering one of his devastatingly accurate floated crosses, a service which yielded Joe Royle, in particular, untold bounty.

Yet the diminutive dreadnought might never have pulled on a blue shirt. On leaving school, he had gone to Anfield, and his £10,000 move across Stanley Park to Goodison in September 1962 caused tumult in the Reds camp. The transfer was sanctioned by the Liverpool board without the agreement of their manager, one Bill Shankly, who made it clear that any further transactions without his blessing would result in his departure. In such circumstances, Johnny's immediate impact for the old enemy must have served to strengthen Shanks' case. After scoring in a pulsating Merseyside derby draw, he notched a hat-trick at home to West Bromwich Albion in the next match and went on to feature prominently as the Toffeemen finished the 1962/63 campaign on top of the First Division.

However, such instant success did not prove an automatic passport to first-team security. During the mid sixties, he found himself frequently in competition with Derek Temple for the left-wing berth, and he missed out on FA Cup glory in 1966. Johnny was a stayer, though, outlasting the England international to strike prime form as the decade drew to a close. Shrugging off the disappointment of Wembley defeat against West Bromwich Albion in 1968 - after his penalty had secured semi-final victory against Leeds - he was at his creative, combative best in 1969/70, richly deserving the reward of a second title medal. One of his most satisfying displays that term came in August against Don Revie's men, then reigning champions, and he tormented Paul Reaney mercilessly, a personal triumph enjoyed by only a select few.

The subsequent season was unexpectedly poor by Goodison standards, yet Johnny continued to operate with undiminished resilience and cunning. In 1971/72, however, he found it more difficult to hold down a regular place, and was transferred to Oldham Athletic in the summer. It wasn't long before injury ended his playing days, but he retained an interest through the progress of his son, also John, who made two senior appearances for Everton before giving admirable service to Tranmere Rovers. The young man must have found his father a hard act to follow; Johnny Morrissey Senior goes down as one of the shrewdest buys the Blues have ever made.

BORN: Liverpool, 18.4.40. GAMES: 311 (2). GOALS: 50.
HONOURS: League Championship 62/3, 69/70.
OTHER CLUBS: Liverpool 57/8-60/1 (36, 6); Oldham Athletic 72/3 (6, 1).

1962/63 - 1971/72

GERRY GLOVER   BARRY REES

GEOFF BARNETT

GERRY HUMPHREYS

STUART SHAW

FRANK D'ARCY

BARRY REES   1963/64 - 1964/65

Wing-half. BORN: Rhyl, North Wales, 4.2.44.
GAMES: 4. GOALS: 2.
OTHER CLUBS: Brighton and Hove Albion 64/5 (12, 1).
DIED: 1965.

STUART SHAW   1964/65 - 1965/66

Outside-right. BORN: Liverpool, 9.10.44. GAMES: 3. GOALS: 0.
OTHER CLUBS: Southport 66/7-68/9 (67, 6); Port Vale 69/70 (3, 0).

GERRY GLOVER   1964/65 - 1965/66

Wing-half. BORN: Liverpool, 27.9.46. GAMES: 2 (1). GOALS: 0.
OTHER CLUBS: Mansfield Town 67/8 (18, 0).

GEOFF BARNETT   1965/66 - 1967/68

Goalkeeper. BORN: Northwich, Cheshire, 16.10.46.
GAMES: 10. GOALS: 0.
OTHER CLUBS: Arsenal 69/70-75/6 (39, 0).

FRANK D'ARCY   1965/66 - 1970/71

Full-back. BORN: Liverpool, 8.12.46. GAMES: 8 (9). GOALS: 0.
OTHER CLUBS: Tranmere Rovers 72/3 (8, 1).

GERRY HUMPHREYS   1965/66 - 1969/70

Winger. BORN: Llandudno, North Wales, 14.1.46.
GAMES: 14. GOALS: 2. OTHER CLUBS: Crystal Palace 70/1 (11, 0);
Crewe Alexandra 71/2-76/7 (193, 30).

HARRY BENNETT   DEREK SMITH

BILLY BRINDLE

DAVID TURNER

TERRY OWEN

AIDEN MAHER

DEREK SMITH   1965/66 - 1966/67

Centre-forward. BORN: Liverpool, 5.7.46. GAMES: 3 (1). GOALS: 0.
OTHER CLUBS: Tranmere Rovers 67/8-68/9 (83, 21).

HARRY BENNETT   1967/68

Centre-half. BORN: Liverpool, 16.5.49. GAMES: 3 (1). GOALS: 0.
OTHER CLUBS: Aldershot 70/1-72/3 (89, 7);
Crewe Alexandra 73/4 (30, 1).

BILLY BRINDLE   1967/68

Midfielder. BORN: Liverpool, 29.1.50. GAMES: 2. GOALS: 0.
OTHER CLUBS: Barnsley 70/1 (1, 0).

AIDEN MAHER   1967/68

Outside-left. BORN: Liverpool, 1.12.46. GAMES: 1. GOALS: 0. OTHER
CLUBS: Plymouth Argyle 68/9-70/1 (64, 3);
Tranmere Rovers 71/2 (7, 1).

TERRY OWEN   1967/68

Winger. BORN: Liverpool, 11.9.49. GAMES: 2. GOALS: 0.
OTHER CLUBS: Bradford City 70/1-71/2 (52, 6);
Chester 72/3-76/7 (176, 40); Cambridge United 77/8 (1, 0);
Rochdale 77/8-78/9 (83, 21); Port Vale 79/80 (18, 3).
Father of Michael Owen (Liverpool, 96/7-).

DAVID TURNER   1967/68

Right-back. BORN: Derby, 26.12.48. GAMES: 1. GOALS: 0.
OTHER CLUBS: Southport 70/1-72/3 (71, 0).

COLIN HARVEY

Some Evertonians' achievements are reflected in the number of great games they played; it is more accurate to measure Colin Harvey's in terms of great seasons. Never have the Blues been blessed with a footballer who combined technical excellence, long-term consistency and sheer open-hearted willingness to a higher degree than the undemonstrative, but monumentally resolute midfielder. Yet, incredibly, there were times when even the Goodison faithful took Colin for granted. Early in his career they tended to overlook the sterling efforts of the local lad while lavishing praise on costly, more glamorous imports; then, after he became established, they were so accustomed to his unflagging standards that a rare indifferent display - perhaps once every three or four years! - would stand out like a red scarf on the Gwladys Street terrace.

It seems hard to credit now, but as a teenager Colin had a trial for Liverpool; the rejoicing in the devotedly Blue Harvey household must have been unconfined when he signed as a Goodison apprentice in October 1962. Thereafter he progressed so rapidly that within 11 months he had made his senior debut, deputising for the injured Jimmy Gabriel in the knee-trembling atmosphere of a European Cup tie at Inter Milan's San Siro stadium. Fireworks, smoke bombs and the baying of 90,000 Italians failed to intimidate Colin as, with determination not to fail etched all over his 18-year-old features, he gave a mature, self-possessed display, Everton losing by a single goal to one of the best sides in the world.

After such a rarified start, he returned to the reserves to consolidate before securing a regular first-team berth in 1964/65. Despite the fans' initial failure to recognise a thoroughbred, people inside the game had no such doubts. Colin had every attribute demanded of a modern midfielder, and indeed, his speed, sharpness of tackle and the awesome stamina which carried him between penalty areas with bewildering frequency are well documented. But his superb close control, accurate and positive distribution, and intelligent positional play were overshadowed too often by the merits, admittedly outstanding, of Messrs Ball and Kendall. In fact, Colin shared all responsibilities, both creative and defensive, with his illustrious colleagues and should never have suffered in comparison.

He wasn't perfect, of course, being a decidedly poor finisher. Even his best-remembered goal, the winner in the 1966 FA Cup semi-final against Manchester United, was mishit, bobbling past Harry Gregg from 15 yards. One that went some way towards balancing the books, however, came on the Goodison afternoon in April 1970 when Everton clinched the title. Veering past two West Bromwich Albion defenders, Colin cracked home a 25-yard piledriver that left team-mates gaping in amazement before they engulfed him in celebration.

Around that time, the Harvey engine was running at its sweetest - there was outrage among many pundits that he was capped only once - but by the mid seventies there were signs of a burn-out. Those who had marvelled at the way his slim frame had coped with the enormous demands he had placed on it for more than a decade were not surprised when fitness became increasingly elusive. Accordingly, in October 1974, a £70,000 deal took Colin to Sheffield Wednesday, whom he served admirably for 13 months before injury forced him to retire.

An enthusiastic character who had always found time for youngsters, he took up coaching and turned out to be a natural. There followed a Goodison homecoming, which was to bring triumph as Howard Kendall's number-two, then despair as manager. His deeds on the field, however, had already guaranteed Colin Harvey an unassailable reputation as one of the most influential players in more than a century of Everton history.

BORN: Liverpool, 16.11.44. GAMES: 380 (4). GOALS: 24.
HONOURS: League Championship 69/70; FA Cup 65/6. 1 England cap (71).
OTHER CLUBS: Sheffield Wednesday 74/5-75/6 (45, 2).
MANAGER: Everton (87-90).

1963/64 - 1974/75

BRIAN LABONE

Everton have been blessed with a veritable cavalcade of great players down the years, a lot of them more naturally gifted than Brian Labone, the majority more spectacular, perhaps all more ruthless. But none have been nobler. Such a description may seem incongruous in the frequently cut-throat, sometimes cynical world of post-war professional football, but when applied to the modest Merseyside-born centre-half, a man who led the Blues through some of their finest hours, it is entirely appropriate.

Yet there is a myth about Brian, whose calm, almost tranquil character was reflected in his play to the extent that he was booked just twice in 530 senior games as a stopper, a position traditionally associated with crunchingly robust tactics; the contention was that he lacked 'devil', and that if he had been tougher both he and Everton would have achieved even more. Such a theory was, however, fatally flawed on two counts: first, Brian had to be true to his own nature; second, although impeccably fair, he *was* hard - no soft touch could have lasted for 14 years at the top level.

In fact, that illustrious Labone career might have been stillborn. As a bright grammar school boy, he planned to go to university, and deliberated carefully before accepting an offer from Goodison Park in July 1957. Thereafter his progress was rapid: after impressing against Dave Hickson in a public trial game, he bypassed the junior sides to claim a place in the reserves. Seven months later he made his senior debut because of injury to Tommy Jones, but it was not until his second outing, against Spurs, that he discovered the harsh facts of top-flight life when he was given a chasing by the rumbustious Bobby Smith.

However, Brian survived and prospered, winning a regular berth in 1959/60 and emerging as one of the League's most promising pivots, commanding in the air, a crisp timer of tackles and an astute reader of the game. On the ball, he was both comfortable and constructive when using his right foot, wisely reserving his left for finding touch in emergencies, and though he wasn't the quickest defender in the land, neither was he the slowest. Star status arrived in 1962/63, when he became the first Evertonian to be capped by England since the war - a startling fact - and was a huge influence on that term's title triumph.

But even after succeeding the disgraced Tony Kay as captain and holding aloft the FA Cup in 1966, there was still something of the reluctant celebrity about Brian. That same year he asked to be excused from the England World Cup party to concentrate on his wedding plans - admittedly he was in the shadow of Jack Charlton at the time - and in 1967, aged 28, astounded the soccer world by announcing his retirement. Having lost both form and confidence, Brian told the club that he would leave in 18 months' time, or as soon as a suitable replacement was found, to enter the family business. Happily, this dramatic move cleared his mind, his anxiety evaporated, and soon he returned to peak form.
With Alf Ramsey continuing to select him, Brian reversed his decision, helped Everton to another Championship in 1969/70 and recovered from injury in time to excel in the subsequent World Cup finals. The monumental Labone career - only Ted Sagar played more League games for the club - was soon to end, though, curtailed by an Achilles tendon injury suffered in 1971.

Now in insurance and still a dedicated Blue, Brian is honoured at Goodison not only as a distinguished and loyal player, but as a man who treated everyone, from chairman to turnstile attendant, with the same kindness and integrity. Harry Catterick once called him 'the last of the great Corinthians'; coming from his late manager, who knew him so well and was never one to dispense fulsome praise, that says everything.

BORN: Liverpool, 23.1.40. GAMES: 530. GOALS: 2.
HONOURS: League Championship 62/3, 69/70; FA Cup 65/6.
26 England caps (62-70).

1957/58-1971/72

GORDON WEST

Gordon West was an Everton institution, the most flamboyant character of the Catterick era, glorying in extrovert antics that kept dressing-room morale bubbling and delighted the fans. He enjoyed a particularly warm relationship with Liverpool's Kopites, to whom he endeared himself after reacting to one of their customary fusillades of abuse by blowing them a kiss; their response was to present him with a handbag, a happy ritual which offered hilarious light relief at several subsequent Merseyside derbies. Yet the charismatic custodian's gift for comedy should not overshadow the professional excellence which, though he never *quite* scaled the heights once predicted for him, marked him out as one of the League's leading net-minders throughout the sixties.

Tall, heftily built and magnificently athletic, Gordon might have been born to keep goal, belying the fact that he had trials with several clubs as a schoolboy centre-half. He was an instinctive performer, breathtaking as a shot-stopper, courageous at close-quarter blocks and usually reliable at claiming crosses. One weakness was a rather inadequate kick - the legacy of a long-standing thigh injury - but he compensated amply with penetrating, constructive throws in the manner of the great Bert Trautmann. His powers of concentration came in for occasional criticism, but it's a telling point that any momentary lapses were sufficiently rare to condemn his accomplished rival, Andy Rankin, to marathon stints in the reserves.

Gordon made his First Division entrance for Blackpool as a 17-year-old, temporarily replacing Tony Waiters, whose own brilliance made it easier for Everton to prise the younger man away from Bloomfield Road in March 1962. Not that the Tangerines didn't strike a hard bargain, Harry Catterick handing over £27,000, then a record fee for a 'keeper, to make his first signing as Goodison boss. It was a bold move and one which paid swift dividends as Gordon, instantly displacing Albert Dunlop, helped the Blues take the League title in his first full season.

There was still improvement to be wrought in the West technique, however, and for the next two campaigns he shared senior duties with Rankin before reasserting himself on the 1966 Wembley trail, excelling in FA Cup clashes with Coventry and Manchester City. He missed only a handful of games over the next four campaigns and picked up a second Championship medal in 1969/70, before slipping out of favour again. But once more he confounded the doubters, returning as an ever-present in 1971/72, then giving way, ultimately, to David Lawson.

Gordon, who despite his ebullient personality was notoriously nervous before a game, was to be missed not only for his footballing ability, but also for the encouragement he gave to youngsters and for the ever-ready wit that had so captivated the Kop. Sandy Brown was frequently the target for good-natured barbs, as in October 1967 when the Scot had deputised between the posts when his 'keeper had been sent off for punching Newcastle's Albert Bennett. Afterwards the assailant, bursting with mock outrage, convulsed his team-mates by berating poor Sandy for failing to save the resultant penalty!

Gordon left Goodison in 1973, having won three caps - there might have been more but for his withdrawal from the 1970 World Cup party for family reasons - and there were some who believed the 30-year-old was retiring prematurely. Their contention was given added weight when, some two years later, he was lured back to the game by neighbouring Tranmere. After shedding some weight, he provided four seasons of first-team cover and, no doubt, added a colourful new dimension to the Prenton Park scene. Meanwhile on the other side of the Mersey, it was not until the arrival of a young man named Neville Southall that Everton were to find a truly satisfactory replacement for Gordon West.

BORN: Barnsley, Yorkshire, 24.4.43. GAMES: 399. GOALS: 0.
HONOURS: League Championship 62/3, 69/70; FA Cup 65/6. 3 England caps (68-69).
OTHER CLUBS: Blackpool 60/1-61/2 (31, 0); Tranmere Rovers 76/7-78/9 (17, 0).

1961/62 - 1972/73

JOE ROYLE

Replacing any popular player at a club the size of Everton is an unenviable task, but to inherit the shirt of an idol can be to sip from a poisoned chalice. Yet when Alex Young reached the end of his glittering Goodison reign, phlegmatic teenager Joe Royle grasped the cup of opportunity, drank deeply, and after an initial hiccup, experienced the heady taste of success. Of course, he never assumed the mantle of 'The Golden Vision' - that was created for only one man to wear and, quite rightly, is mothballed forever in Blues legend - but the strapping striker, so utterly unlike his artistic predecessor in his style of play, covered himself in glory in his own characteristic way.

At 16, Joe was the club's youngest senior debutant when he was called in for the axed Alex at Blackpool in January 1966. Furious fans vilified manager Harry Catterick - he was even manhandled by one misguided delegation - and the raw boy returned to the reserves. Demonstrating for the first but not the last time that his was an old head on young shoulders, he shrugged off subsequent criticism, worked endlessly and with ultimate success to improve his rather clumsy touch on the ball, and come the start of 1967/68, he claimed a well-deserved regular first-team place.

There followed four seasons in which Joe netted 95 times in 158 League and Cup appearances, a sensational sequence that encompassed Wembley defeat in the 1968 FA Cup Final, Championship triumph two years later and a first England cap in 1971. The Royle goal rush owed plenty to majestic aerial power, but also not a little to subtlety and intelligence. His head was big (though only in the physical sense) with a wide, flat forehead that might have been fashioned expressly for making meaningful contact with a football, and he was as adept at using it for acutely judged deflections as high-velocity strikes. As he grew in experience, Joe learnt to time his runs to devastating effect, as he demonstrated at Leeds in November 1968. There seemed little danger when Alan Ball clipped in an apparently innocuous cross, and 'keeper Gary Sprake was poised to gather it comfortably when Joe appeared, horizontal and as if from nowhere, to glance the ball into the corner of the net.

Joe's ground-level skills were underrated and he became a top-class target-man, adept at retaining possession under pressure, linking with co-attackers and roaming to the flanks, where occasionally he displayed the ability to beat a defender and dispatch an accurate centre. Extremely mobile for a big fellow, he was at his most effective when operating in comparative isolation between two wide-men - Jimmy Husband and Johnny Morrissey were ideal - rather than in harness with the likes of Joe Harper or Bob Latchford.

Sadly for all concerned, Joe was not destined to see out his prime with the Toffeemen. In the early seventies his career was threatened by back injuries, and he returned from two spine operations to face strong competition from newly-arrived front-runners for a berth in a much changed team. Though he was merely 25, a fresh start was prescribed, and in December 1974 Joe made a £200,000 switch to Manchester City. Subsequent travels took in Bristol City and Norwich, for whom he scored his final First Division goal at Goodison, eliciting a warm cheer from his former fans.

Thereafter, through his efforts at the helm of Oldham Athletic, Joe personified the acceptable face of soccer management, combining integrity, humour and sound judgement, and many Evertonians expected him to succeed Colin Harvey in November 1990. In fact, his day did not come until 1994, of which more follows a little later.

BORN: Liverpool, 8.4.49. GAMES: 272 (3). GOALS: 119.
HONOURS: League Championship 69/70. 6 England caps (71-77).
OTHER CLUBS: Manchester City 74/5-77/8 (99, 23); Bristol City 77/8-79/80 (101, 18);
Norwich City 80/1-81/2 (42, 9). MANAGER: Oldham Athletic (82-94);
Everton (94-97); Manchester City (98-).

1965/66 - 1974/75

TOMMY WRIGHT

Few club full-back partnerships since the war have approached the sheer quality of Everton's Ray Wilson and Tommy Wright, two men doing the same job for the same team yet, in terms of public recognition, with a huge gulf between them. Quite properly, the peerless merits of England's 1966 World Cup hero have been the subject of unstinting praise, but the sterling attributes of his lesser-known colleague - himself an accomplished international - have tended to receive inadequate attention. That is a gross injustice to the quiet Merseysider, whose combination of all-round talent and ideal temperament would have graced any top side of his era.

There was a time, however, when it looked as though Tommy might not make the grade. In the early sixties, as a member of the Blues' A-team inside trio that also included John Hurst and Colin Harvey, he was making unremarkable progress. Then injuries prompted a reshuffle, he found himself at right-back where he impressed mightily, and by the middle of 1964/65 he had joined the senior ranks as the long-term replacement for Alex Parker.

In the number-two shirt, Tommy was the epitome of efficiency, putting the skills he had learnt as an inside-forward to effective use. He controlled the ball comfortably with foot or chest, was a shrewd tactician who delighted his front-men with his constructive passing and, unlike so many overlapping full-backs, could usually be relied upon not to squander advantage with a poor cross. Indeed, one of Everton's most dangerous attacking options involved Jimmy Husband cutting inside to leave a gaping space for Tommy to charge into, before picking out the head of Joe Royle or - a Wright speciality - creating chaos with a low drive into the six-yard box. Crucially, though, his penchant for getting forward did not detract from his premier duty, that of defence. Superbly athletic, he was rarely stranded upfield, his tackling was flinty and sure, and he was extremely competitive in the air for a small man.

To this array of assets could be added utter commitment, which was never proved more conclusively than in the 1966 FA Cup Final. The Blues, having clawed back a two-goal deficit, had just taken the lead for the first time when, with Sheffield Wednesday launching a last wave of assaults, Tommy was stricken by chronic cramp. Team-mates strove to protect him from the ball but the Owls broke swiftly down their left flank and he was the only man in position to give chase. With an uncharacteristically voluble Brian Labone screaming him on, the plucky right-back ignored the agony, and sprinted. The interception was made, with typical lack of fuss, and in the excitement few supporters noticed who had come to the rescue - and none of them knew at what cost.

That Wembley incident was typical of the fortitude with which Tommy overcame frequent injuries to knees that were naturally nobbly and prone to knocks. Indeed, he missed only seven League games between 1966 and 1971, pocketing a title medal for his pains in 1970. Deservedly, he rose to the England ranks, excelling against Brazil in the 1970 World Cup finals, but his career was to fall prey to knee trouble, and he was forced out of the game - at 29, still at his peak - in 1973.

Tommy, whose nephew Billy was to follow him into Everton's back four towards the end of the decade, never had the polish of Ray Wilson and was not the sort of man to catch the fans' imagination. But no one sums up a player more accurately than his fellow footballers, and they were unequivocal in their judgement of Tommy Wright: to them, quite simply, he was one of the best.

BORN: Liverpool, 21.10.44. GAMES: 370 (1). GOALS: 4.
HONOURS: League Championship 69/70; FA Cup 65/6.
11 England caps (68-70).

1964/65 - 1972/73

ALAN WHITTLE

There was blond hair and bravery, on-the-field arrogance and a fair degree of natural talent; yet to saddle Alan Whittle with the ludicrous tag of 'the new Denis Law' was to place a hideously onerous burden on a young man who was not equipped to shoulder it. But the publicity machine rolled on inexorably: the press wrote their sensational headlines, and Harry Catterick - perhaps in a foolhardy attempt at psychology - said something about 'Everton's greatest discovery of all time'. The impressionable Merseysider gave every appearance of believing the overkill, and the inevitable anti-climax ensued.

In fact, though by no means a 'great', Alan *was* a very good player. That much was evident from a handful of impressive performances in 1968, but it was when he deputised for the injured Jimmy Husband during the second half of the 1969/70 Championship campaign that he leapt to prominence. That term the stocky striker was irresistible, his 11 goals in 15 games infusing the Blues' challenge with renewed zest and giving birth to those wild comparisons with the Manchester United star.

Fast and strong, well endowed with both balance and control, Alan could scythe through a defence, opponents seeming to bounce off him, before applying a deadly finish. He was seen at his best at West Ham in December 1969, taking possession in his own half, beating a man and sprinting some 50 yards through a quagmire before slipping the ball past the 'keeper. That same month, Leeds were on the receiving end of the Whittle opportunism when he latched on to a Joe Royle flick, waltzed through a forest of legs and scored from close range.

However, Alan was not to be the same force again. He never shirked but inconsistency set in, and plainly, that vital ingredient that lifts a capable footballer to a higher plane was missing. In late 1972, unable to command a regular place, he joined Crystal Palace for £100,000; a would-be superstar had found a more realistic level.

BORN: Liverpool, 10.3.50.
GAMES: 86 (3). GOALS: 26.
HONOURS: League Championship 69/70.
OTHER CLUBS: Crystal Palace 72/3-75/6 (108, 19);
Leyton Orient 76/7-79/80 (50, 6); Bournemouth 80/1 (9, 0).

1967/68 - 1972/73

KEITH NEWTON

A move to Everton should have provided the crowning glory of Keith Newton's distinguished career; instead, despite a valuable short-term contribution to the Goodison cause, it led to frustration and premature departure. Like Ray Wilson before him, Keith had signed for the Blues in his late twenties, a mature, cultured full-back who had proved himself at international level and now sought to win top club honours before he passed his peak. But unlike Ray, the £80,000 acquisition from Blackburn Rovers never quite saw eye to eye with Harry Catterick about how the game should be played.

On arrival on Merseyside in December 1969, Keith was drafted into the side as a replacement for the less elegant Sandy Brown. He played 12 League games as Everton stepped up their bid for the title, and although an injury suffered at Tottenham in March kept the tall, lean Mancunian out of the triumphant run-in, he had done more than enough to justify his fee. A splendid tackler, he was strong in the air and adept at shrewd interceptions, but it was his intelligent use of the ball that stood out. Whether playing himself coolly out of trouble at the back or overlapping exhilaratingly down the wing, he revelled in using his creative ability - and that was the bone of contention.

After playing magnificently in the 1970 World Cup finals, Keith's form dipped a little and Harry criticised his habit of dwelling on the ball. That winter the England man was injured, then dropped, and come the end of the following season, after failing to command a regular place in a side that was now struggling, Keith moved to Burnley, whom he helped to regain their top-flight berth.

In retrospect it seems ironic that such an accomplished and versatile footballer - naturally right-footed but equally at home on the left - could not have found fulfilment at Goodison, once dubbed the 'Academy of Soccer Science'. The impasse was a shame for both player and club.

BORN: Manchester, 23.6.41. GAMES: 57 (1). GOALS: 1.
HONOURS: League Championship 69/70. 27 England caps (66-70).
OTHER CLUBS: Blackburn Rovers 60/1-69/70 (306, 9);
Burnley 72/3-77/8 (209, 5).

1969/70 - 1971/72

JOHN HURST

John Hurst could be guaranteed not to turn a drama into a crisis. The tall, leggy centre-back possessed one of the coolest heads in football, and when pressure mounted on the Everton goal, he would be found at the centre of the storm, defusing the danger efficiently and unfussily before seeking a chance to set up the Blues' next attack. Yet 'Gentleman Jack', the quietest man in the Goodison dressing room, did his job so unobtrusively that few public plaudits came his way. Inside the game, however, there was no lack of recognition; amongst his peers, he was respected as an impeccable professional who offered class and consistency in equal and ample measure.

The likeable Lancastrian arrived on Merseyside as a teenage centre-forward who had starred for Blackpool and England schoolboys. Harry Catterick converted him into a defensive wing-half, and after outstanding displays during Everton's 1965 Youth Cup triumph, John made his first senior appearances during the following autumn, providing competent cover for Jimmy Gabriel and Brian Harris. However, by the end of a season in which he had also deputised for striker Fred Pickering, he had found his most effective role, standing shoulder to shoulder with Brian Labone in the heart of defence.

No doubt helped by his early experience as a front-runner, John prospered at the back, being blessed with every footballing asset except outstanding pace. Comfortable in possession, he was an intelligent reader of the game, more likely to make a perceptive interception than be forced into a desperate challenge. Capable of an enterprising part in the fluent passing movements that characterised the Blues' approach in the late sixties, John relished surging forward - usually Howard Kendall was the man who dropped back to plug the gap - and his height was an effective attacking weapon at set pieces. Such sorties did not get in the way of his prime responsibiity, however, and he was a doughty tackler when the need arose.

Having established his credentials in 1966/67 - his immaculate policing of Roger Hunt in the FA Cup victory over Liverpool confirming his progress - he became a reliable bastion of the side. Indeed, he demonstrated the strength and resilience of his constitution in the spring of 1968 when he went down with hepatitis on semi-final eve, yet bounced back in time for the Wembley defeat by West Bromwich Albion. John was ever-present for the next two terms, including the Championship campaign of 1969/70 which he began with the bonus of two crucial goals, a neat close-range hook to secure the points at Highbury and a cracking 20-yarder, after a slick one-two interchange with Alan Ball, to sink Manchester United at Old Trafford.

Over the ensuing half a decade, John continued to play splendidly yet was never given the chance to build on an international career which reached its peak when he captained England's under-23 team. Like Arsenal's similarly underrated Peter Simpson, he was over-shadowed by Bobby Moore, Norman Hunter and Colin Todd, perhaps understandably, although his cultured style might have been well suited to the higher level.

John's Goodison tenure ended, at the age of 29, with a move to Oldham Athletic in the summer of 1976. He had lost his Everton place as Billy Bingham sought unsuccessfully to build a new side capable of emulating the triumphs of the Catterick era, though not one of the manager's favoured replacements was John Hurst's equal as a player. However, the Toffeemen's prodigality proved a windfall for the Latics, and one of English soccer's more polished central defenders spent five enjoyable and effective seasons at Boundary Park before retiring in 1981. Thus did 'Gentleman Jack' depart in typically unassuming fashion, letting his football do the talking to the last. When he returned to Everton for a spell as youth coach during the nineties, the new generation of Blues could not have wished for a more impeccable role model.

BORN: Blackpool, 6.2.47. GAMES: 385 (14). GOALS: 34.
HONOURS: League Championship 69/70.
OTHER CLUBS: Oldham Athletic 76/7-80/1 (170, 2).

1965/66 - 1975/76

TOMMY JACKSON

Chunky midfield toiler Tommy Jackson was never good enough to hold down a regular Everton place, but in times of emergency he was a veritable gem. He proved it when Alan Ball was suspended for the 1968 FA Cup semi-final against Leeds at Old Trafford, the enthusiastic Ulsterman stepping up to excel in a tetchy, demanding encounter. Neither quick nor particularly skilful, he was a dedicated snapper at the heels of more accomplished players, and played a creditable part in a 1-0 victory by harassing the likes of Billy Bremner and Johnny Giles into uncharacteristic errors.

That was an early triumph for Tommy, who had arrived recently from Glentoran at a cost of £9,000, and although he was not required at Wembley, there were honours on the horizon. By the end of the year his dogged work for the Blues had won him a full international breakthrough, and in 1969/70 he deputised for Ball, then Kendall, then Harvey, on enough occasions to pocket a Championship medal.

Tommy left Goodison in October 1970, a makeweight in the transaction that took Henry Newton to Merseyside, later going on to do well in a short spell as a calming influence on Tommy Docherty's newly-promoted and highly precocious Manchester United youngsters.

BORN: Belfast, 3.11.46. GAMES: 34 (4). GOALS: 0.
HONOURS: League Championship 69/70. 35 Northern Ireland caps (68-77). OTHER CLUBS: Glentoran, Northern Ireland; Nottingham Forest 70/1-74/5 (81, 6); Manchester United 75/6-76/7 (19, 1).

1967/68 - 1970/71

JOE HARPER

Scottish international striker Joe Harper will have few fond memories of English football. A spell at Huddersfield during the sixties ended with a hasty return to his homeland, and the chunky, 5ft 6in goal-poacher fared little better after moving to Everton from Aberdeen for £180,000 in December 1972. However, to be fair to a self-assured operator who scored heavily for all his employers north of the border, he arrived at Goodison at a time of travail, with the Blues languishing in the nether regions of the First Division.

After announcing his presence by missing a penalty on his debut at home to Spurs, he atoned swiftly with point-saving strikes in the next two games. Yet as the team continued to struggle, Joe found goals hard to come by. A darting opportunist who, despite his size, generated a powerful shot, he needed precise and early service to be at his most effective; sadly, he was rarely to get it.

After 14 months, with some fans complaining that he had not provided value for money, he accepted a £120,000 move to Hibernian, later shining once more at Aberdeen. In other Everton sides, Joe might have gelled; in the one he joined, though by no means a complete flop, he never lived up to his reputation.

BORN: Greenock, Scotland, 11.1.48. GAMES: 46 (3). GOALS: 14.
HONOURS: 4 Scotland caps (72-78).
OTHER CLUBS: Morton 65/6-66/7;
Huddersfield Town 66/7-67/8 (28, 4); Morton 68/9-69/70;
Aberdeen 69/70-72/3 (103, 68); Hibernian 73/4-75/6 (69, 26);
Aberdeen 76/7-80/1 (105, 57).

1972/73 - 1973/74

JOHN McLAUGHLIN

John McLaughlin was a diminutive, pale, prematurely balding young man who rejoiced in the nickname of 'Tiger'. Understandably, his somewhat fragile appearance took Everton supporters by surprise - he was hardly what they expected a Scottish defender to look like - but to be fair to the enthusiastic left-back for whom Harry Catterick paid £65,000 to Falkirk in October 1971, the nickname was not entirely ironic.

In fact, John was fearless, a harassing, ferret-like marker who was as pluckily effective in the air as a fellow of 5ft 5in could be. At times he was adventurous, too, enjoying a dribble, and could read defensive situations well, but there was a question mark over both his strength - his clearances were apt to lack distance - and his stamina.

On arriving at Goodison he went straight into senior action, replacing the out-of-favour Keith Newton, and by the end of 1971/72 had played in 31 League and Cup games, his highest total in five seasons on Merseyside. But in truth, John - whose sole goal for the Blues was the winner at home to Arsenal in September 1973 - never *really* convinced as an Everton player, and in 1976 he crossed the Atlantic to sample the American scene.

BORN: Stirling, Scotland, 3.1.48. GAMES: 68 (2). GOALS: 1. OTHER CLUBS: Falkirk 67/8-71/2 (108, 10).

1971/72 - 1975/76

STEVE SEARGEANT

A combination of hot competition and lack of height forced Steve Seargeant from his most effective position as a central defender. Unfortunately for the blond Merseysider, although he strove pluckily - and with some initial success - to do justice to himself in the unfamiliar role of left-back, he was unable to carve a long-term niche at Goodison.

Harry Catterick gave the former England schoolboy international his senior breakthrough in the early seventies, calling him in to deputise whenever John Hurst or Roger Kenyon was injured. An aggressive tackler whose control and distribution never let him down, he lacked the stature to dominate opponents in the air, and in March 1974 new manager Billy Bingham switched him to the flank. Despite being exposed, at times, for a deficiency in pace, he retained the number-three shirt throughout an encouraging 1974/75 campaign which saw the Blues finish fourth in the League table. Come the next term, however, the team was less buoyant, Steve suffered an injury and he never recovered a regular berth.

A well-respected, popular individual - 'Sarge' did duty as David Johnson's best man - he left Everton in February 1978 to join Detroit Express, later returning to Liverpool, where he ran a pub.

BORN: Liverpool, 2.1.51. GAMES: 86 (4). GOALS: 1. OTHER CLUBS: Detroit Express, USA.

1971/72 - 1977/78

HENRY NEWTON

When Harry Catterick parted with £150,000 and Irishman Tommy Jackson to sign Henry Newton from Nottingham Forest in October 1970, he was paying a top price - Martin Peters and Allan Clarke were the only two Britons to have cost more - for one of the leading midfielders in the land. Sadly, and through no fault of the talented 26-year-old, it was to prove an ill-fated move.

From the start, Henry had seemed an incongruous addition to a payroll that already included Messrs Ball, Harvey and Kendall; indeed, he was destined to spend the bulk of his Everton service as a replacement for his namesake, Keith, at left-back. Understandably frustrated at being played out of position, though never failing to give a whole-hearted performance, he suffered also from injury and illness and his three terms on Merseyside must go down as an anti-climactic interlude in an accomplished career. In all probability, given better luck and appropriate opportunity to do justice to his ability, the former Forest driving force and captain would have proved equally invaluable to the Blues. Quick and brave, sharp in the tackle and a constructive passer, he was the type of all-purpose footballer who would have slotted productively into the engine-room of any leading side.

Henry was a classy enough defender, too, but the role left him unfulfilled; accordingly, when the chance came for a return to his native Midlands in September 1973, he accepted a £110,000 move to Derby, with whom he was to win a title medal in 1975. In fact, the Rams had wanted to sign him three years earlier, but Forest had not been keen to let another star follow Terry Hennessey and Alan Hinton to the Baseball Ground. An under-23 international who narrowly missed full honours, Henry was a popular figure at Goodison, unfailingly professional in his outlook and helpful to youngsters; what a pity that he never had the chance to show his true mettle.

BORN: Nottingham, 18.2.44. GAMES: 83. GOALS: 6.
OTHER CLUBS: Nottingham Forest 63/4-70/1 (281, 17);
Derby County 73/4-76/7 (117, 5); Walsall 77/8 (16, 0).

1970/71 - 1973/74

ROD BELFITT

With every respect to an honest trier, Everton hardly got the best of the deal in which they signed Ipswich Town front-runner Rod Belfitt and pocketed £50,000 in exchange for the immensely promising David Johnson.

Rod, a tall, strong Yorkshireman best known for his contribution as a reserve during the halcyon days of Don Revie's Leeds United, was valued at £80,000 but never looked remotely comfortable during his 11 months at Goodison, lacking the finesse to succeed at the top level.

To be fair, the odds were always stacked against him. Arriving in November 1972, shortly after Joe Royle suffered a long-term injury, he was paired first with Alan Whittle, then with fellow newcomers Bernie Wright and Joe Harper, all in the space of six weeks. Consequently there was little chance to forge the type of goal-scoring partnership needed to lift the floundering Blues up the League table.

Rod moved on to Sunderland in October 1973, but achieved little on Wearside or with his subsequent clubs. An intelligent man who was qualified as a draughtsman, he returned to his former occupation on retiring from League football in 1976.

BORN: Doncaster, Yorkshire, 30.10.45. GAMES: 16 (2). GOALS: 3. OTHER CLUBS: Leeds United 64/5-71/2 (73, 17); Ipswich Town 71/2-72/3 (40, 13); Sunderland 73/4-74/5 (39, 4); Fulham *on loan* 74/5 (6, 1); Huddersfield Town 74/5-75/6 (34, 8).

1972/73

PETER SCOTT

Gritty full-back Peter Scott was an accomplished athlete who lacked nothing in terms of speed, strength and effort but whose command of the game's more delicate techniques was rather less impressive.

The enthusiastic Merseysider - an England youth international destined to win Northern Ireland caps through parental qualification - made his First Division debut at Ipswich on the opening day of 1971/72, showing his versatility by deputising for the injured Colin Harvey in midfield. In the same match, right-back Tommy Wright damaged his knee and thus was Peter handed an extended run in the number-two shirt.

An unorthodox, penguin-like running style created a misleading impression of laborious movement, but rarely was he outstripped, even by the most fleet-footed of opponents. Unfortunately, his ball control and distribution were not of the highest order, and successive managers, Harry Catterick and Billy Bingham, opted to look elsewhere as they searched for a polished long-term replacement for the ailing Wright. After lingering for several seasons on the fringe of the senior squad, Peter joined York City in December 1975, going on to give worthy service, both at Bootham Crescent, and later at Aldershot.

BORN: Liverpool, 19.9.52. GAMES: 48 (2). GOALS: 2. HONOURS: 10 Northern Ireland caps (75-79). OTHER CLUBS: Southport *on loan* 73/4 (4, 0); York City 75/6-78/9 (100, 3); Aldershot 78/9-82/3 (121, 2).

1971/72 - 1974/75

ARCHIE STYLES

Perhaps he lacked ambition, maybe he was too casual, conceivably he just didn't get the breaks at the right time, but whatever the reason for Archie Styles' failure to forge an illustrious Everton career, it was a crying shame for both club and player.

After winning England caps at schoolboy and youth level, the locally-born left-back was the subject of heady optimism at Goodison Park. Archie had the speed and strength expected of any young defender, but he was endowed also with a glorious talent for controlling a ball and dispatching it accurately with his left foot.

He was adept at setting up attacks by bending long, raking passes around opponents and into the path of his own forwards, a gift which should have guaranteed a golden future. Instead, when his opportunity came, it slipped away.

Archie's most promising run started in December 1972, when he replaced Henry Newton, but after a lacklustre spell in mid 1973/74, he was sold to Birmingham, a £90,000 makeweight in a multiple deal that saw Bob Latchford move the other way. The rest of his playing days produced little of note, and he retired with his potential unfulfilled.

BORN: Liverpool, 3.9.49. GAMES: 26 (1). GOALS: 0. OTHER CLUBS: Birmingham City 73/4-77/8 (74, 3); Peterborough United 78/9 (32, 1); Portsmouth 79/80 (26, 0).

1972/73 - 1973/74

GARY JONES

The glittering talent of Gary Jones flickered tantalisingly across the Goodison stage, only to be lost amid bitter frustration at a time when it should have been burning at its brightest.

When the mercurial Merseyside-born flankman emerged in the early seventies, he was feted by enthusiastic pundits who detected a hint of greatness in his apparently effortless ability to outwit defenders, and the Gwladys Street choir roared hymns of praise for his unpredictable moments of pure theatre. But sager counsels persisted that while Gary could entertain bewitchingly, sometimes it was at the expense of the team effort. Reaching the penalty-spot with a flashy, wrong-footed corner or indulging in a spot of impromptu ball-juggling were acceptable in their place, but team-mates did not always appreciate them in the middle of a well-rehearsed move.

Tactical shortcomings and lapses of concentration apart, Gary had everything. His fabulous skill in both feet was complemented by speed, strength and courage, and the precision of his crosses was tailor-made for centre-forward Bob Latchford. Naturally right-sided, he was arguably most effective on the left wing, from which he relished cutting inside to create mayhem.

The bulk of his senior games were played in mid decade under Billy Bingham, who was once heard to speculate wistfully over the Jones potential to emulate George Best, but the relationship between player and manager deteriorated and ended in acrimony. The situation came to a head when Gary disagreed publicly with his substitution at home to Leeds in March 1976, and that summer he was sold to Birmingham for £110,000. It was an unsatisfactory ending to an Everton tenure that, had a golden gift been harnessed, surely must have produced untold glory. A brief stint at St Andrews was followed by an American interlude before Gary returned to his native city to run a pub.

BORN: Liverpool, 5.1.51. GAMES: 90 (7). GOALS: 14.
OTHER CLUBS: Birmingham City 76/7-77/8 (35, 1);
Fort Lauderdale Strikers, USA.

1970/71 - 1975/76

JOHN CONNOLLY

When spindly flankman John Connolly was bobbing and weaving past a possee of bemused defenders, conjuring up a rare image that hovered somewhere between graceful greyhound and runaway rabbit, he was simply devastating. Indeed, there were days when his marker would be lucky to get a kick of the ball as the blond, curly-haired Scot revelled in his tormenting art.

But John was a player who needed to perform well all the time or his confidence would slump alarmingly. On such occasions - not being the tenacious type who would tackle back and fill in as an extra midfielder when the tide was flowing against him - he tended to become anonymous, a luxury any team could ill afford.

Harry Catterick was in the process of recovering from a heart attack when, anxious to secure John's services before other clubs stepped up their interest, he dashed to a Carlisle rendezvous in March 1972 to conclude a £75,000 deal with St Johnstone. Replacing the departed Johnny Morrissey on the left wing, the newcomer missed only one game in 1972/73, though a rather threadbare Everton attack failed to make the most of his teasing crosses.

Despite an early success against each of the Manchester clubs, John's own contribution to the goal tally was meagre, which was surprising for one who struck the ball so cleanly and who had scored freely for the Saints. Nonetheless, he played well enough to win a Scotland call-up that summer and hopes were high for a fruitful future.

Sadly, the gifted Glaswegian fell victim to injuries, including a broken leg in an FA Cup tie against non-League Altrincham in January 1974 which sidelined him for a year, and he was never quite the same force again. In 1976 his transfer request was agreed and that September a fee of £90,000 took him to Birmingham City, where he was reunited with erstwhile colleague Gary Jones. Soon there followed a move to Newcastle, before he joined Hibernian, whose fans nurse a traditional yen for tricky wingmen. It was an ideal place for John to end his playing days.

BORN: Glasgow, 13.6.50. GAMES: 112 (4). GOALS: 16.
HONOURS: 1 Scotland cap (73).
OTHER CLUBS: St Johnstone 67/8-71/2 (96, 41); Birmingham City 76/7-77/8 (57, 9);
Newcastle United 78/9-79/80 (49, 10); Hibernian 80/1-81/2 (40, 8).

1971/72 - 1975/76

DAI DAVIES

It's strange but true: Dai Davies was to win more than half a century of caps between his country's posts, yet in nearly seven years with Everton - admittedly a period before the bulk of his international experience - he never inspired total confidence. The big Welshman, a former teacher who was not short of self-belief, was technically correct and seemed to have all the attributes required of a top custodian; however, he was prone to inconsistency, collecting crosses expertly in one match, then floundering indecisively in the next.

A £20,000 acquisition from Swansea in December 1970, Dai was given two senior outings in the spring, and when Andy Rankin departed in late 1971, it seemed that the brave, enthusiastic newcomer was being groomed as Gordon West's ultimate successor. But the arrival of David Lawson scotched that theory, and Dai was not given another chance until September 1974. Having waited so patiently, he retained his place for the rest of the season, then shared duties with David for the next two, before making an £8,000 move to Wrexham in September 1977.

Later he struck the finest form of his career, serving Swansea ably in the First Division, and setting an appearance record for a Welsh 'keeper that stood until broken by Neville Southall in 1991.

BORN: Ammanford, South Wales, 1.4.48.
GAMES: 94. GOALS: 0. HONOURS: 52 Wales caps (75-82).
OTHER CLUBS: Swansea City 69/70-70/1 (9, 0);
Swansea City *on loan* 73/4 (6, 0); Wrexham 77/8-80/1 (144, 0);
Swansea City 81/2-82/3 (71, 0); Tranmere Rovers 83/4 (42, 0).

1970/71 - 1976/77

MICK BUCKLEY

No insult is intended to Mick Buckley - it might even be taken as a compliment - but an apt way of describing the diminutive midfielder is as a less inspired version of Colin Harvey. That is not to say the competent Mancunian was not effective, merely that he played in the style of his predecessor without reaching the same standard; after all, very few did.

Mick, a youth international who spurned his home-town clubs to join Everton, was given his senior baptism by Harry Catterick in March 1972, going on to do his best work - and gain England under-23 caps - in three mid-seventies seasons under Billy Bingham. A slick ball-player endowed with stamina and a waspish tackle that belied his slight frame, he was always alive to attacking opportunities and particularly adept at swift inter-changes of short passes. However, although Mick could trick opponents, he lacked the explosive acceleration to leave them in his wake, and also might be faulted for a poor goal tally.

In 1977 he suffered through injuries, and with the likes of Trevor Ross and Andy King pushing him to the fringe of the team, he joined Sunderland for £80,000 in August 1978. Mick had performed with spirit and skill for Everton, but ultimate success had just eluded him.

BORN: Manchester, 4.11.53. GAMES: 149 (7). GOALS: 12.
OTHER CLUBS: Sunderland 78/9-82/3 (121, 7);
Hartlepool United 83/4 (6, 0); Carlisle United 83/4 (25, 2);
Middlesbrough 84/5 (27, 0).

1971/72 - 1977/78

DAVID JOHNSON

Everton signed David Johnson twice, yet never saw the best of the dashing dark-haired striker. Blues fans will recall the promising but unrefined efforts of a quick, brave and eager youth, and the more polished but less productive contribution of a 30-year-old in an unsettled team; unfortunately their only glimpses of the England centre-forward at his formidable peak came when he visited Goodison, first with Ipswich Town and later with Liverpool.

Local lad David signed for Everton on leaving school, rising to make his First Division bow at Burnley in January 1971. That day at Turf Moor he netted the first of a remarkable sequence of debut goals for the club, which was to continue in the FA, League and European Cups. David tasted further success in his first encounter with the Reds, his opportunism securing the points at Goodison in November 1971, and he went on to become the only player to score the winner in a Merseyside derby for both Everton and Liverpool.

During those early years, Bill Shankly made several attempts to lure the raw sharp-shooter to Anfield, but Harry Catterick - who used him often in an unsuitable wide position to accommodate Joe Royle - had no intention of selling to his greatest rival. Instead, in November 1972, David left for Ipswich in exchange for Rod Belfitt and £50,000, a deal that did not represent Harry's finest hour in the transfer market.

The scale of Everton's loss became clear over the next nine years as the much-improved Johnson technique earned him most of the game's top honours, though it was a surprise when Howard Kendall paid Liverpool £100,000 to bring him across Stanley Park in August 1982. The enthusiastic front-man was still a fine athlete and he worked hard, but his most effective days were behind him; the goals did not flow, and in March 1984 he joined Manchester City. David, who went on to fleeting stints at Tulsa and Preston, would go down as the man Everton sold too soon.

BORN: Liverpool, 23.10.51. GAMES: 91 (12). GOALS: 20.
HONOURS: 8 England caps (75-80).
OTHER CLUBS: Ipswich Town 72/3-75/6 (137, 35);
Liverpool 76/7-81/2 (148, 55); Barnsley *on loan* 83/4 (4, 1);
Manchester City 83/4 (6, 1); Tulsa Roughnecks, USA;
Preston North End 84/5 (24, 3).

1970/71 - 1972/73 & 1982/83 - 1983/84

DAVID LAWSON

When Harry Catterick parted with £80,000 in the summer of 1972 to make Huddersfield Town's David Lawson the costliest goalkeeper in British transfer history, the quiet 24-year-old north-easterner was handed an opportunity to forge a top-flight future which, a few years previously, he could hardly have expected. To that date, his career had encompassed early rejection by Newcastle United, a brief stint with doomed Bradford Park Avenue and an unsuccessful trial with Liverpool, before a season and a half of creditable displays for the Terriers had placed him in the shop window. Sadly, the slender custodian - nicknamed 'Bambi' for his leggy, almost fragile appearance - was not destined for glory commensurate with that record fee.

The Blues' manager - who did not, presumably, see his earlier acquisition, Dai Davies, as a worthy successor to the declining Gordon West - made David his undisputed number one, and initial indications were encouraging. The newcomer was courageous and agile, and his constructive throw-outs were the launchpad for many attacks, but as a couple of seasons passed, a lack of consistency emerged. One moment he would make a blindingly brilliant save, then the next he might drop an innocuous cross. Perhaps he lacked self-confidence; certainly he never dominated his penalty area in the manner expected of an Everton 'keeper, his reluctance to shout for the ball tending to create indecision among the men in front of him.

After suffering an injury in September 1974, David could not reclaim his place from his Welsh rival, and spent the rest of that campaign in the reserves. Over the next two terms he shared senior duties with Dai - in 1977 he played in all three League Cup Final encounters with Aston Villa and both FA Cup semi-final clashes with Liverpool - before joining Luton for £15,000 in October 1978. David went on to give stalwart service to Stockport County before leaving the game.

BORN: Wallsend, Tyneside, 22.12.47. GAMES: 150. GOALS: 0.
OTHER CLUBS: Bradford Park Avenue 67/8-68/9 (13, 0);
Huddersfield Town 70/1-71/2 (51, 0); Luton Town 78/9 (5, 0);
Stockport County 78/9-80/1 (106, 0).

1972/73 - 1976/77

MIKE BERNARD

Ball-winners don't come more fearsome than Mike Bernard - well, it is hard to imagine anyone with a *more* vigorous tackle remaining inside the laws of the game - but it would be unjust to brand the heavily-built midfielder cum full-back as a mere hatchet man. Indeed, the vigorous Salopian's all-round ability was widely underrated; his control was sure, his distribution sharp and precise, and it was significant that two such eminent footballing judges as Sir Alf Ramsey and Harry Catterick placed their faith in him early in his career.

The England manager, perhaps seeing something of his old warhorse Nobby Stiles in the Bernard make-up, blooded the Stoke City stripling at under-23 level, while the Everton boss, anxious to rebuild a side that was creaking alarmingly just two terms after taking the title, laid out £140,000 to acquire his services in April 1972. Mike arrived at Goodison just a month after helping the Potters win the League Cup, and could be excused if he thought the move was a prelude to further medals. Alas, another honour was never to come his way.

His first season with the Blues - Harry's last in charge - coincided with a frustrating period of transition, though Mike performed consistently well in harness with Colin Harvey and Howard Kendall, thriving particularly in the rarified atmosphere of high-pressure encounters such as local derbies. However, in April 1974 Billy Bingham moved him to right-back, where he was to remain throughout the mid seventies. Mike let no one down in the number-two shirt - his courage in battling on through extra time while carrying an injury in the first replay of the 1977 League Cup Final against Aston Villa typified his approach - though the new role reduced the scope of his contribution.

In July 1977 - with Everton's latest boss, Gordon Lee, having shown preference for Terry Darracott - Mike joined Olham, whom he served briefly before injury forced an early retirement.

BORN: Shrewsbury, Shropshire, 10.1.48.
GAMES: 161 (10). GOALS: 8.
OTHER CLUBS: Stoke City 65/6-71/2 (136, 6);
Oldham Athletic 77/8-78/9 (6, 0).

1972/73 - 1976/77

| GEORGE TELFER | RONNIE GOODLASS |

On the rare occasions during a football match when George Telfer walked, he appeared to have a perpetual limp, as though one leg was shorter than the other; but when the stocky, powerful forward was sprinting at full stretch - most of the time, it seemed - he could outstrip the majority of defenders. Arguably, however, his high-velocity approach was insufficiently subtle, and he might have been more effective if all that effort had been spiced with a little more deliberation.

George was at his best in the centre as a front-running foil for Bob Latchford in the mid seventies, and his contribution suffered when he was shifted to a wide role. An instinctive finisher with a rasping shot, he scored some eye-catching goals, particularly during 1975/76, his most productive campaign, but he lacked the all-round skills demanded of a striker in a side with Championship aspirations.

The Telfer star began to fall with the advent of Duncan McKenzie in late 1976, but although injury ruined several opportunities to re-establish himself, he remained on the fringe of the squad until 1981. Then, his career going nowhere, George opted for a fresh start in San Diego, later returning to the English game before becoming Football Development Officer for the Merseyside Youth Association.

BORN: Liverpool, 6.7.55. GAMES: 91 (22). GOALS: 22.
OTHER CLUBS: San Diego, USA; Scunthorpe United 81/2-82/3 (36, 11); Altrincham (non-League);
Preston North End 83/4 (2, 0).

Effervescent Scouser Ronnie Goodlass once thrilled millions with a goal that Pele - yes, *that* Pele - would have been proud to claim. The time was April 1977, the setting Upton Park, and the TV cameras were rolling; Bob Latchford knocked the ball back to Ronnie on half-way, it bounced invitingly and, seeing Mervyn Day off his line, the wily left-winger drove it unerringly over the hapless 'keeper's head and into the net. It brought back memories of an effort by the incomparable Brazilian in the 1970 World Cup - only *he* had just missed!

That incident afforded the most colourful moment in an Everton career that had promised much but didn't quite take off. Ronnie, a stocky flankman adept at skipping past tackles and crossing accurately, enjoyed his sole successful season in 1976/77. That term he helped the Blues reach the League Cup Final, and came close to a Wembley appearance in the FA Cup - he outwitted Tommy Smith to set up Bryan Hamilton's controversially disallowed 'goal' in the semi-final against Liverpool - but was ousted in 1977/78 by newcomer Dave Thomas.

Ronnie, a match-winner on his day but lacking consistency, joined Dutch club Breda for £100,000 in October 1977, later continuing his travels in this country and abroad before returning to live and work on Merseyside.

BORN: Liverpool, 6.9.53. GAMES: 47 (4). GOALS: 2.
OTHER CLUBS: NAC Breda and Den Haag, Holland;
Fulham 80/1 (22, 2); Scunthorpe United 81/2 (9, 0);
South China, Hong Kong; Tranmere Rovers 83/4-84/5 (21, 0).

| 1973/74 - 1980/81 | 1975/76 - 1977/78 |

DAVE CLEMENTS

Dave Clements was a man of stature. As a character of strength, integrity and intelligence, he earned widespread respect during his mid-seventies sojourn at Goodison; as a footballer of calmness, skill and solidity, he would surely have achieved much more had he spent his prime in the service of Everton.

The blond, curly-haired Ulsterman was signed for the Blues by his former international boss, Billy Bingham, from Sheffield Wednesday for £60,000 in September 1973. Dave, a teenage winger with Wolves who blossomed into a polished left-sided midfielder with Coventry and showed the versatility to fill in at full-back for the Owls, was a cultured passer who seemed to play the game unhurriedly, in his own time, a sure sign of class. Blessed with a muscular physique, he was adept at retaining possession by shielding the ball, and it was a rare opponent who hustled him out of his rather measured stride. In fact, had Dave been that crucial and oft-quoted 'half a yard' quicker, he would have been a magnificent player; as it was, he would have been a worthy asset to any squad.

Of course, like so many Everton men of his era, he suffered from frequent team changes, and although he played most of his games in his preferred midfield role - from which he struck the goal that 'held' non-League Altrincham to an FA Cup draw at Goodison in January 1975 - he was withdrawn into defence towards the end.

Dave, ever a positive influence on the club's youngsters, thought deeply about his soccer and it surprised few when he took the reins of the Northern Ireland side in March 1975 while still a First Division regular. However, when the opportunity of a transfer to New York Cosmos - Pele *et al* - came up in January 1976, he gave up the early chance of a long-term career in international management to cross the Atlantic.

BORN: Larne, Northern Ireland, 15.9.45. GAMES: 95 (3). GOALS: 8.
HONOURS: 48 Northern Ireland caps (65-76).
OTHER CLUBS: Portadown, Northern Ireland; Coventry City 64/5-71/2 (229, 26);
Sheffield Wednesday 71/2-73/4 (78, 0); New York Cosmos, USA.
MANAGER: Northern Ireland (75-76).

1973/74 - 1975/76

MIKE PEJIC

Mike Pejic was not a man with whom to take liberties. Invariably grim of expression, his boxer's profile jutting pugnaciously above a square, powerful frame, the England international left-back presented a truly daunting prospect for all those brave souls who plied their trade as First Division right-wingers throughout the seventies. Of course, appearances can be deceptive, but in Mike's case they were not, as unwary opponents were apt to discover early in a game as that first ferocious tackle came snapping in. Yet it would be overwhelmingly unfair to pigeon-hole the rugged fitness fanatic as a performer who relied unduly on his formidable strength. He was comfortable in possession, a smooth and reliable passer, and an overlapper who could carry the ball at speed before delivering a precise cross.

With so much to offer, Mike was a natural target for Gordon Lee, who had been quick to identify the need for a classy left-sided defender after taking over an ailing Everton side early in 1977. Accordingly he made the 27-year-old Midlander of Yugoslav parentage his first signing, paying Stoke £150,000, and reaping an immediate dividend as the newcomer played a major role in the Blues' rapid improvement.

In the following season, Mike formed a high-quality left-flank unit with midfielder Martin Dobson and winger Dave Thomas, and an England recall was mooted. But in the winter of 1978 he was hampered by pelvic discomfort, eventually collapsing in severe pain at Leeds, and was sidelined for the rest of the campaign. Significantly, perhaps, it was not long before Everton slumped out of contention for the title.

Thereafter Mike seemed to recover, but with John Bailey doing well in the number-three shirt, he was allowed to join Aston Villa for £250,000 in July 1979. Ten games later his pelvic problem recurred and he was forced to retire. Though often described as a loner, he always found time to help young players, later coaching at Port Vale and managing Chester City.

BORN: Chesterton, Staffordshire, 25.1.50.
GAMES: 93. GOALS: 2. HONOURS: 4 England caps (74).
OTHER CLUBS: Stoke City 68/9-76/7 (274, 6);
Aston Villa 79/80 (10, 0).
MANAGER: Chester City (94-95).

1976/77 - 1978/79

JIM PEARSON

He was blond, he was Scottish and he was a centre-forward, but it was monstrously unreasonable to expect Jim Pearson to offer more telling similarities with the most idolised star in Goodison history. In fact, far from a new 'Golden Vision' - as Alex Young was dubbed so reverently - Jim was more in the nature of a 'Golden Toothpick'; so spare and bony was his frame that his kit seemed to hang on him. Yet when he arrived as a £100,000 signing from St Johnstone in July 1974, largely unknown outside his native land despite being an under-23 international, there were understandable hopes that another gem had been unearthed from the traditionally bountiful seam of talent north of the border.

There were some encouraging signs: Jim possessed delicate close control, laid the ball off deftly, and despite his lack of weight, was an aerial combatant to be feared, as he showed with a brilliant diving header into Derby's net to cap a splendid personal display in a March 1977 FA Cup tie. He was a tireless chaser, too, constantly seeking to harry defenders into mistakes of the type made by Emlyn Hughes in the subsequent semi-final, the Reds' skipper slipping under pressure and allowing his tormentor to cross for Duncan McKenzie to score.

However, Jim lacked the instant burst of acceleration so vital to strikers striving to turn half-chances into goals, and his long-term tally was disappointing. There were times, also, when impetuosity appeared to affect his concentration, and on such occasions his all-round contribution suffered. A string of injuries added to his frustration and it was no surprise when, in August 1978, he sought new pastures, joining Newcastle for £70,000. Jim didn't linger on Tyneside, though, moving first to the United States, and then re-crossing the Atlantic to become player-manager of non-League Gateshead. A friendly, bubbly man who loved to entertain team-mates with a song, he went on to work for a sports-shoe firm in the North West.

BORN: Falkirk, Scotland, 24.3.53. GAMES: 97 (19). GOALS: 19.
OTHER CLUBS: St Johnstone 70/1-73/4 (105, 39);
Newcastle United 78/9-79/80 (11, 3).

1974/75 - 1977/78

ROGER KENYON

The springtime loss of a star centre-half is the sort of debilitating handicap that can shatter a Championship challenge; that Everton shrugged off the enforced absence of Brian Labone for the eight-match climax to 1969/70 - and lifted the crown in glorious fashion - reflected vast credit on the England international's callow deputy, a lean, hard Lancastrian named Roger Kenyon. The 21-year-old was rewarded with lavish praise, one massively mature display at Anfield being singled out for particular attention, and when injury ended Brian's career in 1971, Roger was a ready-made replacement. In fact, no one who had monitored his progress since his apprenticeship days was surprised; already he had passed one searching test, as a stand-in for John Hurst in the 1968 FA Cup semi-final against Leeds, and was clearly the stuff of which top-flight defenders were made.

Roger's method was to attack the ball vigorously, his aerial timing and ruthlessness in the tackle being complemented by exceptional speed, a combination which often enabled him to close down on opponents and snuff out attacks before they had time to develop. He was more than an out-and-out stopper, however, having the control and precision to build imaginatively from the back. With so much ability, Roger seemed bound to play for his country, but the masterly Roy McFarland barred the way, and the nearest he got to a full cap was three sessions on the substitutes' bench in 1975. The year before, he had shown resilience in recovering from serious wounds received in a car crash, and was dogged frequently by niggling injuries, especially in the late seventies when his senior appearances became less regular.

In 1979, Roger left Goodison and took his first winner's medal in senior soccer - he played too few games for a title gong in 1970 - though he had to cross the Atlantic to collect it. Having helped Vancouver Whitecaps to top their league, he put in a brief stint with Bristol City and then retired.

BORN: Blackpool, 4.1.49. GAMES: 289 (17). GOALS: 9.
OTHER CLUBS: Vancouver Whitecaps, Canada;
Bristol City 79/80 (4, 0).

1967/68 - 1978/79

TERRY DARRACOTT

Terry Darracott embodied the spirit of Everton. His dedication to the Royal Blue cause was absolute, and despite enjoying only one season as an undisputed regular during 11 years in the senior squad, his enthusiasm remained undimmed to the end. A rough-hewn defender of limited finesse, Terry had endearingly few illusions about his own ability. If he made a mistake he never offered an excuse, and the fans warmed to the down-to-earth approach of an engaging character who was, after all, one of their own.

He made his debut as a 17-year-old apprentice, coming in at left-back, though he was to make most of his appearances on the opposite flank. Some canny observers, however, maintained that Terry was most effective as a one-on-one marker, and cite an occasion at Goodison when he shackled George Best so effectively that the brilliant Irishman was, for once, reduced to passenger status. The staple constituents of the Darracott game were a jarring tackle and outstanding courage; once he played on after biting through his lip in a collision, the wound so gory that colleague Andy King fainted! It would be unfair, though, to imply that he was bereft of technique. His control was rudimentary, but Terry could bend passes deftly around opponents, and he was a specialist at clipping devilishly curling crosses into the penalty box at pace.

His one term of grace was 1973/74, when he missed only six League games, and the nearest he came to an honour was as a losing League Cup finalist in 1977. Thereafter Terry, his form reliable and his Scouse humour a constant boost to morale, continued to drift in and out of an ever-changing side until, in 1979, he opted for a spell in America. Twice more he returned to Goodison, first helping the youngsters, then serving as Colin Harvey's managerial assistant. In 1991, Manchester City made him youth coach and the Maine Road boss, ex-Evertonian Peter Reid, knew that his boys could not learn the game from a more honest source - with a few laughs along the way.

BORN: Liverpool, 6.12.50.
GAMES: 166 (10). GOALS: 0.
OTHER CLUBS: Tulsa Roughnecks, USA;
Wrexham 79/80 (22, 0).

1967/68 - 1978/79

DAVID SMALLMAN

Amid all the comings and goings and repeated disappointments that afflicted Everton throughout the seventies, the untimely demise of David Smallman's career through a horrendous sequence of injuries attracted comparatively low-key publicity. But however much the media might have underestimated the wider significance of the Welsh international marksman's personal misfortune, there was no danger of anyone at the club missing the point: the Blues had lost a gem of rare potential.

David, who cost £75,000 from Wrexham in March 1975, was dark and lithe in the manner of Roy Vernon, but the similarity with his illustrious countryman did not end there. Like the former skipper, he was quick and deadly, a silken dart of a finisher with the true poacher's instinct for taking up dangerous positions.

Manager Billy Bingham had visions of the left-sided newcomer making the perfect long-term foil for Bob Latchford, but it was not to be. In 1975, David suffered ankle problems, then each time he recovered, he was struck down again. A dislocated shoulder, torn hamstring, phlebitis, wrenched knee and broken leg followed each other in quick succession, destroying his confidence. In 1980 'Smokey' Smallman - how he loved a cigarette - returned to Wrexham, but never played League football again.

BORN: Connah's Quay, North Wales, 22.3.53.
GAMES: 23 (3). GOALS: 7. HONOURS: 7 Wales caps (74-75). OTHER CLUBS: Wrexham 72/3-74/5 (101, 38).

1974/75 - 1976/77

NEIL ROBINSON

Likeable local boy Neil Robinson launched his career on his own initiative. The sandy-haired right-back attended a rugby-playing school but, loving the round-ball game, wrote to Everton asking for a trial. He impressed, signed as an apprentice, then worked his way up through the junior sides to make his first-team debut as an 18-year-old stand-in - both Mike Bernard and Terry Darracott were injured - at home to Burnley in January 1976. The Blues lost that day but Neil let no one down, and manager Gordon Lee had enough faith in the youngster's ability to play him in the second replay of the following season's League Cup Final against Aston Villa.

That was only his fourth senior outing, and he looked set to consolidate his future at the club. Neil was dedicated, tenacious and an enterprising overlapper who could also play in midfield, but competition for places was distinctly warm and he never became established. His potential had been spotted, however, and John Toshack took him to Swansea for £70,000 in October 1979. At the Vetch he played a prominent part in the Swans' rise to the First Division in the early eighties, before going on to contribute ably to the causes of Grimsby and Darlington.

BORN: Liverpool, 20.4.57.
GAMES: 17 (5). GOALS: 1.
OTHER CLUBS: Swansea City 79/80-84/5 (123, 7);
Grimsby Town 84/5-87/8 (109, 6);
Darlington 88/9-89/90 (38, 1).

1975/76 - 1978/79

BRYAN HAMILTON

When Bryan Hamilton's thigh deflected a Duncan McKenzie flick into the Liverpool net, everyone inside neutral Maine Road thought the Irish midfielder had put Everton into the 1977 FA Cup Final. It was to become an infamous slice of Blues folklore, of course, that referee Clive Thomas disallowed the effort for alleged handball; the score remained at 2-2, and the Reds marched on to win the replay. Recollections of that bitter incident - which provokes outrage among Everton fans to this day - will dominate any discussion on the short Goodison sojourn of the chunky, dark-haired link-man without doing justice to his ability.

Bryan, who combined tenacity and skill as he laboured ceaselessly on the right flank, arrived as a £40,000 signing from Ipswich in November 1975. In Suffolk he had forged a reputation for goal-scoring, so there was some disappointment when his tally slumped on Merseyside. Though he compensated by precise passing and mature reading of the game, as well as formidable eagerness and lung-power, Bryan yielded his place in 1976/77 - a period of considerable flux - and moved to Millwall for £25,000 that summer. A knowledgeable student of soccer with wide international experience, he went on to build a career in management.

BORN: Belfast, 21.12.46. GAMES: 47 (7). GOALS: 5. HONOURS: 50 Northern Ireland caps (68-80). OTHER CLUBS: Linfield, Northern Ireland; Ipswich Town 71/2-75/6 (153, 43); Millwall 77/8-78/9 (49, 6); Swindon Town 78/9-80/1 (24, 1); Tranmere Rovers 80/1-84/5 (109, 6). MANAGER: Tranmere Rovers (80-85); Wigan Athletic (85-86); Leicester City 86-87; Wigan Athletic (89-93); Northern Ireland (94-97).

1975/76 - 1976/77

KEN McNAUGHT

The heights to which Ken McNaught eventually rose - winning League Championship and European Cup medals after leaving Everton for Aston Villa - are a tribute to the application, self-belief and willingness to heed wise counsel of a young man whom many believed too raw to make the grade. Indeed, as a teenage striker he seemed bound for imminent obscurity until he moved into central defence on the advice of his father, Willie, once of Raith Rovers and Scotland. Yet even after Ken succeeded as a junior stopper and joined Everton, he was hardly regarded as one of the Blues' brightest prospects.

Nothing daunted, he worked to hone his talents, and in January 1975 won his senior call-up. The following term, as manager Billy Bingham experimented with various back-four combinations, Ken - his aerial dynamism and power in the tackle compensating for a slight pace deficiency - became established. In 1976/77, he didn't miss a match, and battled manfully to combat the threat of Aston Villa's rampant Andy Gray in the twice-replayed League Cup Final. The victorious Brummies must have been impressed: that summer they bought Ken for £200,000, and he became a reliable component in their subsequently successful side. Later, on retirement, he turned to coaching north of the border.

BORN: Kirkcaldy, Scotland, 11.1.55. GAMES: 84 (2). GOALS: 3. OTHER CLUBS: Aston Villa 77/8-82/3 (207, 8); West Bromwich Albion 83/4 (42, 1); Manchester City *on loan* 84/5 (7, 0); Sheffield United 85/6 (34, 5).

1974/75 - 1976/77

DUNCAN McKENZIE

That Duncan McKenzie was blessed with a sublime talent was never in doubt; the most appropriate showcase for his extravagant gifts, however, was the subject of passionate debate. Some saw him as a born entertainer who would grace any team, others reckoned that he would produce his best only for a top club on a glittering occasion, while a third lobby - pragmatic, sceptical and significantly large - maintained stoutly that the natural stage for the distinctive McKenzie blend of bravura, whimsy and sleight of foot was the circus ring.

Certainly any team-mate who sprinted 60 yards on a dummy run to create space for Duncan, only to see him delight the fans but then squander possession by over-indulgence in trickery, could be excused for taking the last-mentioned view. His off-the-pitch stunts - leaping over mini-cars, hurling golf balls for vast distances, gravity-defying feats of juggling - boosted his image as a fairground attraction, leaving the football world to despair for what might have been.

Not that Duncan's career was without success. He netted prolifically for Nottingham Forest, Leeds and Anderlecht, and many applauded Everton boss Billy Bingham for his boldness in signing the wiry striker from the Belgians for £200,000 in December 1976. Perhaps the pair might have prospered together, but Billy was sacked a month later, and Duncan's philosophy never sat comfortably with that of new manager Gordon Lee.

Nevertheless he worked hard and there were some splendid displays - such as in the 1977 FA Cup semi-final draw with Liverpool, when he scored a clinical goal and gulled several defenders to lay on a second - before differences in outlook led to the inevitable split. In September 1978, still only 28, he joined Chelsea for £165,000, but he remained a free spirit who never made the most of staggering ability. Might a ringmaster have helped Duncan McKenzie achieve what a dozen football managers couldn't?

BORN: Grimsby, 10.6.50. GAMES: 61 (1). GOALS: 21.
OTHER CLUBS: Nottingham Forest 69/70-73/4 (111, 41);
Mansfield Town *on loan* 69/70 (10, 3); Mansfield Town *on loan* 72/3 (6, 7);
Leeds United 74/5-75/6 (66, 27); Anderlecht, Belgium; Chelsea 78/9 (15, 4);
Blackburn Rovers 78/9-80/1 (74, 16); Tulsa Roughnecks and
Chicago Stings, USA; Hong Kong.

1976/77 - 1977/78

MARTIN DOBSON

In a perfect world, Everton manager Billy Bingham might have built his side around Martin Dobson. The tall, rather stately Lancastrian was a player of immense skill and refinement, his calm, fluent distribution and impeccable control a delight to the eye. Yet although he enjoyed a highly accomplished career, Martin never attained the heights of which many believed him capable, his cultured talents not quite attuned, somehow, to the furious, ultra-competitive business of the modern game.

Not that the muscular midfielder was soft in the way of some gifted but brittle play-makers. Indeed, he was so strong in possession, so determined and clever a shielder of the ball, that it was a shock if he ever lost it, and team-mates used to joke that they could pass to Martin and take a rest. He was forceful in the air, too, and a perceptive reader of developing situations, a shortage of pace being the only instantly definable defect in the Dobson game. It was inescapable, however, that his most devastating football was played when the Blues were dominating a match, rather than in the heat of a rearguard action.

Martin had made his name as captain and creative hub of the exciting young Burnley side of the early seventies. Having figured crucially in the Clarets' Second Division Championship triumph and their encouraging first term back in the top flight - an England call-up was a fitting reward - he became Britain's first £300,000 player when he moved to Goodison in August 1974. Limited by Trevor Brooking's excellence to one more cap, he graced the Everton midfield for five campaigns, prompting intelligently and contributing some fiercely-struck goals, such as the piledriver that climaxed a 40-yard run at Anfield in October 1976.

In 1979, a £100,000 deal took Martin back to Turf Moor, where he flourished once more. Later, he entered management, impressing at Bury, but not with Bristol Rovers. It is to be hoped that soccer has not seen the last of one of its more gentlemanly and articulate ambassadors.

BORN: Blackburn, Lancashire, 14.2.48. GAMES: 230. GOALS: 40.
HONOURS: 5 England caps (74).
OTHER CLUBS: Burnley 67/8-74/5 (224, 43) and 79/80-83/4 (186, 20);
Bury 83/4-85/6 (61, 4). MANAGER: Bury (84-89); Bristol Rovers (91).

1974/75 - 1978/79

BOB LATCHFORD

The late seventies was a time of sore trial for all those who viewed their football from a Royal Blue perspective. Since winning the Championship as the decade dawned, Everton had floundered in the League and failed to lighten the gloom by lifting a cup; meanwhile, across Stanley Park at Anfield, their all-conquering neighbours were rising to ever-greater heights in both domestic and European competition. Clearly, if trophies were out of reach, then the very least the long-suffering fans needed was a folk-hero in the true Goodison tradition, a man to lift beleaguered spirits, one incontrovertible source of pride in painful arguments with smug friends and workmates who followed the Reds. At last, in 1977/78, he emerged, in the burly shape of Bob Latchford, whose quest to become the first player in six years to net 30 times in a First Division season fired the national imagination.

In fact the modest Midlander, whose brothers Peter and Dave were professional goalkeepers, had been at the club since February 1974, when he left Birmingham City at a cost of £350,000 in a package deal which took Howard Kendall and Archie Styles to St Andrews. That spring he silenced doubts about his speed and subtlety, two assets which he possessed to a higher degree than certain pundits maintained, enjoying a spell of seven goals in as many games and giving birth to a renewed wave of optimism in the Blues' camp.

Bob was a born opportunist, brilliant in the air - his speciality was the diving, near-post header - and capable of striking from every conceivable angle and range. He had an instinct for taking up dangerous positions and his fine touch made him an expert at laying the ball off, though a typical centre-forward's right and proper greed for goals ensured that he passed only when he spotted no opening for himself. There were those who criticised him for lack of graft outside the penalty area, but so productive was his expenditure of energy *inside* the box that none could legitimately cavil at his contribution.

However, as Billy Bingham's frequently-changed team struggled to achieve consistency, Bob's League tally during his initial three full seasons was more respectable than remarkable. A clue to the riches ahead came early in 1977, when his form played a major part in the revival wrought by new manager Gordon Lee, though his goals in both replays of the League Cup Final could not avert defeat by Aston Villa. The golden campaign that followed etched the name of Latchford indelibly on the Blues' roll of honour, and it ended in suitably dramatic fashion. To reach that elusive total of 30, and claim a £10,000 prize put up by the Daily Express, he had to score twice in the final game, at home to Chelsea. Everton romped to victory though Bob left it until the last 18 minutes before a precise nod and a penalty sent Goodison wild. Ironically, the feat brought little personal profit - he shared his award with footballing charities, his team-mates and the groundstaff, pocketing less than £200 himself - but the glory was all his own.

Bob's bountiful spell won him England recognition, but never again was he to taste such heady success. As he approached his thirties, injuries became more frequent and in July 1981 he moved to Swansea for £125,000, proving he was far from finished by netting regularly for the Welshmen. At Goodison, his name will always be synonymous with that 30-goal epic, but the easy-going marksman whom Gordon Lee urged to become more ruthless, was no one-season wonder; indeed, no one had scored more post-war League goals for Everton until his total of 106 was overhauled by Graeme Sharp in 1990. Bob Latchford might rue the fact that his marksmanship produced no silverware, but he can point to one memorable achievement: at a time of Liverpool supremacy, he was the man who enabled Evertonians to hold their heads high.

BORN: Birmingham, 18.1.51. GAMES: 286 (3). GOALS: 138.
HONOURS: 12 England caps (77-79). OTHER CLUBS: Birmingham City 68/9-73/4 (160, 68); Swansea City 81/2-83/4 (87, 35); NAC Breda, Holland; Coventry City 84/5 (12, 2); Lincoln City 85/6 (15, 2); Newport County 85/6 (20, 5).

1973/74 - 1980/81

DAVID JONES

David Jones had the perfect physique and boundless enthusiasm but lacked the necessary finesse to become a top-class defender. A former captain of England Youth, he was the subject of considerable optimism at Goodison when he made his senior debut as a 19-year-old. Subsequent under-21 recognition showed that independent judges nourished similar hopes, but regular exposure to First Division football highlighted too many technical shortcomings.

The brawny Merseysider enjoyed his first settled run at left-back, one of Everton's problem positions, in the final quarter of 1975/76. Though he appeared rather ponderous, his deceptively long stride covered the ground quickly, his tackling was jarringly firm and he was proficient enough in the air to deputise in the centre. On the ball, however, he let himself down too often with wild distribution, tending to opt for a full-blooded kick when a more subtle touch would have been preferable.

After switching to the right to accommodate Mike Pejic in 1977, David held his place until Achilles tendon trouble and a broken elbow laid him low in 1978. On regaining fitness, he was recalled, before moving to Coventry for £275,000 in the summer of 1979, though sadly the rest of his career was dogged by injuries. Subsequently David emerged as one of the most promising young managers in the country.

BORN: Liverpool, 17.8.56. GAMES: 95 (8). GOALS: 2.
OTHER CLUBS: Coventry City 79/80-80/1 (11, 0);
Seiko, Hong Kong; Preston North End 83/4-84/5 (50, 1).
MANAGER: Stockport (95-97); Southampton (97-).

1975/76 - 1978/79

BRUCE RIOCH

Everton fans were exultant when manager Billy Bingham paid Derby County £200,000 for Bruce Rioch in December 1976, and why not? Their club had acquired one of Britain's most admired footballers, a multi-talented midfielder whose combination of flair and steel was expected to become a dominant influence on a side striving with increasing desperation to regain parity with their ultra-successful Anfield neighbours.

Certainly, Bruce was splendidly equipped for the challenge. A precise and imaginative distributor with a scorching left-foot shot, he was ruthless in the tackle - at times excessively so, some might say - and boasted searing acceleration over that vital first ten yards. His playing attributes were capped by a strong personality which commanded respect from colleagues; here, surely, was the man to lift the Blues. Yet somehow, despite several storming displays, it never happened. Admittedly, he was not helped by cartilage problems, and it's possible that he didn't relish the replacement of Billy Bingham by Gordon Lee. Whatever the reason, Everton never saw the best of Bruce and a mere 11 months after his arrival at Goodison, he returned to the Baseball Ground for £150,000. He went on to captain Scotland in the 1978 World Cup, before turning to management in the eighties.

BORN: Aldershot, Hampshire, 6.9.47. GAMES: 39. GOALS: 4. HONOURS: 24 Scotland caps (75-78).
OTHER CLUBS: Luton Town 64/5-68/9 (149, 47); Aston Villa 69/70-73/4 (156, 34); Derby County 73/4-76/7 (106, 34) and 77/8-79/80 (41, 4); Birmingham City *on loan* 78/9 (3, 0); Sheffield United *on loan* 78/9 (8, 1); Seattle Sounders, USA; Torquay United 80/1-83/4 (71, 6).
MANAGER: Torquay United (82-84); Middlesbrough (86-90); Millwall (90-92); Bolton (92-95); Arsenal (95-96).

1976/77 - 1977/78

DAVE THOMAS

Some wingers are lethal when they sprint for the byline, others create greatest havoc by cutting inside. Sensible full-backs soon pick up such preferences and attempt to jockey their opponent towards the area where he is weakest. In the case of Dave Thomas at his best, however, such tactics were to no avail; he could take either option and destroy a defence in the twinkling of an eye.

His method owed much to speed, even more to sleight of foot, but what marked him out as special was his ability to make crosses accurately and with perfect weight from almost any angle. This rare gift was all the more devastating because he could deliver with either foot, thus not having to waste time, as so many players do, in switching the ball to his favoured side.

The Thomas talent was much in demand among Britain's top clubs when he appeared on the market in August 1977, and Everton manager Gordon Lee was cock-a-hoop with his £200,000 capture from Queen's Park Rangers. Dave, a one-time teenage prodigy at Burnley who won England caps and narrowly missed a title medal at Loftus Road, was expected to be a key factor in the Blues' renewed Championship challenge, and so it proved. Although that prize eluded them - they finished a creditable third - the dashing flankman who scorned shinpads and played with socks around his ankles was a source of inspiration, his immaculate service from the left touchline helping Bob Latchford to net 30 League goals.

Much was expected of such a deadly combination in 1978/79, but although Lee's men managed a top-four placing, the anticipated sparkle was missing. Swingeing changes to the playing staff ensued, an unsettled Dave asked for a move, and in October 1979 he was sold to Wolves for £420,000. A quiet man who preferred gardening to socialising, he never hit the heights again as his career wound down at a succession of clubs. Meanwhile Everton were left to ponder on how they had failed to make the long-term most of a brilliant entertainer.

BORN: Kirkby-in-Ashfield, Nottinghamshire, 5.10.50.
GAMES: 84. GOALS: 6. HONOURS: 8 England caps (74-75).
OTHER CLUBS: Burnley 66/7-72/3 (157, 19); Queen's Park Rangers 72/3-76/7 (182, 29); Wolverhampton Wanderers 79/80 (10, 0); Vancouver Whitecaps, Canada; Middlesbrough 81/2 (13, 1); Portsmouth 82/3-84/5 (30, 0).

1977/78 - 1978/79

GEOFF NULTY

Geoff Nulty had every reason to be delighted with his £40,000 move from newly-relegated Newcastle to Everton in the summer of 1978: it enabled him to stay in the First Division, it renewed his link with former Magpies boss Gordon Lee, and it meant a return to his native Merseyside. Sadly, however, Goodison was to be the scene of a personal calamity.

During their days together at St James' Park, Gordon had heaped praise on the utility man and it was no surprise when he acquired his services for the Blues. However, although Geoff was an experienced midfielder, he was most accomplished as a central defender, and it was perhaps unfortunate that much of his time at Everton was spent in the more forward role. A tireless worker and abrasive ball-winner, he was strong in the air and read the game intelligently, but his distribution was too deliberate to thrive in a top-class engine room.

Accordingly Geoff never cemented a regular place, but was proving a useful squad member when he ran out for the fateful home clash with Liverpool in March 1980. A tackle with Jimmy Case resulted in the Evertonian being stretchered off with damaged knee ligaments, and he never played again. Geoff remained in the game for some years, coaching first at Goodison and then, still with Gordon Lee, at Preston.

BORN: Prescot, Lancashire, 13.2.49. GAMES: 32 (6). GOALS: 2. OTHER CLUBS: Burnley 69/70-74/5 (130, 20); Newcastle United 74/5-77/8 (101, 11).

1978/79 - 1979/80

MICKY WALSH

Nothing went right for poor Micky Walsh after his £325,000 transfer from Blackpool to Everton in August 1978. He was fixed in the public mind as the man whose fabulous strike had won him a TV goal-of-the-season award during his Bloomfield Road days, and there were demanding denizens of the Goodison terraces who seemed to believe that he should repeat the feat every time he ran on to the pitch. Manager Gordon Lee was more realistic, merely seeing him as an ideal striking partner for Bob Latchford. Unfortunately, neither expectation was to be met.

It was not for want of trying, though. In his early games, Micky - who was brave, quick and could control the ball at speed - suffered chronic luck and endured the sort of drought that every marksman dreads but which afflicts them all at some time. Several shots struck the woodwork, he missed a hatful of chances, and a couple of efforts that would have rivalled his TV spectacular went narrowly wide.

Seven months after his arrival, having netted just three times in 29 outings, the disillusioned Eire international - his father hailed from the Republic - moved to QPR in a straight swap for Peter Eastoe. After faring little better at Loftus Road, he tasted success in Portugal, a deservedly happy ending for an honest and talented professional.

BORN: Chorley, Lancashire, 13.8.54. GAMES: 26 (3). GOALS: 3. HONOURS: 22 Republic of Ireland caps (76-85). OTHER CLUBS: Blackpool 73/4-77/8 (180, 72); Queen's Park Rangers 78/9-80/1 (18, 3); Porto, Portugal.

1978/79

GEORGE WOOD

If footballers were judged solely on first impressions, then George Wood needn't have turned up for his second match. At least, that was a popular view on the Goodison terraces as the burly, blond Scot endured a traumatic debut following his £150,000 signing from Blackpool in August 1977. The Blues went down 3-1 to Nottingham Forest and the new 'keeper was blamed for all three goals.

Such a dismal introduction might have undermined a less determined individual, but George showed his depth of character in recovering to play the finest football of his life during his first two seasons on Merseyside. In 1977/78 he returned 19 clean sheets, going on to hit even more impressive form in the subsequent campaign, which culminated in well-deserved full international honours.

George cut an imposing figure between the posts, hurling his 6ft 3in frame to all corners of his goal with an athleticism that was due partly to natural ability but also to hard work on the training ground. Perhaps he was better at stopping shots than gathering crosses - an observation that can be made about countless custodians - but his huge hands held on to most of the missiles that came his way, and he won over most of the fans who had once been so critical.

Come 1979/80, however, a series of indifferent performances saw him ousted by Martin Hodge, and during the summer George was sold to Arsenal, his fee unchanged from three years earlier. At Highbury he earned distinction by keeping the great Pat Jennings out of the side on merit for nearly a year, and was rewarded by a Scottish recall in time for the 1982 World Cup. George - whose need for contact lenses would have been fallen on avidly by Gwladys Street comedians had it been general knowledge - went on to extend his senior career into its 21st season, finishing at Hereford in the early nineties.

BORN: Douglas, Lanarkshire, 26.9.52. GAMES: 126. GOALS: 0.
HONOURS: 4 Scotland caps (79-82).
OTHER CLUBS: East Stirlingshire 70/1-71/2 (44, 1); Blackpool 71/2-76/7 (117, 0); Arsenal 80/1-82/3 (60, 0); Crystal Palace 83/4-87/8 (192, 0); Cardiff City 87/8-89/90 (67, 0); Blackpool *on loan* 89/90 (15, 0); Hereford United 90/1 (41, 0).

1977/78 - 1979/80

MICK LYONS

If a footballer's worth was measured solely by his passion for the game and his devotion to one club, then Mick Lyons would have been in a class of his own. The strapping Merseysider, whose single-mindedness never obscured his basic affability, was the type of man who would carry the team kit with the same pride others might feel when walking out at Wembley. Utterly honest - he was ready to admit that he was not over-endowed with natural ability - his most effective station on the field of battle was the last ditch, where his courage and strength, resourcefulness and capacity for toil were priceless assets during a less than illustrious interlude in the Blues' history.

Mick, who spent many of his boyhood Saturdays on the Goodison terraces, did not enjoy and easy path to the top flight. After rising through the junior ranks to the reserves as a teenage striker, he was reduced to A-team status by the progress of David Johnson, a setback which prompted his conversion to central defender and occasional midfielder. His senior debut in 1971 was followed by two in-and-out terms during which he took periodic stick from the club's more demanding fans; but the world loves a trier, and most of Mick's erstwhile critics warmed to him as he became a regular member of the side until the early eighties.

The Lyons technique might have been tailored expressly for the rearguard actions he fought so nobly. Formidably combative in the air and an adhesive close-marker, he was under-estimated at opponents' peril; so often he seemed to be beaten, yet would find something extra, perhaps a desperate long-legged lunge or a kamikaze head-first dive into a maelstrom of flailing boots. Mick could be a potent attacking force, too - invariably he moved forward for the last ten minutes of a game if Everton were losing - and both Billy Bingham and Gordon Lee selected him for emergency spells at centre-forward. In fact, despite jibes that his blunderbuss method made him little more than nuisance value, in 1973/74 he was top scorer with nine goals, a testimony to his versatility.

Despite his failings - his ball control was apt to let him down and his reading of the game appeared over-impulsive at times - Mick had won his spurs by the mid seventies, fully deserving the England under-23 caps, B international recognition and club captaincy that came his way. Such a zealous Blue might have been tempted to trade the lot for a little glory in local derbies against Liverpool, but in that area he seemed to be jinxed. Throughout his clash with the Reds, missing the only two Everton victories. There were moments of despair, too, such as on his 22nd birthday at Goodison in December 1973 when his majestic header found the net only to be disallowed, and even more excruciating, his volleyed 40-yard own-goal past a dumbfounded George Wood at Anfield nearly six years later. After that most wretched of incidents, a surprisingly joyful Toffees supporter approached the demoralised defender in a pub; when asked by a tactful Andy King to go easy on the criticism, the fellow announced that he couldn't be happier - he'd drawn Mick's name in a sweep as the scorer of the first goal and won £40!

It was all to end, the good times and the bad, without a major club honour to his name - the nearest miss being in the second replay of the 1977 League Cup Final, in which a Lyons goal was not enough to secure victory over Aston Villa. Mick parted from his beloved Everton in August 1982, having lost his place to Billy Wright, and joined Sheffield Wednesday, whom he helped gain promotion from Division Two before sampling management at Grimsby. Next came a brief return to Goodsion as a coach under Colin Harvey, then a similar job at Wigan. But whatever the future holds for Mick Lyons, he will be numbered, always, among the very truest of Blues.

BORN: Liverpool, 8.12.51.
GAMES: 434 (26). GOALS: 59.
OTHER CLUBS: Sheffield Wednesday 82/3-85/6 (129,12);
Grimsby Town 85/6-86/7 (50,4).
MANAGER: Grimsby Town (85-87).

1970/71 - 1981/82

ANDY KING

Rarely has an individual exuded the sheer joy of football with such utter abandon as Andy King. The impish midfielder believed passionately that he was born to play the game, and did so with flair, vision and an almost child-like sense of wonder that endeared him to the fans even during those frustratingly inconsistent interludes that punctuated his career. His natural exuberance was like a tonic on the terraces, inspiring a lasting affection for a confirmed southerner who fell in love with Merseyside and made it his spiritual home. Of his bountiful talent, there could be no doubt: Andy's technique was exquisite and, gloriously, he never kicked a ball without attempting to do something creative with it. Yet there remains an enduring sadness that, despite enjoying two spells at Goodison while still a young man, he never managed to do long-term justice to that immense potential.

The former Spurs schoolboy was a precocious 19-year-old when he became an Evertonian for the first time, Billy Bingham paying Luton £35,000 in April 1976. He responded instantly with a trio of livewire displays that inspired victories and won the approval of his team-mates, who had been promised a Spanish holiday if they picked up at least four points from the season's last three games. Thereafter Andy became a fixture in the side, his capacity for the unexpected emerging as a major attraction in a side that languished alarmingly in the ever-lengthening shadow of Liverpool. His masterful control and deft distribution - Bob Latchford was the principal beneficiary - combined with his own predatory finishing ability to win England under-21 recognition, and his future seemed nothing less than golden.

Andy confirmed his stature by scoring one of the most welcome goals in his club's history - ending the Reds' seven-year domination of the local derby with a 20-yard volley past Ray Clemence at Goodison in October 1978 - though for out-and-out artistry there was nothing to cap his winner at Derby the following August. Pounding through the middle, he half-turned to stun a raking pass from Trevor Ross with one touch, simultaneously flicking it over his head, then spinning to lob the ball over the 'keeper, all in one blur of action. It was vintage King, but sadly his form had become patchy and in September 1980, new manager Gordon Lee - who made no secret of his preference for solidity over wayward brilliance - sold him to Queen's Park Rangers for £425,000.

Even that, however, was not to slam the door on his chances of glory with his beloved Blues. In July 1982, Howard Kendall dispatched Peter Eastoe to West Bromwich Albion in exchange for Andy in the hope that the formerly erratic 25-year-old had matured and could, at last, harness his enviable gifts. He started impressively, scoring with a sensational 25-yard curler in the early annihilation of Aston Villa, but his progress was interrupted by a serious knee injury suffered at Sunderland, after which he found it difficult to hold a place in a team that was improving rapidly.

In 1985 Andy, dismayed at being an outsider at a now-vibrant Goodison, drifted into Dutch football, later returning to the British scene. When he retired - to run a soccer school on Merseyside, then rejoining Luton as commercial manager before relishing a stint as boss of Mansfield - he had won no medals or full caps, but he had lived life to the hilt and lit up countless games with his vivacious skills. Let the final word rest with Harry Catterick, who knew a thing or two about footballers: asked in the early eighties which contemporary Everton players he might have coveted for his own outstanding sides, he named only one man - Andy King.

BORN: Luton, Bedfordshire, 14.8.56.
GAMES: 243 (4). GOALS: 68.
OTHER CLUBS: Luton Town 74/5-75/6 (33, 9);
Queen's Park Rangers 80/1-81/2 (30, 9); West Bromwich Albion 81/2 (25, 4);
Cambuur, Holland; Wolverhampton Wanderers 84/5-85/6 (28, 10);
Luton Town 85/6 (3, 0); Aldershot 86/7 (36, 11).
MANAGER: Mansfield Town (93-96).

1975/76 - 1979/80 & 1982/83 - 1983/84

PETER EASTOE

If medals were minted for selflessness, industry and teamwork, then front-runner Peter Eastoe's trophy cabinet would be bulging. The cheerful Midlander's name rarely found its way into the headlines, but in match after match he laboured unobtrusively and efficiently in the common cause.

No matter how many defenders were breathing down his neck, Peter was in his element when the ball was played to his feet. He had neat control, the strength to ride tackles, and a technique for shielding the ball that reminded some observers of Kenny Dalglish. Of course, his overall game was not comparable to that of the Scottish maestro, but Peter was no mere workhorse, possessing the skill and intelligence to unsettle most opponents on his day. The fact that precise lay-offs and dummy runs are not the stuff of personal glory was of no consequence to his fellow professionals, who were well aware of his worth, and many maintain that only a slight deficiency in pace precluded greater achievements.

Peter, an England youth international, began his career at Wolves but he was overshadowed by the club's plethora of star strikers and it was at Swindon that he first shone. A spell with Queen's Park Rangers followed and it was from Loftus Road that he arrived at Goodison in exchange for Micky Walsh just ahead of the March 1979 transfer deadline. His most productive season was 1980/81, when he scored 19 League and Cup goals and was the only Blue to reach double figures, but his help in the development of the young Graeme Sharp during the subsequent term was, arguably, an equally important contribution.

In August 1982, with Howard Kendall striving to find a successful blend, the 29-year-old target man was swapped for Andy King, then with West Bromwich Albion. There followed a spell in Portugal before Peter, still enjoying the game, became player-boss of non-League Bridgnorth.

BORN: Tamworth, Staffordshire, 2.8.53. GAMES: 108 (7). GOALS: 33.
OTHER CLUBS: Wolverhampton Wanderers 71/2-73/4 (6, 0); Swindon Town 73/4-75/6 (91, 43);
Queen's Park Rangers 76/7-78/9 (72, 15); West Bromwich Albion 82/3 (31, 8);
Leicester City *on loan* 83/4 (5, 1); Huddersfield Town *on loan* 83/4 (10, 0); Walsall *on loan* 84/5 (6, 1);
Leicester City *on loan* 84/5 (6, 1); Wolverhampton Wanderers *on loan* 84/5 (8, 0).

1978/79 - 1981/82

COLIN TODD

'Playing Colin Todd at full-back is like asking Lester Piggott to win the Derby on a donkey'; thus did one much-respected ex-Evertonian describe Gordon Lee's policy of deploying the former England sweeper in a flank role. To be fair to the Blues boss, the analogy was rather harsh - after all, Colin had won a third of his caps as a full-back - but the point *was* valid. Indeed, it was the crucial factor, perhaps, in Todd's failure to settle at Goodison following his £300,000 move from Derby County in September 1978, a transaction for which the aggrieved Baseball Ground faithful never forgave their manager, Tommy Docherty.

When differences of opinion with Lee led to the blond north-easterner's £275,000 departure to Birmingham after only a year on Merseyside, the majority of Everton fans were dismayed by his precipitate exit. They recognised a thoroughbred performer whose poise and assurance made the game look deceptively easy, and whose majestic passing and refined ball control were complemented by blistering pace and impeccable timing in the tackle. Many shrewd judges believe that he was the outstanding British defender of his era. What a shame that the inconsistent Blues, so much in need of a player of Colin Todd's stature, couldn't capitalise on that talent.

BORN: Chester-le-Street, County Durham, 12.12.48.
GAMES: 35. GOALS: 1. HONOURS: 27 England caps (72-77). OTHER CLUBS: Sunderland 66/7-70/1 (173, 3); Derby County 70/1-78/9 (293, 6); Birmingham City 79/80-81/2 (93, 0); Nottingham Forest 82/3-83/4 (36, 0); Oxford United 83/4 (12, 0); Vancouver Whitecaps, Canada; Luton Town 84/5 (2, 0). MANAGER: Middlesbrough (90-91); Bolton (96-).

1978/79 - 1979/80

BRIAN KIDD

Few, if any, footballers of the modern era have equalled Brian Kidd's record of playing for four of England's greatest clubs while still in his prime. Yet after the heady experience of helping Manchester United win the European Cup on his 19th birthday, Brian was not to lend his talents to another trophy-winning side, despite an enviable strike rate throughout his travels. After sharing in United's decline, he joined Arsenal in a trough and narrowly missed the title with Manchester City before Everton offered him a last realistic chance of further glory.

The tall, left-sided marksman arrived from Maine Road at a cost of £150,000 in March 1979 with the brief of linking with Bob Latchford and fellow newcomer Peter Eastoe. Immensely skilful and blessed with an explosive shot, he did a highly professional job for the Blues without providing the hoped-for inspiration to lift them above mediocrity. One exception was a brilliantly judged near-post header against Liverpool at Anfield in October 1979, and he will also be remembered as the man who netted a penalty before being sent off in the drawn FA Cup semi-final against West Ham that same season.

In May 1980, by then 31, Brian joined Bolton Wanderers for £150,000. Later he returned to Old Trafford, first as a coach, then as an extremely influential assistant manager.

BORN: Manchester, 29.5.49. GAMES: 51. GOALS: 20.
HONOURS: 2 England caps (70). OTHER CLUBS: Manchester United 67/8-73/4 (203, 52); Arsenal 74/5-75/6 (77, 30); Manchester City 76/7-78/9 (98, 44); Bolton Wanderers 80/1-81/2 (43, 14); Fort Lauderdale Strikers and Atlanta Chiefs, USA. MANAGER: Preston North End (86).

1978/79 - 1979/80

BILLY WRIGHT

When surplus weight cost Billy Wright his Goodison career in 1982/83, it deprived the Blues of their captain and, in terms of all-round footballing ability, their most gifted central defender. Manager Howard Kendall axed Billy, after due warnings, in midwinter for being eight pounds heavier than his prescribed limit; in his absence, Mark Higgins and Kevin Ratcliffe forged a solid partnership and, come the summer, the displaced Merseysider was allowed to join Birmingham on a free transfer.

For club and player alike, it was a prodigious waste of talent. Since making his senior debut in 1978, the young man with the illustrious name and the proud Evertonian family tradition - his uncle is Tommy Wright - had established a reputation for class and versatility. He was skilful in possession, a polished passer and a relentlessly resolute tackler who was admirably effective in the air despite standing only 5ft 9in. These assets enabled him to hold his own at full-back and in midfield, a role for which he was further equipped by a fierce shot, but it was at the heart of the back four that he truly excelled.

So promising was Billy that he won his first England under-21 cap after only ten League games, and pundits spoke in glowing terms of an emerging star. Admittedly, lack of pace was always a weakness, but so keen was his sense of anticipation that it was rare for him to be caught out. When he was, however, sections of the Goodison crowd abused him for his sluggishness, advising him in colourful terms that he might profit by being a trifle slimmer.

Sadly the task proved beyond a player of naturally heavy build, Howard Kendall made his decision, and Billy was Midlands-bound. At St Andrews, by then considerably less bulky, he contributed three terms of distinguished service before joining Carlisle. In 1988 30-year-old Billy slipped into the non-League ranks with Morecambe at a time when, in happier circumstances, he might have been enjoying his Everton prime.

BORN: Liverpool, 28.4.58.
GAMES: 196 (2). GOALS: 10.
OTHER CLUBS: Birmingham City 83/4-85/6 (111, 9);
Chester City *on loan* 85/6 (6, 1); Carlisle United 86/7-87/8 (87, 3).

1977/78 - 1982/83

MARK HIGGINS

The story of Mark Higgins is one of the most poignant in modern Everton history. Here was a young man of unpretentious but undoubted ability, a commanding centre-half and well-respected club skipper, who had learned his trade while grafting through one of the Blues' frustratingly lean periods. Then, having developed to the point where an international future was predicted, and with Howard Kendall's reshaped side on the brink of an avalanche of honours, Mark's glittering prospects were sabotaged, savagely and abruptly, by injury.

His rise through the ranks was no surprise to anyone who had watched him as a youngster. Soccer was in his blood - his father, John, was a member of the formidable Bolton Wanderers defence during the fifties - and he gave full notice of his capabilities by winning a record 19 England schoolboy caps, then going on to captain his country at youth level. An easy-going character whose naturally genial demeanour was belied by an habitual expression of tense concentration on the pitch, Mark was dominant in the air, firm in the tackle and exceptionally quick. With the ball at his feet, he was sensible rather than ambitious, eschewing frills and exuding the type of solidity that managers crave.

After making his senior debut as a teenager in 1976, he proved an apt pupil at the shoulder of Mick Lyons, going on to forge a promising alliance with fellow left-footer Kevin Ratcliffe and emerge as a natural team leader in the early eighties. The first hint of trouble came with an apparent groin strain in November 1983, but further investigation revealed a deep-seated pelvic problem that forced retirement the following year, at 25 and on the threshold of his prime.

Refusing to admit defeat, Mark fought his way back to fitness, and although a top-flight return with Manchester United proved unsuccessful, he held his own in the lower divisions until 1989. It was a spirited riposte to the cruel fates that had robbed him of glories untold.

BORN: Buxton, Derbyshire, 29.9.58.
GAMES: 178 (3). GOALS: 6.
OTHER CLUBS: Manchester United 85/6 (6, 0);
Bury 86/7-88/9 (68, 0); Stoke City 88/9-89/90 (39, 1).

1976/77 - 1983/84

JOHN GIDMAN

For sheer swashbuckling entertainment, there wasn't a full-back in the land to outdo John Gidman. His overlapping exploits down the right flank, executed with a characteristic swagger that both thrilled the fans and warmed them to his cause, were capable of turning a match on its head. Regrettably, as was true of many fine footballers at Goodison in the late seventies, Everton never quite made the most of him.

John's October 1979 move from Aston Villa to the Blues - in exchange for £550,000 and Pat Heard - meant a Merseyside homecoming that doubtless stirred memories of his rejection as a teenager after a year's apprenticeship at Anfield. He had been undeterred, however, going on to sparkle in the Midlands and win an England cap.

Quick, strong and boasting skills that many a midfielder might have envied, John revelled in bursting past opponents and slinging deep crosses into the penalty area. So sure was his touch that he ran with his head up, ever searching for targets, and while such adventure meant that he was caught out of position occasionally, he was usually on hand with a stern tackle if the need arose. When Howard Kendall, seeking to remould his side, swapped John for Manchester United's Micky Thomas in 1981, there was no shortage of supporters who mourned his departure.

BORN: Liverpool, 10.1.54. GAMES: 78. GOALS: 3.
HONOURS: 1 England cap (77).
OTHER CLUBS: Aston Villa 72/3-79/80 (197, 9);
Manchester United 81/2-85/6 (95, 4); Manchester City 86/7-87/8 (53, 1); Stoke City 88/9 (10, 0); Darlington 88/9 (13, 1).

1979/80 - 1980/81

GARRY STANLEY

Gordon Lee paid Chelsea £300,000 for Garry Stanley in the summer of 1979 with the reasonable expectation that the attacking midfielder would reproduce for Everton the type of dynamic displays that had caught the eye during his four campaigns at Stamford Bridge; quite simply, it never happened.

The solidly-built Midlander's mastery of the game's basics - control, passing, tackling - was unquestionable; he was strong and boasted bags of stamina, yet somehow his impact remained negligible. Most disappointing was the lack of fire-power. Garry was a crisp striker of the ball who had scored some stunning goals for the Londoners, but in two terms at Goodison he managed to find the net only once.

Indeed, the main distinction of the Stanley stay was an unwanted one, he and Liverpool's Terry McDermott becoming the first players to be sent off in a Merseyside derby following a petty, out-of-character fracas at Anfield in October 1979.

His Everton career standing still, Garry joined Swansea for £150,000 in October 1981 and played an enterprising part in the Welshmen's initial success in the top flight before seeing out his League days in the Second and Third Divisions.

BORN: Burton-on-Trent, Staffordshire, 4.3.54.
GAMES: 61 (2). GOALS: 1.
OTHER CLUBS: Chelsea 75/6-78/9 (109, 15);
Fort Lauderdale Strikers, USA; Swansea City 81/2-83/4 (72, 4);
Portsmouth 83/4-85/6 (47, 1); Wichita, USA;
Bristol City 88/9 (10, 0).

1979/80 - 1980/81

ASA HARTFORD

For Asa Hartford, Everton was the right club at the wrong time. Here was a high-class performer, a midfield creator cum motivator who would have graced Goodison in any of the Blues' vintage post-war sides; sadly, it was the lot of the blond, stocky Scottish international to parade his talents at the hub of a distinctly lacklustre combination.

Asa combined skill and industry to an impressive degree. Though naturally left-sided, he possessed impeccable touch with either foot and was particularly effective in quickfire short-passing interchanges that could scythe a path through the most congested of areas. Darting urgently hither and thither, his craft and guile underpinned by a biting tackle, indomitable courage and the enthusiasm to drive colleagues to ever-greater efforts, he was a reassuring, sometimes inspirational figure. Unsurprisingly, there is no shortage of former team-mates who rate Asa as the best footballer they ever played alongside and it was entirely appropriate that the fans voted him their player of the year for 1979/80, following his £500,000 signing from Nottingham Forest that August.

In fact, the man who had once earned unwanted fame when his transfer from West Bromwich to Leeds fell through because of a heart condition - how ludicrous his subsequent record made the Yorkshiremen's then-understandable fears seem to be - might have joined Everton from Manchester City two months earlier. However, Brian Clough had proved more persuasive than Gordon Lee and it took a personality clash to remove Asa to Goodison after only three games in a red shirt.

In October 1981, his Merseyside sojourn ended with a £350,000 switch back to Maine Road where, evidently, the 31-year-old play-maker saw greater potential. Ahead lay a varied career as player, manager and coach, notably under Kenny Dalglish at Blackburn.

BORN: Clydebank, Scotland, 24.10.50. GAMES: 98. GOALS: 7.
HONOURS: 50 Scotland caps (77-82). OTHER CLUBS: West Bromwich Albion 67/8-73/4 (214, 18); Manchester City 74/5-78/9 (185, 22); Nottingham Forest 79/80 (3, 0); Manchester City 81/2-83/4 (75, 7); Fort Lauderdale Strikers, USA; Norwich City 84/5 (28, 2); Bolton Wanderers 85/6-86/7 (81, 8); Stockport County 87/8-88/9 (45, 0); Oldham Athletic 88/9 (7, 0); Shrewsbury Town 89/90-90/1 (25, 0). MANAGER: Stockport County (87-89); Shrewsbury Town (90); Manchester City (caretaker, 96).

1979/80 - 1981/82

JIM McDONAGH

Jim McDonagh played well enough during his sole season at Goodison Park to launch an international career, but never demonstrated the dominance necessary to secure a long-term place between the Everton posts.

The former England youth custodian - dubbed 'Seamus' by team-mates when he was called into the Eire side, courtesy of Republican ancestry - joined the Blues from newly-relegated Bolton in July 1980. Gordon Lee, having sold George Wood, drafted his £250,000 acquisition straight into the first team, and he missed only two League games that term.

A muscular six-footer, he proved competent but that was not enough to convince Gordon's successor, Howard Kendall, of his worth and two new 'keepers - Jim Arnold and a certain Neville Southall - were signed. Accordingly, in August 1981 the amiable McDonagh returned to Burnden Park, where he had played a splendid part in the 1978 Second Division Championship triumph, in a deal that saw central defender Mick Walsh travel in the opposite direction.

Jim - who in 1976 spent a spell at Old Trafford on loan from his home-town club, Rotherham, without getting a senior outing - later sampled management across the Irish Sea with Galway United.

BORN: Rotherham, Yorkshire, 6.10.52. GAMES: 48. GOALS: 0.
HONOURS: 24 Republic of Ireland caps (81-86).
OTHER CLUBS: Rotherham United 70/1-75/6 (121, 0);
Bolton Wanderers 76/7-79/80 (161, 0) and 81/2-82/3 (81, 1);
Notts County 83/4-84/5 (35, 0); Birmingham City *on loan*
84/5 (1, 0); Gillingham *on loan* 84/5 (10, 0);
Sunderland *on loan* 85/6 (7, 0); USA; Scarborough 87/8 (9, 0);
Huddersfield Town *on loan* 87/8 (6, 0).

1980/81

EAMON O'KEEFE

In two years, Eamon O'Keefe sprang from the virtual anonymity of the Northern Premier League to the international stage. The combative, squarely-built attacker's quantum leap at the age of 26 was due in part to his own effort and skill, but it would never have been possible had Everton boss Gordon Lee not backed a hunch and paid Mossley £25,000 for his enthusiastic services in July 1979.

Eamon, who had been on Plymouth Argyle's books without tasting senior action and also played in Saudi Arabia before joining the Blues, never looked out of place in the top grade. A 5ft 7in bundle of aggression - he was sent off for a rash challenge on Ronnie Whelan at Anfield in November 1981 - Eamon was both quick and deft enough to turn defenders and packed a fierce shot. He looked most dangerous when foraging alongside a big man, and many believe he could have excelled in tandem with Graeme Sharp if given an extended chance.

However, the blond Mancunian, whose parentage qualified him for the Republic of Ireland, departed the Goodison scene in January 1982 as new manager Howard Kendall made sweeping changes. Eamon joined Wigan for £65,000 before travelling - and scoring - extensively throughout the rest of his career.

BORN: Manchester, 13.3.53.
GAMES: 34 (17). GOALS: 8.
HONOURS: 5 Republic of Ireland caps (81-85).
OTHER CLUBS: Wigan Athletic 81/2-82/3 (58, 25);
Port Vale 83/4-84/5 (59, 17); Blackpool 84/5-86/7 (36, 23);
Cork Celtic, Republic of Ireland;
Chester City 88/9-89/90 (17, 4).

1979/80 - 1981/82

JOHN BARTON

John Barton's unassumingly impressive form as Everton clinched a place in Europe during the spring of 1979 offered persuasive evidence of the vast reserve of untapped talent to be found among the unfashionable outposts of part-time football. Only several months earlier, the lean, athletic right-back had been helping Southern League Worcester City to dump Plymouth Argyle out of the FA Cup; his exploits attracted the attention of Gordon Lee, who gambled £30,000 on raw potential and must have been gratified at the result.

The quiet, 25-year-old Brummie was comfortable on the ball and loved to get forward, his long stride and ability to deliver accurate crosses equipping him admirably as an overlapper. John was competent at the back, too, and after he had played only three games, no less an authority than Colin Todd was predicting an international future. Sadly, in October 1979, he broke his leg at Coventry and was never the same force again. John was freed by Howard Kendall in March 1982 and joined Derby, whom he helped to avoid relegation before returning unexpectedly to the non-League ranks.

BORN: Birmingham, 24.10.53. GAMES: 23 (2). GOALS: 0. OTHER CLUBS: Derby County 81/2-83/4 (69, 1).

1978/79 - 1980/81

GARY MEGSON

Gary Megson was one of the young men around whom Gordon Lee hoped to build a brave new Everton. The manager, beset by critics as his constantly shuffled side floundered, paid Plymouth Argyle £250,000 for the 20-year-old midfielder in February 1980.

For their money, the Blues got a keen, competent all-rounder who tackled with determination and used the ball skilfully, and had they been riding high, the red-headed newcomer might have fulfilled the hopes of his boss. As it was his inexperience showed, and when Howard Kendall took charge, young Gary was out.

In August 1981, a fee of £130,000 took him to Sheffield Wednesday - the club for whom his father, Don Megson, had been a stalwart - and it was at Hillsborough that he played his finest football during two spells. Gary, whose resolution was sometimes employed in the back four, later did well for Manchester City.

BORN: Manchester, 2. 5. 59. GAMES: 23 (2). GOALS 3. OTHER CLUBS: Plymouth Argyle 77/8-79/80 (78, 10); Sheffield Wednesday 81/2-83/4 (123, 13); Newcastle United 84/5-85/6 (24, 1); Sheffield Wednesday 85/6-88/9 (110, 12); Manchester City 88/9-91/2 (82, 2); Norwich City 92/3-94/5 (46, 1); Lincoln City 95/6 (2, 0); Shrewsbury Town 95/6 (2, 0). MANAGER: Norwich City (95-96); Blackpool (96-97); Stockport County (97-)

1979/80 - 1980/81

PAUL LODGE

Paul Lodge was the more promising of two teenage midfielders who forced their way into the Everton first-team reckoning in the early eighties. The dark-haired Merseysider was bountifully blessed with natural ability, his touch, distribution and vision all superior to that of his team-mate and friend. Paul was not the complete player, however, being a little short of pace, and lacking the edge of aggression and all-consuming drive that characterised his pal. Accordingly, he drifted out of contention while the other lad, a certain Steve McMahon, moved from strength to strength, a pointed, poignant illustration that a football career cannot be based on talent alone.

The portents had been so favourable when Paul had enjoyed a creditable first senior run in the spring of 1981. That autumn he impressed again under new boss Howard Kendall, playing with particular maturity in a 2-0 win at Middlesbrough, but then his form declined, his confidence appeared to evaporate, and soon he was gone. After brief service in the lower divisions, Paul left the League at the age of 25.

BORN: Liverpool, 13.2.61. GAMES: 31 (4). GOALS: 0. OTHER CLUBS: Wigan Athletic *on loan* 82/3 (5, 1); Rotherham United *on loan* 82/3 (4, 0); Preston North End 82/3-83/4 (38, 0); Bolton Wanderers 84/5 (4, 0); Port Vale *on loan* 84/5 (3, 0); Stockport County 84/5-85/6 (13, 2).

1980/81 - 1981/82

TREVOR ROSS

The five-year contribution of Trevor Ross to the Everton cause was not without credit, yet for a man who was given more than a century and a half of senior outings, he left an ultimate impression of rather limited significance.

The England schoolboy international, who qualified for Scotland under-21 honours through his father - former Third Lanark forward William Ross - arrived at Goodison as a £170,000 signing from Arsenal in November 1977. Injury to Mike Pejic brought about his debut as an emergency number-three, but it was on the right side of midfield that Trevor specialised. Aggressive in the tackle and an athletic, direct raider down the flank, he passed the ball neatly and possessed a powerful shot which he might have used more often. His form, however, tended to be in and out, and consequently his place in the side was under frequent threat.

Eventually Trevor dropped out of contention early in the managerial reign of Howard Kendall, and after being used unsuccessfully as bait to persuade Sheffield United to part with Terry Curran, he joined AEK Athens. His Greek sojourn was brief, as was a subsequent stint at Bramall Lane, and Trevor rounded off his League career at Bury.

BORN: Ashton-under-Lyne, Lancashire, 16.1.57.
GAMES: 146 (5). GOALS: 20.
OTHER CLUBS: Arsenal 74/5-77/8 (58, 5);
Portsmouth *on loan* 82/3 (5, 0);
Sheffield United *on loan* 82/3 (4, 0); AEK Athens;
Sheffield United 83/4 (4, 0); Bury 84/5-86/7 (98, 11).

1977/78 - 1982/83

IMRE VARADI

His critics denounced him as naive and selfish, while those who thrilled to a dash of cavalier extravagance spiced with moments of genuine quality were inclined to sing his praises. On one point, however, there could be only unanimous agreement: Imre Varadi was never dull.

Indeed, from his teenage years, the swarthy Londoner was to enjoy a career in which convention played little part. After being rejected by a non-League club, he was plucked from a Sunday morning side by a sharp-eyed Sheffield United scout and made an immediate impact at Bramall Lane with his unorthodox forward play. Imre loved to put his head down and run with the ball, boasting the skill and speed to panic defenders and bring fans to the edge of their seats, though he seemed unaware, at times, that football was a passing game.

Everton boss Gordon Lee, excited by this unusual talent, gambled £80,000 on signing him in March 1979, but despite some invigorating moments - including a goal in the FA Cup triumph over Liverpool in January 1981 - Imre didn't quite fit in. That summer he joined Newcastle for £125,000 before wandering from club to club for a further 15 years.

BORN: Paddington, London, 8.7.59. GAMES: 28 (6).
GOALS: 7. OTHER CLUBS: Sheffield United 78/9 (10, 4);
Newcastle United 81/2-82/3 (81, 39); Sheffield Wednesday
83/4-84/5 (76, 33); West Bromwich Albion 85/6 (32, 9);
Manchester City 86/7-88/9 (65, 26); Sheffield Wednesday
88/9-89/90 (22, 3); Leeds United 89/90- 92/3 (26, 5),
Luton Town *on loan* 91/2 (6, 1); Oxford United *on loan* 92/3 (5,
0; Rotherham United 92/3-94/5 (67, 25); Mansfield Town
95/6 (1,); Scunthorpe United 95/6 (2, 0).

1979/80 - 1980/81

JOE McBRIDE	MARTIN HODGE

Anyone who watched Joe McBride give the chasing of a lifetime to Ivan Golac, Southampton's formidable Yugoslavian full-back, would bear witness to the skill and pace of the wiry flankman. That afternoon at Goodison Park in October 1980, Joe excelled himself, taking the eye as the outstanding creator on view and capping his sparkling exhibition of dribbling and crossing by scoring both goals in a 2-1 victory. Unfortunately, although he strove unstintingly in the Royal Blue cause, such match-winning inspiration was too rare to ensure the left-sided Glaswegian a long-term niche at the club.

Youth international Joe - named after his father, who led Scotland's attack during the sixties - joined Everton straight from school and spent two seasons in the Central League before receiving his senior call-up on Boxing Day 1979. For the visit to Bolton, manager Gordon Lee had decided to revert to the use of an orthodox winger, and Joe did well enough to retain his place for a run of 18 matches. During 1980/81 he played his most convincing football and might have become established had Lee not been sacked. However, he could not win a regular place under Howard Kendall and in August 1982 moved on to Rotherham, later returning to his homeland with some success.

BORN: Glasgow, 17.8.60.
GAMES: 64 (6). GOALS: 11.
OTHER CLUBS: Rotherham United 82/3-83/4 (45, 12);
Oldham Athletic 83/4-84/5 (36, 5);
Hibernian 84/5-88/9 (81, 11);
Dundee 88/9-90/1 (49, 5).

Martin Hodge was an underrated 'keeper who emerged from the shadow of one Everton rival, only to find himself upstaged by three more. Gordon Lee signed the tall, brave Lancastrian, whose apparent ungainliness was belied by considerable agility, from Plymouth for £135,000 in July 1979. George Wood was Goodison's top custodian at the time, yet by November the newcomer had ousted the Scottish international and went on to play in that term's FA Cup semi-final against West Ham.

The breakthrough was temporary, however. George departed but first Jim McDonagh, then Jim Arnold and Neville Southall, kept Martin on the sidelines. Predictably, after four loan periods with other clubs, he opted for a fresh start, accepting a £50,000 move to Sheffield Wednesday in August 1983.

Hillsborough proved the making of him. In his first Owls campaign he played a major part in securing promotion from the Second Division, he didn't miss a League match for more than four seasons, enjoyed a spell as skipper, and was placed on standby for England's 1986 World Cup party. Martin's former Blues team-mates, who had long admired his unswerving dedication in the face of adversity, rejoiced at his overdue success. He went on to serve Leicester City and others with distinction.

BORN: Southport, Lancashire, 4.2.59. GAMES: 31. GOALS: 0.
OTHER CLUBS: Plymouth Argyle 77/8-78/9 (45, 0);
Preston North End *on loan* 81/2 (28, 0); Oldham Athletic *on loan* 82/3 (4, 0); Gillingham *on loan* 82/3 (4, 0); Preston North End *on loan* 82/3 (16, 0); Sheffield Wednesday 83/4-87/8 (197, 0); Leicester City 88/9-90/1 (75, 0); Hartlepool United 91/2-92/3 (69, 0); Rochdale 93/4 (42, 0); Plymouth Argyle 94/5 (17, 0).

1979/80 - 1981/82	1979/80 - 1980/81

BILL KENNY Snr   1970/71 - 1974/75

Midfielder. BORN: Liverpool, 23.10.51. GAMES: 10 (2). GOALS: 0.
OTHER CLUBS: Tranmere Rovers 74/5-76/7 (54, 6).

BERNIE WRIGHT   1971/72 - 1972/73

Forward. BORN: Birmingham, 17.9.52. GAMES: 10 (1). GOALS: 2.
OTHER CLUBS: Walsall 71/2 (15, 2) and 72/3-76/7 (152, 38);
Bradford City 76/7-77/8 (66, 13); Port Vale 78/9-79/80 (76, 23).

ALAN WILSON   1971/72 - 1972/73

Midfielder. BORN: Liverpool, 17.11.52. GAMES: 2. GOALS: 0.
OTHER CLUBS: Southport 75/6-77/8 (134, 13); Torquay United 78/9 (42, 2).

DAVE IRVING   1973/74 - 1975/76

Forward. BORN: Workington, Cumberland, 10.9.51 GAMES: 6 (2). GOALS: 1.
OTHER CLUBS: Workington Town 70/1-72/3 (65, 16);
Sheffield United 75/6 (2, 0); Oldham Athletic 76/7-77/8 (21, 7).

JOHN SMITH   1973/74

Midfielder. BORN: Liverpool, 14.3.53.GAMES: 2. GOALS: 0.
OTHER CLUBS: Carlisle United 76/7 (5, 0);Southport *on loan* 76/7 (18, 2)

CLIFF MARSHALL   1974/75 - 1975/76

Winger. BORN: Liverpool, 4.11.55. GAMES: 7 (1). GOALS: 0.
OTHER CLUBS: Southport 76/7 (13, 0).

DREW BRAND   1975/76 - 1976/77

Goalkeeper. BORN: Edinburgh, 8.11.57. GAMES: 2. GOALS: 0. OTHER CLUBS:
Crewe Alexandra *on loan* 76/7 (14, 0) and 78/9 (1, 0); Hereford United 80/1-81/2 (54, 0);
Wrexham *on loan* 82/3 (1, 0); Blackpool 83/4 (3, 0).

ROSS JACK   1978/79

Forward. BORN: Inverness, Scotland, 21.3.59.
GAMES: 1. GOALS: 1.
OTHER CLUBS: Norwich City 80/1-82/3 (56, 10);
Lincoln City 83/4-84/5 (60, 16); Dundee 85/6-87/8 (38, 4);
Dunfermline Athletic 87/8-90/1 (130, 46);
Kilmarnock 91/2-92/3 (55, 13); Montrose 92/3 (6, 2).

BILL KENNY Snr   ALAN WILSON   JOHN SMITH

DAVE IRVING   DREW BRAND   ROSS JACK

BERNIE WRIGHT   CLIFF MARSHALL

STEVE McMAHON

When Steve McMahon left Goodison in May 1983, it was apparent that the Blues were losing a youthful gem with an abrasive cutting edge; what was not then apparent was the creative lustre that, in maturity, would illuminate his game and transform the born-and-bred Evertonian into one of Anfield's brightest stars.

Looking at the powerful Liverpool play-maker in his late-eighties pomp, it was hard to recall the slim individual who had graduated from Goodison ball-boy to apprentice professional before winning a regular first-team berth as a 19-year-old under Gordon Lee in 1980/81. Most noticeable for his eagerness and brisk tackling, Steve appeared skilful enough without being outstanding, usually opting for short, safe passes and displaying little sign of the long-range vision he was to employ later to such devastating effect.

Nevertheless, he thrived in a nondescript team, seldom looking more committed than when pitted against Graeme Souness in local derbies. The fans voted him player of the year for 1981/82, he was capped by England at under-21 level, and before long his relentless ambition was demanding a better chance of club honours than he believed Everton could offer. New manager Howard Kendall was reluctant to part with a player of such potential, but after much heart-searching - and rejecting an offer from Liverpool - Steve signed for Aston Villa in a £250,000 deal that was to finance the arrival of Trevor Steven.

Ironically, had he hung on for another season, surely Steve must have played a leading role in the glorious Kendall-inspired revival. Had that transpired, the name of McMahon would by now surely occupy a revered place in Blues annals. Instead he spent two terms at Villa before becoming Kenny Dalglish's first signing. The Reds nurtured and maximised his ability to scintillating effect, and the Blue half of Merseyside was left to heave a collective sigh.

BORN: Liverpool, 20.8.61. GAMES: 119 (1). GOALS: 14. HONOURS: 17 England caps (88-90).
OTHER CLUBS: Aston Villa 83/4-85/6 (75, 7);
Liverpool 85/6-91/2 (204, 29);
Manchester City 91/2-94/5 (87, 1);
Swindon Town 94/5- (42, 0).
MANAGER: Swindon Town (94-).

1980/81 - 1982/83

ALAN BILEY

Alan Biley was a flamboyant front-runner who became an instant favourite with the Gwladys Street choir, only to fade frustratingly from the Goodison scene.

Something of a lower-division cult figure with his first club, Cambridge United, Alan did nothing to dent his racy image at Derby before becoming the first signing of newly-appointed Everton boss Howard Kendall in July 1981. The £300,000 newcomer made a dramatic bow in the season's opener at home to Birmingham, deceiving goalkeeper Jeff Wealands with the cutest of chips, then confirmed his promise by netting at Leeds in his second game.

The fans warmed to the blond marksman's perky demeanour - dubbing him 'Spike' on account of his Rod Stewart-type hair-do - and the manager enthused about his ability, citing his dangerous, darting penalty-area presence, his explosive turn of speed and splendid timing in the air.

But when a goal drought followed his initial success, Alan's confidence nosedived; he was dropped, and, after a loan spell with Stoke, joined Portsmouth just 13 months after his arrival on Merseyside. He flourished on the south coast, but was never again to return to the top level.

BORN: Leighton Buzzard, Bedfordshire, 26.2.57.
GAMES: 18 (3). GOALS: 3. OTHER CLUBS: Cambridge United 75/6-79/80 (165, 74); Derby County 79/80-80/1 (47, 19); Stoke City *on loan* 81/2 (8, 1); Portsmouth 82/3-84/5 (105, 51); Brighton and Hove Albion 84/5-85/6 (35, 8); New York, USA; Cambridge United 86/7 (3, 0)

1981/82

MICK FERGUSON

Mick Ferguson's Everton ambitions were shattered by injury within months of his £280,000 signing from Coventry City in August 1981. Manager Howard Kendall needed the lean, bearded Geordie to provide height and power as a contrast to nippier fellow strikers Peter Eastoe and Alan Biley, and banked on Mick reproducing the prolific form that had made him such a threat in partnership with Ian Wallace at Highfield Road.

Alas, the quiet Geordie suffered a succession of ankle problems and apart from one spell during his first Goodison autumn - in which he notched six goals in eight outings - he never had the chance to prove his worth.

Mick, a big man with noticeably small feet whose rather deliberate running style earned him the nickname of 'The Ice Skater', returned to contention the following year, but by then the young Graeme Sharp had thrust himself into the reckoning and the number-nine shirt was no longer vacant. In November 1982, a move to Birmingham might have revived the Ferguson fortunes, but fitness proved elusive once more, and neither with City nor several subsequent clubs did Mick make appreciable impact. After retirement he worked for Football In The Community in his native north-east.

BORN: Newcastle, 3.10.54. GAMES: 10 (2). GOALS: 6.
OTHER CLUBS: Coventry City 74/5-80/1 (127, 51); Birmingham City 82/3-84/5 (22, 9); Coventry City *on loan* 83/4 (7, 3); Brighton and Hove Albion 84/5-85/6 (17, 6); Colchester United 85/6-86/7 (26, 11).

1981/82

JIM ARNOLD

When Jim Arnold left Blackburn to rejoin his former Ewood Park boss, Howard Kendall, at Goodison in August 1981, the tall, rather spidery custodian had every reason to expect several seasons of uninterrupted senior service. After all, the one-time England semi-professional international was a reliable, unshowy performer at the peak of his powers, and if the arrival a month previously of a raw young Welshman represented a tiny cloud on his horizon, well, 'keepers were notoriously slow to mature, weren't they?

Unluckily for the worthy Arnold but to the lasting good fortune of the Blues, that callow newcomer, name of Neville Southall, made prodigiously rapid strides and the older man was faced with a battle for his place. For three months, he won it, but was then evicted before returning for 32 games in 1982/83 and a creditable stint at the start of the subsequent campaign. There was no doubt about the eventual outcome, however, and to his eternal credit, Jim - a splendid shot-stopper whose dexterity at taking crosses did not always match his agility on the line - offered genial and expert encouragement to the emerging star.

Jim continued to provide high-quality cover until August 1985, when he moved on to Port Vale to complete his League career.

BORN: Stafford, 6.8.50.
GAMES: 59. GOALS: 0.
OTHER CLUBS: Blackburn Rovers 79/80-80/1 (58, 0);
Preston North End *on loan* 82/3 (6, 0);
Port Vale 85/6-86/7 (53, 0).

1981/82 - 1983/84

MICK WALSH

Mick Walsh - not to be confused with the Everton striker of the same name - had established his credentials as a sound First Division central defender when he left Bolton for the Blues in August 1981. Unhappily for the big, blond left-footer, who was exchanged for 'keeper Jim McDonagh and a £90,000 cheque, his opportunities were limited at a time of sweeping change and after two unfulfilling terms he left to try his luck in the United States.

The strapping stopper started well enough at Goodison, but lost his place to the promising Mark Higgins early in his first Merseyside winter and never regained it. His only subsequent appearances were made in the number-three shirt, a role that did not make the most of his greatest asset, his power in the air.

Some observers felt that Mick - a Mancunian who won Eire caps through Republican ancestry - had more to offer than he was allowed to produce and regretted his departure, not least for his good-humoured contribution to dressing-room banter. On returning to Britain, he sojourned briefly at Maine Road before offering doughty service to Blackpool, and then managing Bury.

BORN: Manchester, 20.6.56.
GAMES: 22. GOALS: 0.
HONOURS: 5 Republic of Ireland caps (82-83).
OTHER CLUBS: Bolton Wanderers 74/5-80/1 (177, 4);
Norwich City *on loan* 82/3 (5, 0); Burnley *on loan* 82/3 (3, 0);
Fort Lauderdale Strikers, USA; Manchester City 83/4 (4, 0);
Blackpool 83/4-88/9 (153, 5).
MANAGER: Bury (90-95).

1981/82 - 1982/83

MICKEY THOMAS

The Everton career of Mickey Thomas was a casualty of self-destruction. In October 1981, a mere two months after the scurrying left-sided midfield attacker had arrived from Manchester United in exchange for John Gidman, he refused to play in a reserve match. Mickey had been injured against Ipswich and in his absence the Blues had won twice, so manager Howard Kendall opted to keep an unchanged side. The Welsh international's reaction - the product of frustration rather than arrogance - was a daft breach of discipline that resulted in his prompt departure to Brighton for £400,000.

It was a shame for both player and club. Mickey was blessed with far more flair than his critics perceived, boasting a splendid first touch and an ability to make telling crosses. He was tenacious, too, offering more than nuisance value when he tackled back inside his own half, and with a more considered approach might have become a part of the Goodision success story that was soon to unfold.

Instead Mickey set off on a whistle-stop tour of clubs that continued into the early nineties, when he was plagued by personal problems and served a short term in jail.

BORN: Mochdre, North Wales, 7.7.54. GAMES: 11. GOALS: 0.
HONOURS: 51 Wales caps (76-86). OTHER CLUBS: Wrexham 71/2-78/9 (230, 33); Manchester United 78/9-80/1 (90, 11); Brighton and Hove Albion 81/2 (20, 0); Stoke City 82/3-83/4 (57, 14); Chelsea 83/4-84/5 (44, 9); West Bromwich Albion 85/6 (20, 0); Derby County *on loan* 85/6 (9, 0); Wichita, USA; Shrewsbury Town 88/9 (40, 1); Leeds United 89/90 (3, 0); Stoke City 89/90-90/1 (43, 7); Wrexham 91/2-92/3 (34, 2).

1981/82

BRIAN BORROWS

Howard Kendall was beset by too many problems for comfort in the early eighties, but he had one, at least, that most managers would have relished. Brian Borrows and Gary Stevens offered the Everton boss an exceptionally high-quality choice at right-back, and, at that time, there was little to choose between the skilful Merseysider and the future England international.

In fact, in 1981/82, many shrewd judges saw Brian as the more complete all-round footballer, his touch and distribution markedly superior to that of his rival. Rather than hoofing the ball hopefully upfield, he could deliver it low and accurately to the feet of his forwards, and had the ability to trick his way past defenders when overlapping into attack. However, although 'Bugsy' was no slowcoach, the athletic Gary was even quicker, and Howard must have surmised - rightly, as it turned out - that the Stevens technique could be improved immensely.

Accordingly, after scrapping for the number-two shirt for two seasons, Brian bowed out of Goodison in 1983, signing for Bolton. Happily his class did not wither in the lower divisions and he returned to the top flight to excel for Coventry. In different circumstances, it is fair to speculate, he might have served the Blues with equal distinction.

BORN: Liverpool, 20.12.60.
GAMES: 29. GOALS: 0.
OTHER CLUBS: Bolton Wanderers 82/3-84/5 (95, 0); Coventry City 85/6-96/7 (409, 11); Bristol City *on loan* 93/4 (6, 0); Swindon Town 97/8- (37, 0).

1981/82 - 1982/83

ALAN AINSCOW

Alan Ainscow was the type of footballer of which his profession could be justly proud. Not extravagantly gifted and never remotely approaching star status, he was honest, down-to-earth and dedicated, an indefatigable humorist who kept morale bubbling during hard times, and who inspired genuine respect and affection among his team-mates.

The blond, right-sided midfielder arrived at Goodison in August 1981 in the vanguard of a wave of signings by new manager Howard Kendall, most of which were to prove of short-term value. He repaid the first instalment of his £250,000 fee by scoring in a home victory over Birmingham City, his former employers, in the season's curtain-raiser, but thereafter the Blues' fortunes ebbed rather than flowed.

However, 28-year-old Alan offered doughty service, buzzing athletically up and down his beat, tackling briskly, never hiding from the ball and often liable to pop up with a fiercely driven shot at goal. Sadly, a broken leg suffered at Notts County that November removed him from contention, and as the manager experimented with a host of permutations, he never regained a regular berth.

Alan was freed in May 1983 and he tried his luck in Hong Kong, before returning to extend a worthy Football League career until the age of 37.

BORN: Bolton, Lancashire, 15.7.53. GAMES: 25 (5). GOALS: 3.
OTHER CLUBS: Blackpool 71/2-77/8 (192, 28); Birmingham City 78/9-80/1 (108, 16); Barnsley *on loan* 82/3 (2, 0); Hong Kong; Wolverhampton Wanderers 84/5-85/6 (58, 5); Blackburn Rovers 85/6-88/9 (65, 5); Rochdale 89/90 (20, 0).

1981/82 - 1982/83

ALAN IRVINE

Alan Irvine's Goodison career was characterised by constant striving that fell tantalisingly short of concrete achievement. He was a hard-running winger whose favoured gambit was to push the ball past his full-back and race for the byline; the problem was that sometimes he travelled at a velocity too great for his own good, making impractical the delivery of a measured cross.

Nevertheless the wiry Glaswegian, recruited from Queen's Park as an amateur in May 1981, was a resilient competitor who was not deterred by hard knocks, and although he never quite became established - despite two lengthy stints of senior action in the early eighties - he contributed a number of spirited performances.

Old Trafford provided a grand stage for Alan at his most adventurous in March 1983, when he tortured the Manchester United defence in an FA Cup quarter-final, coming agonisingly close to forcing a breakthrough before the Red Devils stole an undeserved injury-time winner. He did reach Wembley the following term, however, appearing in the two League Cup Final clashes with Liverpool before fading out of the first-team reckoning. That August he joined Crystal Palace for £50,000, later sampling the Scottish League once more before adding his enthusiasm to the Blackburn cause in the early nineties.

BORN: Glasgow, 12.7.58.
GAMES: 70 (10). GOALS: 6.
OTHER CLUBS: Queen's Park 77/8-80/1 (88, 9); Crystal Palace 84/5-86/7 (109, 12); Dundee United 87/8-88/9 (24, 3); Blackburn Rovers 89/90-91/2 (59, 3).

1981/82 - 1983/84

JOHN BAILEY

A Scouser by birth and a comedian by inclination, John Bailey rejoiced in the genuine affection of fans and team-mates alike. On the terraces the dark, curly-haired left back was loved for his buccaneering style, extravagant gestures and total emotional involvement in the game; in the dressing room, he was a one-man variety act, a never-ending source of wisecracks who would bounce in for training no matter how dire a defeat had just been suffered. John's party piece was winding up Welshmen, and he delighted in proclaiming to the likes of Messrs Southall and Ratcliffe that his one appearance for England 'B' was worth at least 50 of their full international caps. Managerial status offered scant immunity from the club jester, either, as Howard Kendall was to discover on the occasion of a kissogram girl arriving at the team hotel!

But endearing as John's humour was, he needed more than jokes to make his way at Everton; indeed, he possessed footballing qualities in abundance, as he demonstrated with gusto after Gordon Lee had prised him from Blackburn with a £300,000 fee in April 1975. Though a capable tackler, John was at his best when using his speed and control to raid deep into enemy territory. Blessed with what is commonly, if curiously, described as an ability to open cans with his left foot, he was an accurate passer who was especially adept at wicked, low crosses into the six-yard box.

After playing an important part in the Blues' rise from their turn-of-the-decade doldrums, it was fitting that John, who was at his uplifting best in the 1984 Milk Cup Final draw against Liverpool, should gain compensation for the replay defeat by sharing in that term's FA Cup triumph over Watford. The following season he played enough games to win a title medal before being replaced by the more abrasive Pat Van den Hauwe. Thereafter Everton progressed to greater glory, but when an £80,000 deal took John to Newcastle in October 1985, the Merseyside soccer scene was immeasurably the poorer. Happily for all concerned, in 1992 he returned to the Blues as a coach; John's youthful charges could expect to work hard, but they would be guaranteed a laugh to lighten their labours.

BORN: Liverpool, 1.4.57. GAMES: 219 (1). GOALS: 3. HONOURS:
League Championship 84/5; FA Cup 83/4.
OTHER CLUBS: Blackburn Rovers 75/6-78/9 (120, 1);
Newcastle United 85/6-87/8 (40, 0);
Bristol City 88/9-90/1 (80, 1).

1979/80 - 1985/86

PAT HEARD   1978/79 - 1979/80

Left-back/midfielder. BORN: Hull, 17.3.60. GAMES: 10 (1). GOALS: 0.
OTHER CLUBS: Aston Villa 79/80-82/3 (24, 2); Sheffield Wednesday
82/3-84/5 (25, 3); Newcastle United 84/5 (34, 2); Middlesbrough 85/6
(25, 2); Hull City 85/6-87/8 (80, 5); Rotherham United 88/9-89/90 (44, 7);
Cardiff City 90/1-91/2 (46, 4).

PAT HEARD

GLENN KEELEY   1982/83

Central defender. BORN: Barking, Essex, 1.9.54.
GAMES: 1 (on loan). GOALS: 0.
OTHER CLUBS: Ipswich Town 72/3-73/4 (4, 0);
Newcastle United 74/5-75/6 (44, 2);
Blackburn Rovers 76/7-86/7 (370, 23); Oldham Athletic 87/8 (11, 0);
Colchester United on loan 87/8 (4, 0).

GLENN KEELEY

STUART RIMMER   1981/82 - 1983/84

Forward. BORN: Southport, Lancashire, 12.10.64.
GAMES: 3. GOALS: 0.
OTHER CLUBS: Chester City 84/5-87/8 (114, 68);
Watford 87/8-88/9 (10, 1); Notts County 88/9 (4, 2);
Walsall 88/9-90/1 (88, 31); Barnsley 90/1 (15, 1);
Chester City 91/2- (247, 67); Rochdale on loan 94/5 (3, 0);
Preston North End on loan 94/5 (2, 0).

STUART RIMMER

IAN BISHOP   1983/84

Midfielder. BORN: Liverpool, 29.5.65. GAMES: 0 (2). GOALS: 0. OTHER
CLUBS: Crewe Alexandra on loan 83/4 (4, 0); Carlisle United 84/5-87/8
(132, 14); Bournemouth 88/9 (44, 2); Manchester City 89/90 (19, 2); West
Ham United 89/90-97/8 (254, 12); Manchester City 97/8 (6, 0).

ROBBIE WAKENSHAW

DARREN HUGHES   1983/84 - 1984/85

Left-back. BORN: Prescot, Liverpool, 6.10.6
GAMES: 3. GOALS: 0.
OTHER CLUBS: Shrewsbury Town 85/6-86/7 (37, 1);
Brighton and Hove Albion 86/7 (26, 2); Port Vale 87/8-91/2 (184, 4);
Northampton Town 94/5-95/6 (21, 0); Exeter City 95/6-96/7 (62, 1).

DARREN HUGHES

ROBBIE WAKENSHAW   1983/84 - 1984/85

Winger. BORN: Ponteland, Northumberland, 22.12.65.
GAMES: 2 (3). GOALS: 1.
OTHER CLUBS: Carlisle United 85/6 (8, 2);
Doncaster Rovers on loan (8, 3); Rochdale 86/7 (29, 5);
Crewe Alexandra 87/8-88/9 (22, 1).

IAN BISHOP

DEREK WALSH

JASON DANSKIN

DARREN OLDROYD

PETER BILLING

DEREK WALSH   1984/85

Midfielder. BORN: Hamilton, Scotland, 24.10.67. GAMES: 1. GOALS: 0. OTHER CLUBS: Hamilton Academical 87/8 (2, 0); Carlisle United 89/90-92/3 (121, 7).

IAN ATKINS   1984/85 - 1985/86

Midfielder. BORN: Birmingham, 16.1.57. GAMES: 6 (3). GOALS: 1. OTHER CLUBS: Shrewsbury Town 75/6-81/2 (278, 58); Sunderland 82/3-83/4 (77, 6); Ipswich Town 85/6-87/8 (77, 4); Birmingham City 87/8-89/90 (93, 6); Birmingham City 91/2 (8, 0); Cambridge United 92/3 (2, 0); Doncaster Rovers 93/4 (7, 0).
MANAGER: Colchester United (90-91); Cambridge United (92-93); Doncaster Rovers (94); Northampton Town (95-).

JASON DANSKIN   1984/85

Midfielder. BORN: Winsford, Cheshire, 28.12.67. GAMES: 1. GOALS: 0. OTHER CLUBS: Mansfield Town 86/7 (10, 0); Hartlepool United *on loan* 87/8 (3, 0).

JOHN MORRISSEY JNR   1984/85

Winger. BORN: Liverpool, 8.3.65. GAMES: 1 (1). GOALS: 0. OTHER CLUBS: Wolverhampton Wanderers 85/6 (10, 1); Tranmere Rovers 85/6- (446, 50).

DARREN OLDROYD   1984/85

Right-back. BORN: Ormskirk, Lancashire,1.11.66. GAMES: 0 (1). GOALS: 0. OTHER CLUBS: Wolverhampton Wanderers 86/7 (10, 0).

NEIL RIMMER   1984/85

Midfielder. BORN: Liverpool, 13.11.67. GAMES: 0 (1). GOALS: 0. OTHER CLUBS: Ipswich Town 85/6-87/8 (22, 3);Wigan Athletic 88/9-95/6 (190, 10).

PETER BILLING   1985/86

Central defender. BORN: Liverpool, 24.10.64. GAMES: 1. GOALS: 0. OTHER CLUBS: Crewe Alexandra 86/7-88/9 (88, 1); Coventry City 89/90-92/3 (58, 1); Port Vale 92/3-94/5 (26, 0); Hartlepool United 95/6 (36, 0); Crewe Alexandra 96/7 (15, 0).

JOHN MORRISSEY Jnr

IAN ATKINS

NEIL RIMMER

GARY STEVENS

More naturally talented footballers than Gary Stevens have achieved far less than the lean, blond greyhound who wore the number-two shirt throughout Everton's era of mid-eighties eminence. A magnificent athlete with the capacity to learn quickly, he saw off the challenge of the skilful Brian Borrows in the early part of the decade and went on to reach the pinnacle of his profession, winning a regular England place and netting the Blues £1.25 million when he moved to Glasgow Rangers in the summer of 1988.

Gary, who had been converted from midfielder to right-back as he rose through the Goodison youth system, made his senior debut in the autumn of 1981, taking the eye with his speed and stamina. If a winger managed to elude his tackle, usually the boy from Barrow was so quick to recover that he could make a second challenge before a cross was delivered.

What let Gary down at that stage of his career was his work on the ball, especially his service to the front line, which tended to be wayward and almost entirely of the aerial variety. The shortcoming was most noticeable when he had plenty of time, and it was an aspect of his game - along with a question-mark over his positional play - that threatened to preclude further progress. However, he practised hard, learned to do the simple things extremely well and reaped the benefit.

In attack, where his long throw was a telling weapon, Gary became increasingly effective as his all-round expertise developed, the quality of his crosses showing particular improvement. There were a few goals, too, none more memorably significant than the deflected 20-yard left-footer that won a League Cup clash at Anfield in October 1987.

However for much of that term, during which he and manager Colin Harvey had their differences, Gary seemed a little stale, and he was further hindered by injury problems. Consequently his move to Ibrox, where he was to excel, turned out to be in the best interests of all concerned.

BORN: Barrow-in-Furness, 27.3.63.
GAMES: 284 (1). GOALS: 12.
HONOURS: European Cup Winners' Cup 84/5;
League Championship 84/5, 86/7; FA Cup 83/4.
46 England caps (85-92).
OTHER CLUBS: Glasgow Rangers 88/9-93/4 (187, 8);
Tranmere Rovers 94/5-97/8 (127, 2).

1981/82 - 1987/88

TERRY CURRAN

Everton needed two balls when Terry Curran was playing - one for him and another for the rest of the team. That, at least, was the irreverent verdict on the flamboyant, fabulously skilful wingman delivered by a contingent of team-mates whose admiration for his ability to outwit four defenders on a mazy dribble would be tempered by their frustration when he lost possession to a fifth.

The much-travelled Terry spent two spells with the Blues, the first on loan from Sheffield United in the winter of 1982/83 when Howard Kendall was desperate for an entertainer to lift the club during a period of chronic under-achievement. He did so well, creating a plethora of chances for a hitherto goal-shy attack and becoming a darling of the terraces, that the Blues boss tried to make the signing permanent.

The two men could not agree terms, however, and Terry returned to Bramall Lane, not committing himself to Everton until a £90,000 deal was completed the following September. The second time around, he suffered from injuries, his flair was muted, and in 1985 he was freed. Thus did a rare but ill-disciplined talent drift towards oblivion.

BORN: Kinsley, Yorkshire, 20.3.55. GAMES: 23 (5). GOALS: 1. OTHER CLUBS: Doncaster Rovers 73/4-75/6 (68, 11); Nottingham Forest 75/6-76/7 (48, 12); Bury *on loan* 77/8 (2, 0); Derby County 77/8 (26, 2); Southampton 78/9 (26, 0); Sheffield Wednesday 78/9-81/2 (125, 35); Sheffield United 82/3 (33, 3); Huddersfield Town 85/6 (34, 7); Panionis, Greece; Hull City 86/7 (4, 0); Sunderland 86/7 (9, 1); Grantham (non-League); Grimsby Town 87/8 (12, 0); Chesterfield 87/8 (1, 0).

1982/83 & 1983/84 - 1984/85

IAN MARSHALL

Ian Marshall always believed that centre-forward was his best position; the problem was in convincing Howard Kendall. The Everton manager insisted that the tall, burly Oxonian was more suited to the middle of the back four, and it was in that role that his handful of first-team appearances were made. Only several years later, at three other clubs, was he able to prove his point.

An injury to Derek Mountfield provided Ian with his senior Blues break in August 1985, but after several outings alongside Kevin Ratcliffe he returned to the outer fringe of the squad. He was strong in the air and struck the ball with satisfying crispness, but attracted some criticism from fans who saw him as ponderous. In fact, that was a mistaken impression created by a naturally relaxed gait which reflected neither his true pace, nor the effort he was putting in.

Come March 1988, with little prospect of advancement, he moved to Boundary Park, still as a defender. However, an injury crisis at his new club offered a front-line chance and he grabbed it, his goals playing a leading part in the Latics' cup exploits in 1990 and their promotion to the top flight a year later. He went on to strike successfully for Ipswich and Leicester, begging the question: what might have happened if Everton had handed Ian Marshall their number-nine shirt in the late eighties?

BORN: Oxford, 20.3.66. GAMES: 10 (7). GOALS: 2. OTHER CLUBS: Oldham Athletic 87/8-92/3 (170, 36); Ipswich Town 93/4-96/7 (84, 32); Leicester City 96/7- (52, 15).

1985/86 - 1987/88

KEVIN RICHARDSON

Unobtrusive but infinitely capable, midfielder Kevin Richardson is one of those footballers who attract far more plaudits from fellow professionals than either fan or pundits. The blond Geordie beavers away enthusiastically, tackling briskly, passing sensibly and denying more feted adversaries the space in which to play, perhaps going through an entire season without performing one spectacular act, yet of crucial value to his team.

Probably Arsenal and Aston Villa enjoyed Kevin's peak performances, but his contribution to Everton, his first club, should not be overlooked. After being handed his senior chance by Howard Kendall as an 18-year-old in November 1981, the left-sided, 5ft 7in forager worked hard to establish a niche in an expensively assembled squad that was destined for high achievement.

Without securing a regular place, between 1982 and 1985 Kevin played in more matches than he missed, often filling in for injured colleagues with a distinction that was deservedly rewarded with an FA Cup winner's medal in 1984 and a Championship gong the following year. Some of his most telling contributions came in knockout competitions: there were goals in the 1984 Milk Cup semi-final against Aston Villa - in which he played with a broken wrist - and the FA Cup quarter-final clash with Notts County, and Kevin it was who supplied the left-wing cross that led to Graeme Sharp's Wembley opener against Watford.

He was versatile, too, sometimes sweeping in front of his back four to stem the flow of opposition attacks, on other occasions resembling an out-and-out winger. However, Kevin had to live with the fact that when everyone was fit he would be on the sidelines, and in September 1986 he accepted a move to Watford. From Vicarage Road, his talents took him to Highbury and a second title medal, then on to Villa Park, where his evergreen excellence earned him an unexpected but deserved England call-up. Four years on in 1998, no fewer than 17 seasons after his Everton debut, Kevin Richardson was still offering value for money in the top flight.

BORN: Newcastle, 4.12.62. GAMES: 120 (19). GOALS: 20.
HONOURS: League Championship 84/5; FA Cup 83/4.
OTHER CLUBS: Watford 86/7 (39, 2); Arsenal 87/8-89/90 (96, 5); Real Sociedad, Spain, 90/1 (37, 0); Aston Villa 91/2-94/5 (143, 13); Coventry City 94/5-97/8 (78, 0); Southampton 97/8- (28, 0).

1981/82 - 1986/87

PAUL BRACEWELL

When paeans of praise are sung to Everton's most revered combination of modern times - the men who brought League, European and, so very nearly, FA Cup glory to Goodison in 1984/85 - the name of Paul Bracewell tends to languish in the shadows, perhaps mentioned only as an afterthought. Yet that is a gross injustice to the Wirral-born midfielder whose career was moving into overdrive just when a mysterious injury knocked it out of gear.

Paul, a £250,000 recruit from Sunderland in May 1984, was only 23 and a current England international when he limped off at Newcastle on New Year's Day, 1986, suffering severe pain in his right ankle. X-rays proved inconclusive and he saw out the rest of that campaign, often in agony yet unable to prove it with medical evidence. Eventually the trouble was traced to a piece of loose bone, but by the time Paul had recovered - following a series of operations and having made only one senior start in two seasons - the team had changed radically, and in August 1989 he returned to Roker Park.

Thus did the Blues lose an unobtrusive but well-balanced all-round talent, a brisk tackler who occupied centre-field alongside Peter Reid, and helped to keep moves flowing with accurate first-time passes, much in the manner of Liverpool's Ronnie Whelan. Lacking from the Bracewell game were both pace and goal-power, the former mattering little in view of his sharp footballing brain, the latter irrelevant while his service created so many chances for team-mates. In fact, he did manage one crucial strike - rendered even more memorable because it was a rare headed effort - to earn a first-leg win in Bratislava in October 1984.

Before injury sabotaged his progress, he was maturing into a performer of ever-increasing influence. How Everton could have used Paul Bracewell at his peak in the frustrating seasons that lay ahead. Instead he performed outstandingly for Sunderland and others, notably in 1992, when the Wearsiders staved off the threat of relegation and reached the FA Cup Final.

BORN: Heswall, Merseyside, 19.7.62. GAMES: 132 (2). GOALS: 10.
HONOURS: European Cup Winners' Cup 84/5; League Championship 84/5.
3 England caps (85). OTHER CLUBS: Stoke City 79/80-82/3 (129, 5);
Sunderland 83/4 (38, 4) and 89/90-91/2 (112, 2); Newcastle United
92/3-94/5 (73, 3); Sunderland 95/6-97/8 (77, 0); Fulham 97/8- (36, 0).

1984/85 - 1988/89

ANDY GRAY

When Andy Gray breezed into Goodison in November 1983, his £250,000 signing from Wolves was dismissed by many as a mark of managerial desperation. The Blues were five places off the foot of the First Division and goals were in depressingly short supply, but, the argument went, where was the logic in acquiring a burnt-out striker with dodgy knees? Eighteen months and three major trophies later, the Scottish gladiator had routed his doubters and Howard Kendall was being hailed for the most inspired transaction of his life.

Inescapably, Andy Gray played a crucial part in revitalising Everton, not just the team but the whole club. On the pitch, he sent morale soaring with his boldness and hunger for the ball; team-mates marvelled at his aerial majesty, backed up by oft-underrated skill at retaining posession, and they goggled at a bravery that sometimes defied belief.
Yet the upbeat Gray influence was even more marked in the dressing room, where he doubled as arch-motivator and social secretary; exuding confidence, he replaced tension with belief and became the catalyst that helped to transform a squad of top-notch individuals into the best side in England.

And yet Andy's impact was neither instant nor uninterrupted. In fact, he was dropped for an FA Cup replay against Gillingham in January 1984 and considered walking out on his new employers. It was a temporary setback, however, and the raw-boned, blond marauder - his spiritual home might have been the prow of a Viking warship - was at his most effective as the Blues marched on to victory at Wembley. But then, in 1984/85, he recovered from an early-season knock only to be consigned to the bench, from which he watched in frustration as Graeme Sharp and Adrian Heath spearheaded a stirring surge to the top of the table.

Was Andy - an idol of the fans, whose loyalty and adulation he never took for granted - surplus to requirements after all? The answer was to be 'no', or rather 'not yet'. Come the autumn, poor Adrian was injured and the Glaswegian struck a vein of sensational form that won him an international recall as Everton lifted both League title and European Cup Winners' Cup. However, with the silverware barely tucked away in the Goodison trophy cabinet, the Gray sojourn on Merseyside was to end, abruptly and controversially. Howard Kendall announced his intention of signing Gary Lineker, and suddenly there was no place for the popular hero of the recent euphoric campaign. Accordingly that summer, despite petitions from outraged supporters, Andy returned to Aston Villa - who had once sold him for almost £1.5 million - for a knock-down £150,000.

The memories of his derring-do in blue positively queue up to be trotted out: the courageous header against Notts County in the 1984 FA Cup quarter-final, so low that his nose was scraping the turf; the rumbustious challenge on the Watford 'keeper that resulted in his Cup-clinching strike; the brace of spectacular diving efforts against Sunderland on the run-in to the 1985 Championship; the European hat-trick that sunk Fortuna Sittard, and the volleyed opener against Rapid Vienna in the subsequent final; they all clamour for attention.

But Andy's value could not be measured in goals alone. Indeed, there are those who maintain that saving his presence, Howard Kendall would have been hard pushed to avoid the sack, and that but for his uplifting example, Graeme Sharp might never have developed into the top target-man he became. But whatever the scale of his contribution, there can be no doubt that Andy - who went on to double as broadcaster and Villa's assistant manager - was a glorious, much-loved talisman during a brief but matchlessly rousing period of Everton history.

BORN: Glasgow 30.11.55. GAMES: 61 (7). GOALS: 22.
HONOURS: European Cup Winners' Cup 84/5; League Championship 84/5;
FA Cup 83/4. 20 Scotland caps (75-85). OTHER CLUBS: Dundee United 73/4-75/6 (62, 36);
Aston Villa 75/6-78/9 (113, 54); Wolverhampton Wanderers 79/80-83/4 (133, 38);
Aston Villa 85/6-86/7 (54, 5); Notts County 87/8 (4, 0);
West Bromwich Albion 87/8-88/9 (34, 10);
Glasgow Rangers 88/9 (13, 5).

1983/84 - 1984/85

ALAN HARPER

If a caricaturist set out to capture the essence of Alan Harper, the substitutes' bench would provide the inevitable setting. There would slump the blond utility man, glum of countenance, wondering desperately if he would be called from the sidelines. It would be a fitting illustration of a worthy, but frequently frustrating career, the bulk of which was spent on his native Merseyside.

After leaving school, Alan did not have to wait long before suffering his first disappointment. Born into a Reds-mad family, he faced the mortification of not making the grade at Anfield, and so signed for the Blues in June 1983. Immediately, he began to do justice to his undoubted talent, and he enjoyed a lengthy run at right-back during his initial Goodison campaign. Yet having gained a place in Howard Kendall's rapidly improving squad and impressing in most defensive and midfield roles, he could never cement a regular berth in the team. Indeed, he wore six different numbers on the way to picking up a title medal in 1986/87, but if everyone else was fit, then poor Alan would be the man to stand down.

Ironically, he would have walked into most First Division sides. He was an impeccably consistent technician, passing, tackling, heading and shooting to a high degree of competence, though it was rare for him to turn a game with a flash of inspiration. Not that Alan didn't enjoy his moments of glory, notably netting from 30 yards to earn a point at home to Liverpool in March 1984, and opening the score against Sheffield Wednesday in the 1986 FA Cup semi-final with the sweetest of lobs.

Nothing could disguise his craving for first-team football, however, and in July 1988 he accepted a move to Hillsborough, later reuniting with Howard Kendall at Manchester City. August 1991 saw Alan follow his mentor back to Goodison for £300,000, but after a splendid run at right-back, sweeper and in midfield, he was handed that familiar number-12 shirt. Characteristically he fought back to reclaim his place, but was freed to join Luton Town as he approached the veteran stage in September 1993.

BORN: Liverpool, 1.11.60. GAMES: 185 (43). GOALS: 5. HONOURS: League Championship 84/5, 86/7.
OTHER CLUBS: Sheffield Wednesday 88/9-89/90 (35, 0); Manchester City 89/90-90/1 (50, 1).; Luton Town 93/4 (41, 1); Burnley 94/5-95/6 (31, 0); Cardiff City *on loan* 95/6 (5, 0).

1983/84 - 1987/88 & 1991/92 - 1992/93

GARY LINEKER

It seems difficult to grasp now, with Gary Lineker a national hero of Boys' Own Paper proportions, but there was a time when he was *unpopular* with a sizeable section of Everton supporters. The problem, in the months after his arrival from Leicester in July 1985, was that he had replaced the much-loved Andy Gray and the Gwladys Street end, in particular, was not amused.

It was not as if the amiable Gary, who had cost £800,000 plus a percentage of any future fee, presented a natural target for the terrace critics. Admittedly, he failed to find the net on his first three appearances, but then the goals came in a veritable deluge, 38 of them - including three hat-tricks - in a mere 52 outings. Incredibly, it was nearly Christmas before the resentment abated and the fans settled back to enjoy the exploits of a master marksman.

Gary's golden assets, which were to become renowned the world over, were searing pace and instinctive anticipation of developing situations. Though not a man to initiate his own opportunities by taking opponents on - he relied wholly on service from Messrs Sharp, Sheedy and company - he timed his runs to perfection, and was the most clinical of executioners.

As the season neared its climax, the Blues looked a fair bet to clinch the League and FA Cup double, and Gary's gargantuan contribution was recognised by awards from both players and football writers. Sadly, the subsequent crushing anti-climax - which saw Liverpool take both trophies, despite a Lineker goal at Wembley - removed something of the gloss from a fabulous individual achievement.

That summer, Gary top-scored in the World Cup finals before stunning Evertonians by joining Barcelona for £2.5 million. Howard Kendall was less than enthusiastic about the deal but could not stand in the way of such a dream move, and in the event it was hardly a disaster. The following term the Blues shared out the goals - and won the title.

BORN: Leicester, 30.11.60. GAMES: 52. GOALS: 38.
HONOURS: 80 England caps (84-92).
OTHER CLUBS: Leicester City 78/9-84/5 (194, 95);
Barcelona, Spain 86/7-88/9 (99, 44);
Tottenham Hotspur 89/90-91/2 (105, 67).
Grampus Eight, Japan, 92-94.

1985/86

PAT VAN DEN HAUWE

Pat Van den Hauwe took to the pitch growling, scowling and stubbly, like some villainous refugee from a low-budget spaghetti western - and there is no shortage of opposing players and fans who reckoned he continued in similar vein once the game started. The brawny left-back positively oozed aggression and earned the reputation of one of the hardest men in the First Division. Occasionally his methods seemed at odds with the spirit of the game, yet there was no denying that the man dubbed 'Psycho-Pat' by a gleefully ghoulish element on the Goodison terraces was a footballer of considerable ability.

As well as his clattering tackles - which, it must be said, were of immense value to the Everton rearguard - Pat offered pace aplenty, sure-footed control and distribution that was accurate and, at times, imaginative. In addition, his aerial power was such that he could double as a central defender and also offer a potent far-post attacking threat.

The Belgian-born Welsh international - unknowingly, he scuppered his chances of playing for his own country by opting out of national service - was enlisted from Birmingham City at a cost of £100,000 in September 1984. Immediately, Howard Kendall pitched him into the first team at the expense of John Bailey, and he became a fixture in the side that finished the season with two trophies.

Pat took a vigorous part in Everton's impressive, though ultimately unrewarded 1985/86 campaign - he was to make up for the disappointment of Wembley defeat at the hands of Liverpool by pocketing an FA Cup winner's medal with Spurs in 1991 - and his place was not in question until a blood infection limited his appearances in 1986/87. He returned at the death, though, netting the goal at Norwich that clinched the title, then serving in midfield before moving to White Hart Lane in a £575,000 deal in August 1989. At Goodison, the name of Van den Hauwe is still uttered with wicked relish by some, with considerable reservation by others.

BORN: Dendermonde, Belgium, 16.12.60. GAMES: 189 (1). GOALS: 3.
HONOURS: European Cup Winners' Cup 84/5; League Championship 84/5, 86/7.
13 Wales caps (85-89).
OTHER CLUBS: Birmingham City 78/9-84/5 (123, 1);
Tottenham Hotspur 89/90-92/3 (116, 0);
Millwall 93/4-94/5 (27, 0).

1984/85 - 1988/89

DEREK MOUNTFIELD

Everton fans can be over-critical at times, but when they recognise a footballer of high quality and take him to their hearts, they brook no argument about his merits. Such was the case concerning central defender Derek Mountfield, a quiet Merseysider whose exemplary contribution at either end of the pitch as the Blues sought glory on three fronts in 1984/85 won him unreserved admiration on the terraces. Consequently, when he was axed in favour of expensive new signing Dave Watson following a serious injury, outraged supporters berated manager Colin Harvey and waved banners calling for their hero's reinstatement. Some went as far as to proclaim that the club had been blessed with no more accomplished middle-of-the-back-four performer since the far-off days of Labone and Hurst - and they could offer persuasive evidence to make their point.

Certainly Derek, a £30,000 capture from Tranmere Rovers in June 1982, must rate as one of Howard Kendall's most astute purchases. Seen originally as a long-term investment, he won early promotion as a result of Mark Higgins' heartbreaking ill fortune, and impressed hugely with his speed, strength in the air and comfort on the ball. He was rewarded by an FA Cup winner's medal in 1984, but it was during the following season that he came into his own. By then, having formed a masterly defensive partnership with Kevin Ratcliffe, he had acquired the confidence to move forward and scored 14 goals in senior competitions. These included a late equaliser in the FA Cup quarter-final against Ipswich, an extra-time winner over Luton in the semi-final, and the strike against Queen's Park Rangers that effectively clinched the Championship on a sunny May day at Goodison.

It seemed that the athletic 22-year-old could look forward to a glowing Blues future, but a torn cartilage sabotaged his 1985/86 campaign and the subsequent arrival of Watson prevented a comeback. Reluctantly - he was a passionate Evertonian - Derek accepted that he must leave, and in June 1988 joined Aston Villa, with whom his fortunes were to be mixed.

BORN: Liverpool, 2.11.62. GAMES: 142 (6). GOALS: 24.
HONOURS: European Cup Winners' Cup 84/5; League
Championship 84/5, 86/7; FA Cup 83/4.
OTHER CLUBS: Tranmere Rovers 80/1-81/2 (26, 1); Aston Villa
88/9- 91/2 (90, 9); Wolverhampton Wanderers 91/2-93/4 (83, 4);
Carlisle United 94/5 (31, 3); Northampton Town 95/6 (4, 0);
Walsall 95/6- (97, 2).

1982/83 - 1987/88

KEVIN RATCLIFFE

Gwladys Street wags reckoned any visitor to Goodison on the day after a match could tell at a glance whether Kevin Ratcliffe had played - when the Welshman had been on duty, the scorchmarks on the turf were a dead giveaway! It was a typical Scouse tribute to the phenomenal pace of the Blues' skipper, the First Division's fastest central defender during his mid-eighties pomp and one of the bulwarks around whom Howard Kendall built his finest side to date.

Yet there was a time when Kevin's Everton future was clouded with uncertainty, his relationship with the manager under severe strain. After impressing on his first senior appearance - subduing the fearsome Joe Jordan in a goalless draw at Old Trafford in March 1980, towards the end of the Gordon Lee era - the young 'Rats' spent two terms in and out of the team, and most of his games were at left-back. Upset by such apparent lack of recognition, and by being played out of position, Kevin confronted Howard and at one stage there was talk of a move to Ipswich.

To the immeasurable long-term benefit of the Goodison cause, no deal took place, and in December 1982 Kevin's fortunes took a decisive upturn when he ended a spell on the sidelines by replacing the overweight Billy Wright alongside Mark Higgins in the middle of the back four. Within a year he had succeeded the injury-ravaged Mark as captain, the following March he was leading his country, and in May 1984, aged 23, he became the youngest man since Bobby Moore 20 years earlier to receive the FA Cup. That signalled the start of the Blues' purple period, and Kevin was a constant, monumentally reassuring figure, excelling alongside first Derek Mountfield and then Dave Watson as the silverware piled up.

Understandably, it was Kevin's velocity in sprints both long and short that attracted most attention - even when Everton's offside trap was sprung, his recovery could be so rapid that Neville Southall might be reduced to the role of spectator - yet the Ratcliffe speed of thought could be equally crucial. He read the game with instinctive shrewdness, 'closing down' opponents instantly in moments of danger and frequently averting crises by clever positional play. His tackle was scything when necessary, but he preferred to remain on his feet, well-balanced and ready to cope with any new threat.

Thus Kevin - a schooldays team-mate of Ian Rush, who troubled him more than most centre-forwards during his professional career - took an effective overview of the action, making nonsense of the fact that his god-given footballing talent was negligible. Heavily biased towards his left side, he excelled despite aerial ability that was combatively competent without being outstanding, and a distinctly average touch on the ball. This last was rarely exposed because he concentrated on doing the simple things well, invariably shying away from any form of elaboration.

Of course, Kevin's natural leadership qualities played a significant part in his continued eminence. A tough-minded, quietly spoken individual who was accustomed to let his deeds on the pitch do his talking for him, he was respected and liked by his colleagues. The fans, too - some of whom had given him an unreasonably rough ride during his formative first-team years - warmed eventually to a man who had been an Everton supporter as a boy and went on to serve the club so nobly.

Only as the nineties dawned, and that renowned Ratcliffe acceleration began to lose its edge, was his place in the side open to question. In the spring of 1992 Kevin was given a free transfer, but such a downbeat departure could not diminish his stature as one of Goodison's most revered sons, an accolade both hard earned and thoroughly deserved.

BORN: Mancot, North Wales, 12.11.60. GAMES: 469 (3). GOALS: 2.
HONOURS: European Cup Winners' Cup 84/5; League Championship 84/5, 86/7; FA Cup 83/4. 59 Wales caps (80-93).
OTHER CLUBS: Dundee 92/3 (4, 0); Cardiff City 92/3-93/4 (25, 1); Derby County 93/4 (6, 0); Chester City 94/5 (23, 0). MANAGER: Chester City (95-).

1979/80 - 1991/92

GRAEME SHARP

For the man who holds the record as Everton's top post-war goalscorer, Graeme Sharp has been accorded curiously scant public recognition. Yet while he lacked the charisma that won Andy Gray the fans' undying affection, and never matched the sensational strike rate that earned universal admiration for Gary Lineker, there is no doubting his stature among the most demanding and perceptive judges of all. In the estimation of his peers, the steely Glaswegian is a veritable giant; indeed, many nominate him as the First Division's most able target-man of the eighties, and sceptics would do well to ponder the testimony of a certain Ian Rush, who knows a bit about the business of leading an attack. When asked in 1987 by his new club, Juventus, which player in the world he would like for a partner, the Welshman named Graeme Sharp.

Of course, no deal ensued, but it is easy to see why Ian would have relished linking up with his long-time rival from the opposite side of Stanley Park. As well as netting his own quota of goals, Graeme was a supremely unselfish provider whose positional sense was remarkably acute. Tall and strong, he was an aerial play-maker who combined power and deftness, and was able to distribute as accurately with his head as numerous contemporaries could with their feet. He could control the ball instantly with chest, thigh and most other areas of his anatomy, usually retaining possession no matter how stringent the physical intimidation - Andy Gray taught him a thing or two about looking after himself - before making an intelligent lay-off. Outright pace could not be numbered among his assets, but opponents let him run free at their peril; his ability to trick his way past defenders in tight situations was underrated.

Such all-round excellence was not immediately apparent when Gordon Lee paid Dumbarton £120,000 for the strapping teenager in April 1980, although lively interest from Aberdeen's Alex Ferguson was a telling clue to his potential. For more than a season, Graeme was unsettled, and was so slow to break into a struggling team that he considered moving on. But his career blossomed under new boss Howard Kendall and he enjoyed a series of fruitful combinations, first with little Adrian Heath, progressing through Messrs Gray and Lineker, then reuniting with 'Inchy' before Everton's mid-eighties flood of honours finally dried up. He offered each partner impeccable service - Lineker, perhaps, owed him the greatest debt, as the England star acknowledged readily - and along the way picked up a dozen caps, though some muttered darkly of so-called bias against 'Anglo' Scots costing him many more international outings.

Highlights of Graeme's decade as a Blue include the opening goal in the 1984 FA Cup Final victory over Watford and the headed equaliser against Bayern Munich in the 1985 European Cup Winners' Cup semi-final. But surely the most spectacular and satisfying strike of his life came at Anfield in the autumn of 1984 on the way to the title. Gary Stevens sent a long, high pass out of defence that dropped obligingly into the path of the sprinting centre-forward; he took it down on his left instep, wrong-footing Liverpool's Mark Lawrenson in the process, and the ball sat up perfectly for Graeme to hit a dipping right-foot volley from 25 yards; Bruce Grobbelaar arched his back valiantly, but the picturesque salmon-leap was in vain, the net bulged, and the Merseyside derby was won.

It was a supreme moment, and one which was revived with a mixture of glee and sadness in the memories of countless Evertonians when it was announced in July 1991 that Graeme was joining Oldham for £500,000. Though he was 30 and his goal tally had deteriorated in recent seasons, there were those who reckoned he was released too soon. His new team-mates at Boundary Park, however, were not complaining.

BORN: Glasgow, 16.10.60. GAMES: 412 (20). GOALS: 150.
HONOURS: European Cup Winners' Cup 84/5; League Championship 84/5, 86/7; FA Cup 83/4. 12 Scotland caps (85-88).
OTHER CLUBS: Dumbarton 78/9-79/80 (40, 17); Oldham Athletic 91/2-94/5 (109, 31). MANAGER: Oldham Athletic (94-97).

1979/80 - 1990/91

ADRIAN HEATH

A tiny man with skilful, scurrying feet and a mighty heart that didn't shrink from the most daunting of physical challenges, Adrian Heath overcame a crisis of confidence to play an exhilarating part in some of the Blues' most heady triumphs. He arrived on Merseyside from his native Stoke for £700,000 in January 1982, not quite 21 and looking more like a little boy lost than the costliest signing Everton had ever made.

Perhaps hindered by switches between midfield and the front line, and not helped by senseless barracking, he took time to settle. Gradually, however, Howard Kendall's judgement was vindicated. Adrian was a workaholic who unsettled opponents with his close skills and darting speed, ever available to receive the ball, running hither and thither among defenders like some hyperactive fieldmouse in a room full of cats.

He was in his element when attacking alongside big Graeme Sharp. Their partnership was never demonstrated to more devastating effect than at Maine Road in 1982 when 'Inchy' skipped over a through-pass before scampering into space, whereupon Graeme clipped the ball into the path of his nippy partner, who drove it home from 20 yards. In 1983/84 Adrian was the club's top scorer, two of his most important strikes being the late Milk Cup equaliser at Oxford - which appeared to revitalise the Blues' flagging fortunes - and the FA Cup semi-final winner against Southampton. The following term he struck peak form, only to be sidelined in December by a wrenched knee, thus being deprived not only of taking further part in Everton's League and European conquests, but also, maybe, a full England cap to add to his under-21 honours.

He recovered to play a telling role in the 1986/87 title-winning campaign, but the next season was disappointing both for Adrian and Everton, and in late 1988 he opted to try his luck in Spain. Soon he returned to England, but while he served Manchester City well, there seemed little doubt that Goodison had seen the best of 'Inchy'. Thus it was not surprising that when he returned to the Toffees as Kendall's number-two in 1997, his welcome was as enthusiastic as it was genuinely warm.

BORN: Stoke, Staffordshire, 11.1.61. GAMES: 267 (26). GOALS: 89.
HONOURS: League Championship 84/5, 86/7; FA Cup 83/4.
OTHER CLUBS: Stoke City 78/9-81/2 (95, 16); Espanyol, Spain; Aston Villa 89/90 (9, 0); Manchester City 89/90- 91/2 (71, 4); Stoke City 91/2 (6, 0); Burnley 92/3-95/6 (115, 29); Sheffield United 95/6 (4, 0); Burnley 95/6-96/7 (5, 0).
MANAGER: Burnley (96-97).

1981/82 - 1988/89

IAN SNODIN

The loss of Ian Snodin for the better part of two seasons was a handicap beyond measure as Everton lurched painfully into the nineties. At his peak arguably the most complete all-round footballer at Goodison, the vigorous Yorkshireman - whose career was jeopardised by a chronic hamstring problem and other injuries - was an inspirational performer in midfield, the centre of defence or, most effectively of all, at right-back. Indeed, when he was laid low in 1989/90, his performances in the number-two shirt had earned an England call-up and there was every reason to believe that a long-term international stint was in the offing.

Ian made his first favourable impression on Howard Kendall when playing for Doncaster against Everton in a 1984 League Cup tie, but it was not until after a spell with Leeds United - whom he captained - that he arrived on Merseyside, spurning the advances of Liverpool to sign on at Goodison for £840,000 in January 1987. Soon his midfield style was being likened to that of Bryan Robson, and he was a major factor in that term's Championship success.

A magnificent athlete, he boasted pace and a biting tackle - the five-a-side team he led in training were known as 'Snodin's Snarlers' - while his ball control and passing, both long and short, were in the thoroughbred class. The one knack he did not possess was scoring goals and it was a frequent frustration to see him blast wide after powering into a menacing position.

Deservedly, however, Ian - whose brother, Glynn, played for an assortment of Yorkshire clubs - became a terrace favourite, especially after demonstrating his versatility as a deputy for centre-half Dave Watson, then slotting in so effectively at right-back.

When misfortune struck, he earned widespread admiration by refusing to give in, fighting a two-year battle to regain fitness. Eventually Ian returned to battle once more under the Blues banner, proving to be a major if no longer dominating force, before being freed to join Oldham in January 1995.

BORN: Rotherham, Yorkshire, 15.8.63. GAMES: 131 (4). GOALS: 5.
HONOURS: League Championship 86/7.
OTHER CLUBS: Doncaster Rovers 79/80-84/5 (188, 25);
Leeds United 85/6-86/7 (51, 6); Sunderland *on loan* 94/5 (6, 0);
Oldham Athletic 94/5-96/7 (57, 0); Scarborough 97/8- (35, 0).

1986/87 - 1994/95

WAYNE CLARKE

Wayne Clarke cost Everton £300,000 in March 1987; two months later he had repaid the investment with interest. By season's end the slender, round-shouldered marksman, bought from Birmingham City as an emergency replacement for the injured Graeme Sharp, had netted five times and the Championship had been secured. His first strike, an impudent 25-yard lob to take the points from Arsenal at Highbury, was particularly telling, and a smoothly-dispatched hat-trick at home to Newcastle underlined Howard Kendall's wisdom in signing a proven scorer at a bargain price.

While Wayne was a lesser talent than his more famous older brother, Allan, he shared the family instinct for tucking away chances, precisely and economically, and if his overall class was insufficient to carve a long-term Blues career, it hardly mattered in the circumstances.

Before leaving for Leicester in 1989 - as makeweight in the deal that took Mike Newell to Merseyside - Wayne enjoyed two further moments of glory. His goal decided the 1987 Charity Shield clash with Coventry, and the following spring he sent Goodison into ecstasy with an opportunist poke to end Liverpool's 29-match unbeaten run. For the Clarkes, it was doubly satisfying: had the Reds not lost they would have claimed the record held by the Leeds United of Allan's prime.

BORN: Wolverhampton, 28.2.61. GAMES: 50 (22). GOALS: 19.
HONOURS: League Championship 86/7.
OTHER CLUBS: Wolverhampton Wanderers 77/8-83/4 (148, 30); Birmingham City 84/5-86/7 (92, 38); Leicester City 89/90 (11, 1); Manchester City 89/90-91/2 (21, 2); Shrewsbury Town *on loan* 90/91 (7, 6); Stoke City *on loan* 90/1 (9, 3); Wolverhampton Wanderers *on loan* 91/2 (1, 0); Walsall 92/3 (39, 21); Shrewsbury Town 93/4-94/5 (59, 22).

1986/87 - 1988/89

NEIL POINTON

A fearsome expertise at press-ups made some of his more stately team-mates cringe, and turf-gouging slide-tackles earned good-natured rebukes from the Goodison groundsmen, yet Neil Pointon was a popular addition to the Blues squad when he arrived as an unknown quantity from Scunthorpe United in November 1985. Certainly, Howard Kendall was delighted when the curly-haired left-back - pressed into First Division action only two days after his £50,000 transfer because regular number-three Pat Van den Hauwe had measles - made an efficient debut in a 6-1 home victory over Arsenal. Soon he was rewarded with a 19-match senior spell as Pat deputised in the centre for the injured Derek Mountfield, and a long-term Everton future seemed to be the likely Pointon destiny.

The 21-year-old newcomer proved a commendably sound all-rounder. When his winger gained possession, Neil would be on him in an instant, denying space and challenging crisply. While not prone to dally in the danger area, he could pass constructively and a combination of speed and crossing ability stood him in good attacking stead. In the summer of 1990, however, after five seasons at Goodison in which he was rarely *quite* sure of his place, he joined Manchester City as part of the package that took Andy Hinchcliffe in the opposite direction.

BORN: Warsop Vale, Nottinghamshire, 8.11.64.
GAMES: 117 (10). GOALS: 5.
HONOURS: League Championship 86/7.

OTHER CLUBS: Scunthorpe United 81/2-85/6 (159, 2); Manchester City 90/1-91/2 (74, 2); Oldham Athletic 92/3-95/6 (94, 3); Heart of Midlothian 95/6- (67, 3).

1985/86 - 1989/90

PAUL POWER

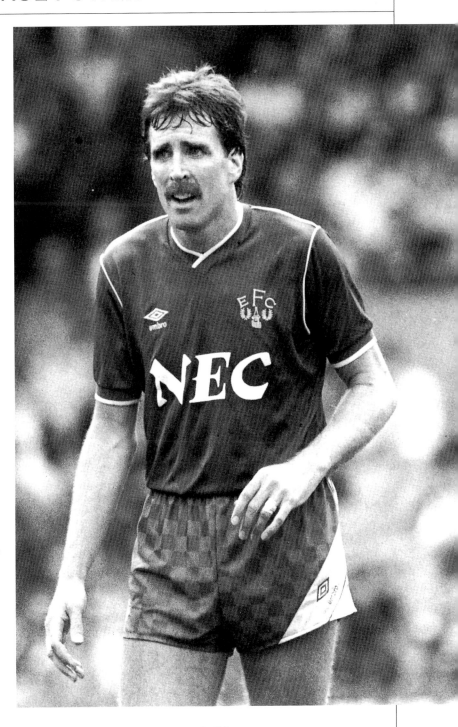

Few purchases bore more impressive testimony to the managerial acumen of Howard Kendall than that of Paul Power. In the summer of 1986, after 11 trophy-starved seasons as a professional at Maine Road, the 32-year-old Manchester City captain and England 'B' international was presumed to be nearing his First Division sell-by date. But the Everton boss saw something others had missed, snapped up the dark, rather gangling Mancunian for a mere £65,000, and made him a first-team regular as the Blues lifted the League crown.

Admittedly, a spate of injuries was instrumental in Paul's instant inclusion, first filling in for Pat van den Hauwe at left-back, later excelling as Kevin Sheedy's left-flank deputy and occasionally operating in central midfield. However, it was up to the versatile newcomer to make the most of his opportunity, which he did to such effect that he shared the supporters' player of the year award with Kevin Ratcliffe.

Part of the Power secret was his dedication to fitness, a factor which must have weighed heavily in Kendall's decision to acquire his services, but his all-round competence should not be underrated. Competitive in the air and firm in the tackle, Paul used the ball constructively and carried a fierce shot, which many fans - especially those who witnessed his venomous 25-yarder that secured the points at home to Southampton in February 1988 - maintained he should have unleashed more frequently.

During 1987/88 he celebrated his 34th birthday and it was hardly surprising that his appearances became sporadic. Soon, he joined the Blues' coaching staff, although he was not destined for a long-term Goodison future. Instead Paul, an articulate man who had studied for a law degree before making the grade at his first club, became north-west regional manager of the Football In The Community scheme. What a stirring tale of belated but richly deserved achievement he could tell to encourage his new clients.

BORN: Manchester, 30.10.53. GAMES: 63 (2). GOALS: 6. HONOURS:
League Championship 86/7.
OTHER CLUBS: Manchester City 75/6-85/6 (365, 26).

1986/87 - 1987/88

PETER REID

As Howard Kendall led the Blues to unprecedented glory in the mid eighties, his predecessor, Gordon Lee, could be excused if he gazed wistfully at the diminutive on-the-field director of his former charges and mouthed the most poignant, oft-repeated words in football: 'If only . . .' The fact was that Gordon had bid £600,000 for Peter Reid in the summer of 1980, but any hope of enlisting Bolton's midfield controller was dashed by a continuation of the player's appalling catalogue of injuries. Thereafter, Everton's decline became ever more distressing, Lee's sacking ushered in the Kendall era, and in December 1982 Peter, whose influence on the side's subsequent success simply cannot be overstated, checked in at Goodison for one tenth of the earlier offer.

Not that the battle-scarred newcomer, who had recovered from two broken legs, torn knee ligaments and a cartilage operation, was an overnight sensation. Indeed, in the spring of 1983 he looked to be losing his battle for fitness and his manager feared the worst; even when Peter reported ready for the fray in 1983/84, Kendall - beleaguered by critics as the Blues made a stuttering start - left his most inspirational creator on the sidelines.

Soon, however, the Reid option became irresistible, and the turnaround in the club's fortunes during the second half of the campaign was due in no small measure to the perceptive promptings of the pugnacious Lancastrian. His method owed everything to superb skill and vision, yet it was simple in the extreme. Peter rarely needed more than two touches of the ball: he would get it, give it, move into space and demand it back, forever bringing colleagues into the game and opening fresh avenues of attack. His lack of pace was rendered irrelevant by a keenly honed sense of anticipation that invariably made him first to loose balls, and by the precision of his passing, often in brisk, short triangular manoeuvres but also over long distances, as his 50-yard chip to set up Gary Lineker's 1986 FA Cup Final strike demonstrated vividly.

Of course, Peter's outstanding technique represented only part of his immense contribution to Everton's avalanche of honours. His sheer vitality and strength of will, later to stand him in splendid stead as a manager, were of incalculable value in driving on his team-mates, and evoked memories of the equally irrepressible Bobby Collins.

It is not to be wondered at that Peter's most injury-free term, that of 1984/85, should coincide with his club's finest hours - coming so excruciatingly close to the treble of League, FA Cup and European Cup Winners' Cup - or that he should end it as the players' player of the year. Nor was there any escaping the fact that when he replaced the luckless Bryan Robson in the 1986 World Cup finals, the hitherto ineffective England side took on new stature, and there can be little doubt that had he spent less time with limbs in plaster, Peter would have become a major force at international level.

In the 16 months from September 1985, ankle trouble limited him to only 11 League starts, but his return in February 1987 proved a telling factor in the Blues' second title triumph in three seasons. That June, on the departure of Howard Kendall, the increasingly grizzled veteran - notwithstanding a period when the grey around his temples turned jet black - became player-coach, a role he fulfilled until joining Queen's Park Rangers in 1989. Though by then he was 32, there is a persuasive school of thought that he was allowed to leave too soon, and that his experience would have been invaluable to the likes of young John Ebbrell. Peter Reid had achieved more than enough already, however, to ensure his enshrinement in Goodison folklore. Kendall had once called him Everton's most important signing since the war; nothing more need be said.

BORN: Huyton, Lancashire, 20.6.56. GAMES: 222 (6). GOALS: 13.
HONOURS: European Cup Winners' Cup 84/5; League Championship 84/5, 86/7; FA Cup 83/4. 13 England caps (85-88). OTHER CLUBS: Bolton Wanderers 74/5-82/3 (225, 23); Queen's Park Rangers 88/9-89/90 (29, 1); Manchester City 89/90-92/3 (99, 1); Southampton 93/4 (7, 0); Notts County 93/4 (5, 0); Bury 94/5 (1, 0).
MANAGER: Manchester City (90-93); Sunderland (95-).

1982/83 - 1988/89

NEIL ADAMS

After one season of high promise with Stoke City, his home-town club, Neil Adams was snapped up by Howard Kendall in the summer of 1986 as an investment for the future. In the short term, the Everton boss used the sandy-haired attacking midfielder to strengthen his squad, and Neil was given 12 League outings as the Championship was claimed in his first Merseyside campaign. But it seemed likely that the youngster, whose speed and skill were well suited to a wide position, would need more time in the reserves to continue learning his trade.

Sure enough, Neil had few senior opportunities in 1987/88 - his most memorable moment was heading a late winner, from a Pat Van den Hauwe corner, against Oldham in a League Cup replay at Goodison - but when he did step up the feeling grew that, for all his potential and his England under-21 recognition, he might lack the spark to make the grade at Goodison.

Colin Harvey, Kendall's successor, was clearly of that mind, for he allowed Neil - a popular character who excelled as master of ceremonies during team sing-songs - to join Oldham in January 1989. At Boundary Park he made an instant impression and helped Joe Royle's club into the top flight, later finding a productive First Division niche with Norwich City.

BORN: Stoke, Staffordshire, 23.11.65.
GAMES: 21 (3). GOALS: 1.
HONOURS: League Championship 86/7.
OTHER CLUBS: Stoke City 85/6 (32, 4);
Oldham Athletic 88/9-93/4 (129, 23);
Norwich City 93/4- (164, 22).

1986/87 - 1987/88

PAUL WILKINSON

When Paul Wilkinson visited Goodison as Grimsby's centre-forward in November 1984, he presented Howard Kendall with the most eloquent of calling cards. After striving long and manfully against a masterful defence in a game dominated by the hosts, Paul popped up with a shock 89th-minute strike to dump the Blues out of the League Cup. Four months later, after further form-checks, a highly-impressed Howard signed the 20-year-old six-footer for £250,000.

By the end of that term, Paul had scored the only goal in a Merseyside derby and the omens were favourable for the hard-running front-man, an all-knees-and-elbows type of competitor who could control the ball on the ground and battle for it in the air. Alas, he was not to make the grade with Everton.

A combination of early-season injuries and the fabulous form of Messrs Lineker and Sharp limited Paul's chances in 1985/86, and the following season, while enjoying enough outings to win a title medal and scoring freely in the League Cup, he could not count on a place. A transfer seemed the only way forward and that March he joined Nottingham Forest for £200,000, later assisting Middlesbrough's advance into the new Premier League.

BORN: Louth, Lincolnshire, 30.10.64. GAMES: 25 (12).
GOALS: 14. HONOURS: League Championship 86/7.
OTHER CLUBS: Grimsby Town 82/3-84/5 (71, 27);
Nottingham Forest 86/7-87/8 (34, 5); Watford 88/89-90/1
(134, 52); Middlesbrough 91/2-95/6 (166, 49); Oldham
Athletic on loan 95/6 (4, 1); Watford on loan 95/6 (4, 0); Luton
Town on loan 95/6 (3, 0); Barnsley 96/7-97/8 (49, 9); Millwall
97/8- (30, 3).

1984/85 - 1986/87

KEVIN LANGLEY

Three months to the day after making his First Division debut, Kevin Langley played his final senior game for the Blues. However, the tall, rather slight Lancastrian's contribution at the outset of the 1986/87 campaign was enough to earn him a Championship medal. Midfielder Kevin, a £120,000 acquisition from Wigan during the summer, had impressed with his skill and composure during pre-season fixtures, and with both Peter Reid and Paul Bracewell sidelined by long-term injuries, Howard Kendall opted to give the newcomer an early opportunity.

Though the team stuttered, Kevin made a promising start. Constructive use of the ball was his forte, as he showed at home to Manchester United, his delicate chip setting up Adrian Heath for the subtle glancing header that capped an emphatic victory. But he was neither the quickest mover nor the most biting of tacklers, and when the inevitable critics raised their voices his confidence and form deserted him.

Dropped by Everton, he joined Manchester City, returning to Goodison with his new club that May and revelling, no doubt, in a splendid personal performance against his former colleagues. Yet Kevin failed to consolidate his place in the top flight, and after two and a half years at Birmingham, he retraced his steps to Wigan.

BORN: St Helens, Lancashire, 24.5.64. GAMES: 20. GOALS: 3. HONOURS: League Championship 86/7. OTHER CLUBS: Wigan Athletic 81/2-85/6 (160, 6); Manchester City 86/7 (9, 0); Chester City *on loan* 87/8 (9, 0); Birmingham City 87/8-89/90 (76, 2); Wigan Athletic 90/1-93/4 (157, 6).

1986/87

BOBBY MIMMS

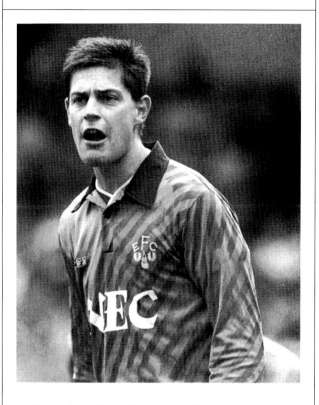

If ever a footballer was handed a thankless task, it was poor Bobby Mimms when he was called up to deputise for the injured Neville Southall in the spring of 1986. However well he might have played - and he let no one down - his chances of permanent promotion were, shall we say, limited.

Undeterred, the England under-21 custodian - a £150,000 signing from Rotherham the previous summer - signalled his intentions with clean sheets in his first six League outings. There followed competent, indeed blameless performances in the FA Cup Final and Charity shield encounters with Liverpool, and a steady spell in the opening months of 1986/87.

Of course, the peerless Nev returned and Bobby, who could hardly have done more to demonstrate his ability, was back in the Central League. After a similar experience early in the following term - one display which salvaged a point against Nottingham Forest was quite breathtaking - the Yorkshireman concluded, understandably, that he needed fresh pastures and joined Spurs in January 1988. However, Bobby did not become established at White Hart Lane, settling instead at Blackburn before returning to the lower divisions.

BORN: York, 13.10.63. GAMES: 33. GOALS: 0. HONOURS: League Championship 86/7.OTHER CLUBS: Rotherham United 81/2-84/5 (83, 0); Notts County *on loan* 85/6 (2, 0); Sunderland *on loan* 86/7 (4, 0); Blackburn Rovers *on loan* 86/7 (6, 0); Manchester City *on loan* 87/8 (3, 0); Tottenham Hotspur 87/8-89/90 (37, 0); Aberdeen *on loan* 89/90 (6, 0); Blackburn Rovers 90/1-95/6 (128, 0); Crystal Palace 96/7 (1, 0); Preston North End 96/7 (27, 0); Rotherham United 97/8- (42, 0).

1985/86 - 1987/88

TREVOR STEVEN

Trevor Steven was a captivating combination of excitement and consistency, equally capable of destroying a defence with a moment of scintillating touchline brilliance or toiling dutifully as a competent cog in the Blues' midfield machine. No manager would *want* to part with such a player, a man who had delighted the Goodison faithful more than most throughout the never-to-be-forgotten trophy crusades of the mid eighties, but come the summer of 1989, Colin Harvey had no choice. The quiet, but strong-willed Trevor had made it clear he was Ibrox-bound, Everton's reluctant manager asked a British record of £2.5 million, and a tribunal decided that a fairer figure would be almost £1 million less.

Only two years later, as the Steven talents were exported to France for three times Glasgow Rangers' outlay, the Merseysiders could claim justifiably that their original valuation had not been fanciful. However, they too had made a tidy profit from the fair-haired north-easterner whom Howard Kendall had coveted for two seasons before securing his £300,000 transfer from Burnley in July 1983.

At first Trevor, a confirmed perfectionist, seemed a mite over-anxious to impress at his first big-city club. Understandably, his form suffered and he was dropped for a midwinter spell, from which he emerged with renewed confidence as the thrilling performer Kendall knew him to be. His most exhilarating assets, beloved of the fans, were the pace and deft footwork that left opponents stranded in his wake and the thundering shot which, at first, he had seemed loth to employ. By 1984/85 that reticence had been comprehensively overcome, as he demonstrated emphatically at home to Sunderland on the title run-in, outwitting his full-back, sprinting into the penalty box and testing the durability of the net's roof with a crashing shot. Trevor was a canny crosser, too - he laid on Andy Gray's 1984 FA Cup Final clincher with a typically tantalising delivery - and he was quick to assess the ever-changing options for a pass.

But for all those eye-catching skills, a significant part of his value related to less spectacular merits such as versatility and work-rate. Though at his best on the right, Trevor was effective on either wing and also could step in as an enterprising deputy striker, as he did in the first leg of the 1985 European Cup Winners' Cup semi-final against Bayern Munich. Equally admirable was the stamina and tactical nous which facilitated his long, raking runs backwards and forwards along his flank, denying space to the opposition and covering for Gary Stevens when the right-back ventured into attack.

Trevor, who top-scored with 14 goals as Everton regained the Championship in 1986/87, suffered few losses of form, although his contribution was unusually wan during the autumn of 1987 when his willingness to run at defenders became decreasingly apparent. Characteristically, though, he recovered to enjoy a vintage spring as his penultimate season at Goodison drew to a close.

On the international scene, his contribution was compared with that of Steve Coppell, and it perplexed many sound judges that he was not an England regular. Leading Continental coaches held Trevor in especially lofty regard - no doubt swayed by his splendid showings and vital goals during the Blues' victorious European campaign - and his stock was sky-high with one impeccable authority much closer to home, a certain Kenny Dalglish. Indeed, during the ex-Liverpool boss's brief sabbatical from management, he was asked by mega-rich Marseille to name *the* player to buy; his first choice, Lothar Matthaus, was unavailable; next on his list was Trevor Steven. References don't come more gilt-edged than that.

BORN: Berwick, Northumberland, 21.9.63. GAMES: 279 (4). GOALS: 58.
HONOURS: European Cup Winners' Cup 84/5; League Championship 84/5, 86/7;
FA Cup 83/4. 32 England caps (84-92).
OTHER CLUBS: Burnley 80/1-82/3 (76, 11);
Glasgow Rangers 89/90-91/2 (55, 6);
Marseille, France, 91/2, (27, 3);
Glasgow Rangers 92/3-96/7 (81, 10).

1983/84 - 1988/89

IAN WILSON

Ian Wilson was a current Scottish international when Everton paid Leicester City £300,000 for his services in September 1987, yet the stylish midfielder was destined to make minimal impact on the Goodison scene. During his two campaigns on Merseyside, in which he was employed most often as deputy for the injury-plagued Kevin Sheedy on the left flank, he was invariably competent yet failed to stamp authority on a side that, under new manager Colin Harvey, strove unavailingly to match the standard of the Kendall years.

On arrival from Filbert Street, where he had flourished for eight seasons, the balding Aberdonian had slotted comfortably into the team pattern, looking at ease on the ball and scoring on his senior debut at home to Rotherham in the League Cup. He proved versatile, too, doing a sound job at left-back, a role in which his along-the-touchline distribution took the eye.

However in August 1989, having passed 30 and with little likelihood of a regular berth, Ian - remembered warmly for his enthusiastic General Custer impersonation at the players' Christmas fancy dress party in 1987 - decided to try his luck in Turkey, later returning to complete his career in the Football League.

BORN: Aberdeen, 27.3.58. GAMES: 36 (12). GOALS: 2.
HONOURS: 5 Scotland caps (87).
OTHER CLUBS: Leicester City 79/80-87/8 (285, 17);
Kocaelispor and Besiktas, Turkey; Derby County 90/1 (11, 0);
Bury 91/2 (24, 1); Wigan Athletic 92/3 (5, 0).

1987/88 - 1988/89

NORMAN WHITESIDE

How the Goodison faithful would have relished Norman Whiteside in his pomp; sadly, the 24-year-old Irish dreadnought who swapped the red shirt of Manchester United for the blue of Everton in the summer of 1989 was a rather sad travesty of the one-time prodigy whose teenage exploits had startled the soccer world. Norman, who during his Old Trafford days was a World Cup hero at 16 and scored in a succession of Wembley showpieces, was a perverse cocktail of delicate skill and wild aggression.

Lack of pace precipitated his conversion by United from front-runner to midfielder, and by the time of his £600,000 transfer, a series of knee injuries had emphasised that deficiency. Nevertheless, Colin Harvey found him a productive role just behind the strikers, and from time to time during that first term there were flashes of the old Whiteside flair. But as his knee condition deteriorated, he slowed still further and his physical ruthlessness became more pervasive, sometimes unacceptably so. In 1991, still only 26, he was invalided out of football, though soon he returned to the game as a physiotherapist with non-League Northwich Victoria. Thus Everton fans' most vivid memory of Norman Whiteside will remain the 1985 FA Cup Final goal for United that deprived the Blues of a historic treble.

BORN: Belfast, 7.5.65. GAMES: 35 (2). GOALS: 13.
HONOURS: 38 Northern Ireland caps (82-89).
OTHER CLUBS: Manchester United 81/2-88/9 (206, 47).

1989/90 - 1990/91

MARTIN KEOWN

Throughout his three-and-a-half term tenure in the Everton rearguard, Martin Keown could fairly be described as the most successful of Colin Harvey's 11 major purchases. Like many expensive newcomers, the dark, curly-haired Oxonian made a shaky start in the demanding atmosphere of Goodison, but acceptably soon after his £750,000 arrival from Aston Villa in July 1989 - the fee was determined by a transfer tribunal - he matured into one of the League's most effective middle-of-the-back-four performers. Indeed, throughout the Blues' disappointing 1991/92 campaign, he excelled consistently, and was rewarded deservedly with full England caps.

Though often unfairly maligned, both during and since his Evertonian days, Martin was, and remains, the very epitome of a high-quality modern defender. Cool and intelligent, he is extremely quick, despite a deceptively awkward, scuttling gait; he tackles with determination, he jumps well at either end of the pitch - his near-post flick-ons offer an effective attacking option - and he controls the ball efficiently. The picture is completed by competent distribution which was arguably over-audacious in his early Everton days, but was refined later into a reliable asset. The raking crossfield pass that abruptly switched the angle of assault and led to a goal for Mike Newell at home to Arsenal in October 1989 was a perfect illustration of this underrated ability.

But for a contract dispute, Martin might never have left the Gunners, his first club, with whom he made a richly promising start before moving to Villa Park in 1986. Highbury fans were dismayed at the sale of a gifted youngster who had seemed the ideal partner for David O'Leary. In the event he didn't settle in the Midlands and was happy to join his third major club at the behest of Colin Harvey, a decision with which the Blues were delighted.

However, after missing the first two months of 1992/93 through injury, then regaining fitness to boost a struggling side, Martin made an unexpected £2 million return to Arsenal that February. Since then he has risen above frequent fusillades of misguided flack to earn belated widespread respect.

BORN: Oxford, 24.7.66. GAMES: 115 (5). GOALS: 0.
HONOURS: 16 England caps (92-).
OTHER CLUBS: Arsenal 85/6 (22, 0);
Brighton and Hove Albion *on loan* 84/5-85/6 (23, 1);
Aston Villa 86/7-88/9 (112, 3); Arsenal 92/3- (165, 2).

1989/90 - 1992/93

TONY COTTEE

Retrospective wisdom is notoriously easy to dispense, but there is no escaping that, as career moves go, Tony Cottee's decision to spurn Arsenal in favour of Everton in the summer of 1988 was roughly on a par with shooting himself in the foot. Thereafter the Gunners won the title twice while the Blues marked time, and the fortunes of the chunky, chirpy little striker dipped accordingly.

Despite starting his Goodison sojourn with an exhilarating hat-trick at home to Newcastle, and topping the club scoring charts in five of the six seasons following his British record £2.3 million move from West Ham, Tony was destined for ultimate disillusionment on Merseyside.

The inescapable conclusion is that Everton and this instinctively predatory marksman, who won his first full England cap at 21, should have achieved far more together - and they should share the blame for their comparative failure. Surely the Blues could have made more of their expensive investment had they employed a truly creative midfielder to feed him. Equally, there were times when Tony might have been less sedentary outside the penalty box and shown a tad more resolve during lean spells. Sadly, when he was dropped - a pretty common occurrence - he appeared to regard himself as a scapegoat, which helped nobody.

Of course, Tony's footballing attributes were legion. He was blessed with an astute positional sense, a real poacher's nose for the main chance that might have earned him adulation at Everton. He excelled at staccato one-two passing movements, boasted a splendid first touch and was both strong and supple enough to worm his way through tiny chinks in packed defences.

Yet although he fizzed at times alongside the likes of Sharp and Newell, Beardsley and Rideout, Tony never found his ideal foil and strained unavailingly to fulfil himself. Thus in September 1994 it came as something of a relief to all concerned when he returned to Upton Park in the exchange deal which took David Burrows to Goodison.

BORN: West Ham, London, 11.7.65. GAMES: 122 (28). GOALS: 55. HONOURS: 7 England caps (86-89).
OTHER CLUBS: West Ham United 82/3-87/8 (212, 92) and 94/5-96/7 (67, 23); Selangor, Malaysia, 96/7; Leicester City 97/8 (20, 4); Birmingham City *on loan* 97/8 (5, 1).

1988/89 - 1994/95

STUART McCALL

Both the red hair and blazing commitment of midfielder Stuart McCall were reminiscent of two erstwhile Everton workaholics, Tony Kay and Alan Ball; sadly, however, it was exceedingly rare that his influence on a game approached that of his distinguished predecessors. Though his enthusiasm was underpinned by substantial skill, he was severely lacking in composure, and uncharitable terrace comparisons to a headless chicken were not always inappropriate.

The Yorkshire-born son of a Caledonian footballing father - Andy McCall, who came south to play for Blackpool alongside Stanley Matthews - Stuart won youth caps for England, then under-21 honours for Scotland, before joining the Blues from Bradford City in June 1988. Having played a dynamic part in the Valley Parade club's revival, the £875,000 newcomer was expected to bring new impetus to the Goodison bandwagon, which had begun to splutter under the guidance of Colin Harvey.

Certainly, neither Stuart's effort nor his all-round ability could be faulted as he helped his new side reach the all-Merseyside 1989 FA Cup Final in the emotional wake of the Hillsborough disaster. Coming on as substitute, he equalised twice - with a close-range stab and a looping 20-yard volley - but had to settle for a loser's medal. Despite that bittersweet experience, he seemed on the verge of a lengthy Everton career, and the following year he won his first full Scottish cap.

Yet still there persisted the feeling that the McCall energy - it made people tired just watching him - should be channelled more creatively. He could pass fluently, but often didn't give himself time, and there were occasions when his chasing down of every loose ball pulled the team out of shape. Accordingly, after assessing him for half a season, Howard Kendall surprised many fans by selling Stuart to Rangers for £1.2 million in August 1991. In the frequently more frenetic environment of Scottish football, he found his true niche, playing a zestfully integral role as the Glaswegians continued to dominate their domestic secene.

BORN: Leeds, 10.6.64. GAMES: 126 (6). GOALS: 10. HONOURS: 40 Scotland caps (90-).
OTHER CLUBS: Bradford City 82/3-87/8 (238, 37); Glasgow Rangers 91/2- (194, 14).

1988/89 - 1990/91

NEVILLE SOUTHALL

The word 'great' is used too glibly - great goals, great players, great matches, the description has become devalued - yet in the case of Neville Southall it was wholly apt. Deservedly, his name was synonymous with goalkeeping excellence, and by the late eighties his equal could not be found anywhere in the world. Indeed at his best, which was most of the time in those days, the inspirational Welshman exuded a confidence that nodded towards omnipotence, lifting the hearts of his team-mates and driving thwarted marksmen to distraction.

Neville's mastery owed much to god-given talent, but the effect of his near-fanatical application was equally immense and those misguided opponents who reckoned that his frequently rather rumpled appearance denoted a casual attitude were only gulling themselves. The one-time brick-carrier and binman was a perfectionist whose preparation extended to voluntary extra training sessions, minute study of the game in all its aspects and rigorous attention to detail, right down to practising with the precise type of ball to be used in his next match. The dividends of such devotion were plain for all to see.

Indeed, Neville was once described by no less an authority than Pat Jennings as a 'keeper without a weakness, an assertion emphasised by a breakdown of the Southall game at its peak. Like many of his contemporaries, he was a magnificent shot-stopper, but what gave him the edge was an astonishing capacity to change direction at the last moment, sometimes even in mid-air, and an instinct for improvising unorthodox saves. The Southall superiority was even more marked when dealing with high balls, a chronic failing with countless custodians. In this area, decisiveness was Neville's trademark; either he punched positively or caught adhesively, but never dithered. Equally crucial was fabulous fitness, which enabled him to leap athletically into position as the focus of an attack changed and to recover instantly after an abortive dive. Mental agility was important, too, and legion were the times that he emerged triumphant from a one-on-one confrontation, seemingly having psyched the advancing forward into faulty judgement.

Remarkably, an early opportunity to acquire the Southall services was passed up by Everton when they watched him in 1980, and he left non-League football for Bury instead. A season later, his vast potential now evident, Howard Kendall recruited him for £150,000, and by December 1981 he had ousted the more experienced Jim Arnold from the senior side. For more than a year the two men held sway alternately, then Neville was axed after a 5-0 drubbing at Anfield and loaned to Port Vale. Some feared the somewhat diffident younger man would not cope with the reverse, but he returned from the Potteries with a new spring in his step and by the end of 1983 had become the Blues' unopposed number-one.

Two brilliant saves from John Barnes contributed massively to the 1984 FA Cup Final win against Watford, and over the next few glorious terms Neville established a peerless reputation, in 1985 being voted the football writers' player of the year. Towards the end of the decade, however, with his own powers undiminished but Everton in comparative decline, disillusionment set in, and at one time he seemed destined for a move. His part in one bizarre incident - a goalmouth sit-in after walking out of a half-time harangue by manager Colin Harvey - did him less than credit, even though Neville, ever his own man, was acting out of frustration rather than malice. By 1991/92 he seemed settled once more, but as the decade wore on his brilliance became punctuated by sequences of alarmingly erratic displays. Repeatedly Neville was written off but invariably he made nonsense of rashly premature epitaphs by regaining prime form, notably in the 1995 FA Cup Final victory over Manchester United. However, come 1997/98, with his 40th birthday on the horizon, one of the finest 'keepers in British football history had finally to step aside, his lasting stature in the game untarnished by a handful of late aberrations.

BORN: Llandudno, North Wales, 16.9.58. GAMES: 726. GOALS: 0.
HONOURS: European Cup Winners' Cup 84/5; League Championship 84/5, 86/7;
FA Cup 83/4, 94/5. 91 Wales caps (82-97). OTHER CLUBS: Bury 80/1 (39, 0); Port Vale
on loan 82/3 (9, 0); Southend United *on loan* 97/8 (9, 0); Stoke City 97/8 (11, 0).

1981/82 - 1997/98

KEVIN SHEEDY

Evertonians may be loth to admit it, but they owe a vast debt to the likes of Ray Kennedy and Graeme Souness, Terry McDermott and Jimmy Case. Admittedly that majestic Anfield midfield quartet did more than most to enphasise the chasm between Red achievement and Blue frustration in the late seventies and early eighties, yet also they performed a crucial, if unwitting, service to the Goodison cause. Such was their excellence that a gifted young fellow named Kevin Sheedy, unable to break into Bob Paisley's side, became so unhappy that he was swayed by the overtures of Howard Kendall and, after much heart-searching, he changed allegiance.

Even in August 1982, when that first transaction between the two clubs in nigh-on 20 years was completed and when the creative youngster was scarcely known away from Merseyside, there was a feeling that Everton had put one over on the old enemy. The clue was in the reaction of the Anfield boss, a superb judge of a footballer's potential, who resisted the deal and was unhappy with a transfer tribunal's £100,000 valuation. Bob was not yet ready to break up his all-conquering combination, but he was well aware of the near-magical properties invested in the Sheedy left foot, and knew in his heart that he was allowing a player of sheer quality to slip through his fingers. So it was to prove, as Kevin became one of the principal architects of the Blues' mid-eighties success.

Here was a performer who could change the course of a match with a single, sophisticated touch. Taking over the left-flank role once intended for the recalcitrant Mickey Thomas, Kevin invested the attack with much-needed imagination, stroking the ball with a precision that, at its best, invited comparison with the work of fellow Eire star Liam Brady. The younger man - who was qualified to play for Wales, also, but believed the Republic offered better prospects - lacerated defences with his satisfyingly comprehensive methods of distribution. Penetrating, long-distance through-balls - his exquisitely timed passes over the top of square reargards added immeasurably to Gary Lineker's bountiful tally in 1985/86 - were mixed with slick short-range exchanges, and his viciously curling crosses were a widely feared speciality.

Yet for all his delicacy, Kevin could strike the ball savagely, often catching opponents unawares by volleying venomously with negligible backlift. He was devastating with a dead ball, too, never demonstrating his mastery more conclusively than at home to Ipswich in a 1985 FA Cup quarter-final. First, he drove a free kick over the defensive wall and into the net to 'keeper Paul Cooper's right; Blues fans were dismayed as the referee signalled an infringement and ordered a retake, but their self-possessed number-11 was undeterred, simply re-spotting the ball and clipping it home again, this time to the hapless custodian's left!

Kevin contributed many important goals - he reached double figures in both successful title campaigns and chipped home the clincher in the European Cup Winners' Cup Final - though his critics maintained that there was a price to pay. They proclaimed that he could not tackle, was poor in the air, employed his right foot for standing purposes only and was short of pace. Valid points all, but in the context of the finely balanced side that lifted four trophies in three years, in which there was no lack of vigour to offset his artistry, it just didn't matter.
Come the early nineties - with the team under reconstruction and a 32-year-old Kevin suffering the consequences, perhaps, of the extensive injuries which cost him so many outings over the years - his flaws were more noticeable. Even so, he was capable still of introducing vision and variety into an increasingly metronomic game and, in any case, should be honoured for a decade of refined effort. Certainly, Kevin Keegan recognised his pedigree and had no hesitation in recruiting him for Newcastle in February 1992. It would be a sad day, indeed, when there was no longer room in football for the likes of Kevin Sheedy.

BORN: Builth Wells, Wales, 21.10.59. GAMES: 337 (12). GOALS: 93.
HONOURS: European Cup Winners' Cup 84/5; League Championship 84/5, 86/7.
45 Republic of Ireland caps (83-93). OTHER CLUBS: Hereford United 75/6-77/8 (51, 4);
Liverpool 80/1-81/2 (3, 0); Newcastle United 91/2-92/3 (37, 4); Blackpool 93/4 (26, 1).

1982/83 - 1991/92

DAVE WATSON

To the modern generation of Everton footballers, fans and managers, Dave Watson has been an unchanging source of strength and inspiration through troubled times. A rock-like, combatively passionate, endlessly resilient stopper, he has seen central defensive partners come and go in seemingly endless procession since his £900,000 arrival from Norwich City in August 1986. He has remained, majestic in moments of triumph and the staunchest of bulwarks on those far more numerous occasions when the tide has flowed relentlessly against the Goodison cause. Come the mid nineties, when desperate rearguard actions went with the territory of wearing the blue shirt, he battled on unflinchingly with desire undiminished, somehow not worn down by the constant adversity.

Had Dave Watson not been made of stern stuff, his football career would have perished on the vine. After failing to reach the first team as a teenager at Anfield, the disappointed but unbowed Merseysider joined the Canaries, with whom he made such enormous strides that he won full England caps. Thus, when Everton paid a club record £900,000 to bring him back to his native city, the move had all the hallmarks of a triumphant homecoming. Initially, however, nothing could have been further from the truth.

Brought in as a replacement for injured local hero Derek Mountfield, Dave appeared indecisive and clumsy, and was caught out of position too often for comfort. His fellow Scousers on the Gwladys Street terraces were not slow to express their scorn, and the gutsy six-footer was subjected to a withering examination of his character. At one stage in the autumn of '86 he was dropped in favour of the fit-again Mountfield, but after coming to terms with the Blues' zonal marking system - Norwich had favoured the more straight-forward man-to-man method - the Watson confidence returned and he played a full part in lifting the title as well as extending his international career. Indeed, so dramatic was his continued improvement that those fickle fans voted him 1987/88 player of the year.

Thereafter, Dave developed into a true Blues stalwart and if even his most enthusiastic advocate could never claim he has been the quickest or most skilful of Evertonians, there has been ample compensation in his formidable aerial power, decisive tackling and single-minded determination to do the simple thing well. After bedding into the side and growing in confidence, he became more positive in attack, too, acquiring a welcome knack of chipping in with priceless goals, notably in the FA Cup. For instance, there was a fifth-round second replay winner against Liverpool in February 1991 and a subsequent quarter-final strike against West Ham. Even more memorable was Dave's header that shaded the 1995 quarter-final against Newcastle, after which his defensive powers had to be at their doughtiest as the Magpies stormed back. Two months later, at Wembley, the Watson game was at its most impeccable once more as he dealt unshowily but effectively with the increasingly frustrated Manchester United attack and earned the man-of-the-match accolade for his pains.

Back in 1991 Peter Reid, then manager of a buoyantly ambitious Manchester City - how long ago that seems - offered £1 million to take his former team-mate to Maine Road. With Dave in his playing pomp it was a significant career crossroads and, happily for Everton, but not for the sky-blue half of Manchester, he appended his name to a new Goodison contract. Soon he was handed the job of skipper and went on to enjoy his most influential years, even stepping up to become caretaker manager after Joe Royle's departure and steering the club safely through a relegation dogfight in the spring of 1997.

In recent years there have been irksome back and knee problems and he needed a cartilage operation soon after his 36th birthday, though normal service was resumed quickly. Inescapably, though, Everton must face a future without Dave Watson at the heart of their rearguard - and the prospect is truly daunting.

BORN: 20.11.61. GAMES: 476 (3). GOALS: 34. HONOURS: League Championship 86/7; FA Cup 94/5. 12 England caps (84-88). OTHER CLUBS: Norwich City 80/1-85/6 (212, 11). MANAGER: Everton (acting, 97).

1986/87 -

MIKE NEWELL

The heart of any true football fan would have bled for Mike Newell as he kicked in before one Everton home game in October 1991. The gangling striker - a born trier who, like his team, had been enduring a lean time - was subjected to a withering chorus of abuse from the terraces. The faceless critics were not even willing to let him perform before venting their spleen! During the match, he reacted with typical spirit, coming on as a substitute and battling manfully, but the abuse must have been hurtful to a Merseysider whose transfer to Everton from Leicester in summer 1989 - at a cost of £1.1 million plus Wayne Clarke - had represented a dream homecoming.

In fact, Mike had made an encouraging start to his Blues tenure, netting in each of his first four League outings at Goodison and impressing with his zest, bravery and power, both in the air and on the ground. While not daintily skilful, he could play his part in swift passing interchanges and there was much optimism for his future. Then injury struck, and on his return to a struggling side it was as though a spell had been broken; now he seemed over-anxious and his strike rate slumped. Come November 1991, he accepted a £1.1 million switch to Blackburn, with whom he regained his best form.

BORN: Liverpool, 27.1.65. GAMES: 62 (27). GOALS: 19.
OTHER CLUBS: Crewe Alexandra 83/4 (3, 0); Wigan Athletic 83/4-85/6 (72, 25); Luton Town 85/6-87/8 (63, 18); Leicester City 87/8-88/9 (81, 21); Blackburn Rovers 91/2-95/6 (130, 28); Birmingham City 96/7 (15, 1); West Ham United *on loan* 96/7 (7, 0); Bradford City *on loan* 96/7 (7, 0); Aberdeen 97/8- (18, 4).

1989/90 - 1991/92

MIKE MILLIGAN

Mike Milligan endured a season of footballing misery with the Blues, yet none could have cavilled at Colin Harvey's decision to pay £1 million for the effervescent Mancunian on the eve of the 1990/91 campaign. Fresh from exerting an inspirational midfield influence during two rousing cup runs, the Boundary Park version of 'Captain Marvel' was seen as one of the most desirable commodities on the mid-summer transfer market.

Yet once in situ at Goodison, the irrepressible, almost hyperactive figure of the previous term paled into a wan reflection of his former hard-tackling, constructive self. From the start, Mike looked out of his depth in the top flight and the confidence that had been his trademark evaporated rapidly. Wandering ineffectually on the edge of the action, he seemed almost bemused, and hopes that he might grow into a new Peter Reid-type controller were summarily dashed.

Inevitably he was axed, but salvation beckoned for the man who had been rejected by Manchester City as a teenager. Joe Royle knew his true worth and took him back to newly-promoted Oldham in the summer of 1991 for £600,000. Soon, with his self-belief restored, 'Millie' was buzzing again, and his dipping 25-yarder that found Everton's net that December must have been especially sweet.

BORN: Manchester, 20.2.67. GAMES: 17 (2). GOALS: 1.
HONOURS: 1 Republic of Ireland cap (92).
OTHER CLUBS: Oldham Athletic 85/6-89/90 (162, 17) and 91/2-93/4 (117, 6); Norwich City 94/5- (111, 5).

1990/91

RAY ATTEVELD

It was hardly fair to saddle Dutchman Ray Atteveld with expectations based on the deeds of his illustrious countrymen. But when any footballer is imported from overseas there is - or there used to be - inevitable expectation that he must be just a little bit special. In fact, utility man Ray, while being a competent all-rounder, had nothing more to offer than hundreds of British professionals and, in that sense, proved something of a disappointment after his arrival in late 1989.

However, that is not to denigrate the ability of the right-back cum right-sided midfielder who could also step into central defence at need. Cool and resourceful, he packed both a fearsome tackle and a powerful shot, was comfortable on the ball and turned well. At his best he linked fluently with right-winger Pat Nevin, and his creativity was rarely better illustrated than when he started and finished a flowing five-man passing sequence in a February 1991 FA Cup replay against Liverpool; his firm drive was saved by Bruce Grobbelaar but his part in the move had demonstrated commendable enterprise.

Apparently, though, Ray was peripheral to returned manager Howard Kendall's plans, and in March 1992 he joined Bristol City for £250,000.

BORN: Amsterdam, Holland, 8.9.66.
GAMES: 53 (12). GOALS: 2.
OTHER CLUBS: Haarlem, Holland;
West Ham United *on loan* 91/2 (1, 0);
Bristol City 91/2-92/3 (14, 1).

1989/90 - 1991/92

NEIL McDONALD

The case of Neil McDonald illustrates vividly the truism that football is a game of opinion. Just weeks after the Blues boss Howard Kendall had unloaded his fellow Tynesider to Oldham for £500,000 - presumably on the basis of performances in 1990/91 - the 26-year-old utility man returned to Merseyside to collect an Everton player of the year award from the local newspaper.

It was an ironic footnote to Neil's three-year sojourn, which began in August 1988 when Colin Harvey paid Newcastle £525,000 for the England under-21 international as a replacement right-back for the recently departed Gary Stevens. Unfortunately it was a role in which the newcomer never looked comfortable, appearing rather ponderous and indecisive. Soon he was attracting the inevitable bile from impatient fans and was dropped, later returning on the left flank, then shuttling between the number-two and three shirts.

But it wasn't until a spell in central midfield in autumn 1990 that he found his optimum position. Cutting out several opponents at a time with penetrative passes of the highest quality and demonstrating the power of his shot, he looked a different player. The manager went for other options, however, and Neil McDonald was on his way.

BORN: Wallsend, Tyneside, 2.11.65. GAMES: 100 (14).
GOALS: 7. OTHER CLUBS: Newcastle United 82/3-87/8 (180, 24); Oldham Athletic 91/2-93/4 (24, 1); Bolton Wanderers 94/5 (4, 0); Preston North End 95/6-96/7 (33, 0).

1988/89 - 1991/92

JOHN EBBRELL

How poignant it is to recall that, before his star was dimmed by a cruel catalogue of injuries, John Ebbrell was the living embodiment of Everton's hope for the future. Talented, level-headed and never one to moan in adversity, the personable Merseysider exuded a clean cut aura reminiscent of a young Brian Labone. Indeed, at the dawn of the nineties it seemed fair to speculate that if his continued development matched his youthful promise, then the Blues would be blessed with an influential, stable figure as crucial to their quest for success during the remainder of the century as was the stalwart centre-half three decades earlier.

The raw materials to forge an outstanding career were all in place for the solidly-built graduate from the FA School of Excellence, whose stint as England under-21 captain demonstrated clearly that he was officer material. The Ebbrell expertise was most apparent when he was operating in the centre of midfield, whether as deep-lying anchorman or fetch-and-carry forager between penalty areas, his control, strength and high endeavour fusing together compellingly.

When John's confidence was high, his passing, particularly with his right foot, was crisp and accurate, and at all times his work-rate was enormous. His tackling was resolute, too, as Liverpool's Steve McMahon discovered when his rather wild challenge in a 1991 FA Cup tie was met unflinchingly by the youngster; the Anfield stands seemed to shake as the two clashed, but it was McMahon who was forced to withdraw from the field.

True, there remained room for progress: John needed to capitalise on his fierce shot and to assert his authority more consistently. Such details, though, seemed sure to be righted as maturity fostered self-belief, but time was to bring heartache rather than fulfilment. As the decade ticked on, John was sidelined for lengthy swathes of each term - he missed the 1995 FA Cup triumph - and during his absences the likes of Joe Parkinson and Barry Horne prospered. In March 1997, frustrated beyond belief, he opted for a fresh beginning with Sheffield United, who paid £1 million for his services only for the Ebbrell injury jinx to strike yet again. Just when he should have been in his prime, John missed the whole of 1997/98, though there were high hopes that he would be fit for the following campaign.

BORN: Bromborough, Merseyside, 1.10.69.
GAMES: 253 (12). GOALS: 19.
OTHER CLUBS: Sheffield United 96/7- (1, 0).

1988/89 - 1996/97

PETER BEAGRIE

Once described memorably by Joe Lovejoy, then of *The Independent,* as 'the archetypal blue-assed-fly winger', Peter Beagrie had it within him to be one of the League's most exciting attackers. But - and it's an old story - too often he failed to harness his extravagant but distinctly wayward natural talent.

Colin Harvey paid Stoke City £750,000 for the England under-21 flankman in November 1989, pitching him straight into the side at the expense of Pat Nevin. Before long, however, Peter's inconsistency became apparent and soon he was reduced to the status of an in-and-out squad member. At his best he thrilled the fans with his dash, control and sudden changes of direction. They gloried in his knack of dragging the ball away just as a defender was poised to claim it, making space through pure skill, then delivering a devastatingly flighted cross from near the left touchline.

The other side of the Beagrie coin was the frustrating solo performer who destroyed the impetus of attacks by over-elaboration, then distributed the ball inaccurately or, alternatively, loitered anonymously on the game's outer fringe. At first he was shot-shy, too, though when he did break his duck after 30 games, the supporters revelled in his celebratory party-piece, an exuberant back somersault.

With only this chequered pedigree behind him, Peter looked to have ruined his long-term chances at Goodison by a wild escapade involving a motor-bike on Everton's 1991 pre-season tour of Spain. He joined Sunderland on loan but such was the disappointing form of Howard Kendall's side that, come October, he was recalled and embarked on his lengthiest senior sequence to date. Perhaps chastened by his experience, he seemed a more disciplined player and started by scoring twice in the League Cup defeat of Wolves.

However, this compelling but unchangingly brittle talent continued on his erratic way until the arrival of Anders Limpar in March 1994 made his Everton exit inevitable. Later that month Peter joined Manchester City for £1.1 million. His return on loan from Bradford City, at the age of 32 in March 1998, was a surprise and appeared to illustrate the paucity of the funds at Howard Kendall's disposal. His performances were adequate but, in all honesty, the best of Beagrie was well behind him.

BORN: Middlesbrough, 28.11.65. GAMES: 106 (30). GOALS: 16.
OTHER CLUBS: Middlesbrough 84/5-85/6 (33, 2);
Sheffield United 86/7-87/8 (84, 11); Stoke City 88/9-89/90 (54, 7);
Sunderland *on loan* 91/2 (5, 1); Manchester City 93/4-96/7 (52, 3);.
Bradford City 97/8 (34, 0).

1989/90 - 1993/94 & 1997/98

PAT NEVIN

Pat Nevin played his football with a jaunty air, like some bright-eyed little bird in flight. At his best he could send the senses soaring; first he surged forward then checked and feinted, before darting off again with predatory defenders floundering in his wake. But, far too often for comfort, the Scottish wingman fluttered ineffectively on the fringe of the action, more like a frustrated moth outside a lighted window.

There was never any doubt about his natural gifts; certainly Chelsea were loth to lose him when he headed north in July 1988, his £925,000 fee settled by a transfer tribunal after bitter wrangling. After all, to his spectacular dribbling skills, Pat added a shot of surprising power for such a slight figure, and an enviable knack of lifting high, hanging crosses into the box with either foot. His touch and vision were never seen to better advantage than at home to Liverpool in September 1989 when he set up a goal for Mike Newell with a sudden outside-of-the-foot backspin chip that paralysed the Reds' defence. And he could go it alone, as Arsenal discovered a month later at Goodison when he waltzed around O'Leary and Lukic to net with panache.

Naturally, Pat was at his most dangerous and entertaining when pushed forward. Not that he was unwilling to beaver in midfield, but frequently that area proved the graveyard of his talents as he was reduced to denying space to opponents. On such occasions, despite his misleadingly frail appearance, he proved his courage placing himself in situations where hard knocks were inevitable, and he suffered his share of injuries.

Already an international at Stamford Bridge, he was recalled by Andy Roxburgh in 1990 and his form was so persuasive that he missed only one League match in 1990/91. But the following term, with Warzycha, Ward and Beagrie in contention for wing berths, his appearances were sporadic and after a successful springtime loan stint at Prenton Park, he joined Tranmere for £300,000 in August 1992. A sensitive, articulate man who keeps sport in its proper perspective, Pat might have much to offer football when his playing days are over.

BORN: Glasgow, 6.9.63. GAMES: 103 (35). GOALS: 20.
HONOURS: 28 Scotland caps (86-96).
OTHER CLUBS: Clyde 81/2-82/3 (73, 17); Chelsea 83/4-87/8 (193, 36);
Tranmere Rovers 91/2-96/7 (201, 30);
Kilmarnock 97/8- (31, 5).

1988/89 - 1991/92

PETER BEARDSLEY

So bright and nimble, cunning and creative, Peter Beardsley lost little time in becoming Everton's most influential attacker after his £1 million move from Liverpool in the summer of 1991.

The deal went through after the Reds pipped Howard Kendall for the signature of Dean Saunders, and there was no shortage of carpers who declared that the Blues were wrong to accept an 'Anfield cast-off', a 30-year-old whose best days were probably behind him. Of course, Liverpool fans made the most of it, chanting 'What a waste of talent' as Peter, still adjusting to his new team, cut a somewhat forlorn figure as his former colleagues triumphed comfortably in that August's Merseyside derby.

But after a spell of six goalless games, the Geordie whose hunched run and gawky expression belied handsome natural gifts, netted nine times in the next eight outings as Everton flickered tantalisingly on the verge of an autumn renaissance. The winter brought anti-climax for Kendall's men, but Peter, at least, did not disappoint. Operating most frequently in an advanced midfield role, just behind the main strikers, he combined flair with industry, guile with dash, an inventive fulcrum to a side which, to be blunt, were not good enough to capitalise on his artistry.

Whether skipping past opponents on an exhilarating dribble or splitting a defence with an instant, visionary pass - such as the left-foot half-volley that set up a chance for Tony Cottee to spurn at home to Leeds in February 1992 - the former Anfield hero remained the consummate entertainer. Though finishing was never his strongest suit, he magnified his value to his new club by completing his first Goodison campaign as top scorer, a feat he came close to equalling in his second and farewell term. As he proved conclusively after his £1.4 million return to St James Park at the age of 32 in July 1993, Peter Beardsley could have offered plenty more to Everton. If only the manager had provided a viable framework to support the sprightly veteran's special ability . . .

BORN: Newcastle, 18.1.61. GAMES: 48. GOALS: 19. HONOURS: 59 England caps (86-96). OTHER CLUBS: Carlisle United 79/80-81/2 (104, 22); Vancouver Whitecaps, Canada, 82; Manchester United 82/3 (0, 0; *one game in League Cup);* Vancouver Whitecaps 83; Newcastle United 83/4-86/7 (147, 61); Liverpool 87/8-90/1 (131, 46); Newcastle United 93/4-96/7 (129, 47); Bolton Wanderers 97/8 (17, 2); Manchester City *on loan* 97/8 (6, 0); Fulham *on loan* 97/8 (8, 1).

1991/92 - 1992/93

MAURICE JOHNSTON

As autumn turned to winter in 1991, Howard Kendall found himself in urgent need of Maurice Johnston's talents for the second time in his managerial career. On the first occasion, in the early eighties, the blond striker was a precocious youngster on the rise, grabbing attention through his scoring feats with Partick Thistle, while Howard was increasingly beleaguered in his first stint at Goodison. However, Watford's Graham Taylor outbid the Blues and Mo went to Vicarage Road.

This time around the prolific Scot, still only 28 but looking a trifle travel-weary, was unable to command a place with Rangers and Howard was desperate for a star who would score goals and placate discontented fans. A deal was struck, £1.5 million securing Everton the services of a marksman with a proven record, but with what some observers described as a questionable temperament. However, he had reacted with maturity to the furore his Catholic faith had caused in the Protestant stronghold of Ibrox, so the omens were good.

Mo's footballing assets were legion: control, speed, heart, strength, industry, heading ability and, above all, sharp reflexes; he had the lot. But could he harness this cornucopia of gifts to the Blues' benefit? Three goals in five games, including one which earned a draw in the Merseyside derby, raised hopes but then injury intervened and momentum was lost. The arrival of Paul Rideout restricted Mo's opportunities in 1992/93 and he departed to Hearts on a free transfer. An enterprising but expensive gamble had not quite paid off.

BORN: Glasgow, 30.4.63. GAMES: 31 (7). GOALS: 10. HONOURS: 38 Scotland caps (84-91). OTHER CLUBS: Partick Thistle 81/2-83/4 (85, 41); Watford 83/4-84/5 (38, 23); Celtic 84/5-86/7 (99, 52); Nantes, France, 87/8-88/9 (66, 22); Glasgow Rangers 89/90-91/2 (76, 31); Hearts 93/4-94/5 (35, 5); Falkirk 94/5-95/6 (41, 6); Kansas City, USA, 97.

1991/92 - 1992/93

MARK WARD

Howard Kendall paid £1 million to make Mark Ward an Everton player - nearly a decade after the feisty little flankman was considered not good enough to make the Goodison grade. As a Blues apprentice in the early eighties, Mark had looked distinctly lively and several shrewd judges were surprised when he was discarded. Disappointed but not deterred, he joined non-League Northwich Victoria, with whom he became an England semi-pro international before returning to the League with Oldham. Thereafter, he excelled with West Ham, prompting Kendall to enlist him for Manchester City's successful fight against relegation in 1990 and then to bring him 'home' in the summer of 1991.

For Mark, it was the realisation of a dream, and he announced his intention of completing his career with his first club. He started with a booking on his debut - he is not a man to dust himself down and walk away from a heavy tackle, his determination bordering on petulance at times - but performed with zest and skill on the Blues' left wing.

In his second game, at home to Arsenal, he confirmed his pedigree with two splendid goals and it was clear that Mark had the quality to play in a top team. At his confident best, he was a penetrative runner adept at lightning breaks, a precision passer and a disruptive crosser. But as Everton progressed numbingly through the early nineties, he suffered injuries and turned in too many nondescript displays, although his effort never flagged. With his peak behind him, Mark was sold to Birmingham for £500,000 in March 1994.

BORN: Prescot, Liverpool, 10.10.62. GAMES: 92 (1). GOALS: 7. OTHER CLUBS: Oldham Athletic 83/4-84/5 (84, 12); West Ham United 85/6-89/90 (165, 12); Manchester City 89/90-90/1 (55, 14); Birmingham City 93/4-95/6 (63, 7); Huddersfield Town 95/6 (7, 1); Wigan Athletic 96/7 (5, 0).

1991/92 - 1993/94

ROBERT WARZYCHA

One moment brilliant, the next apparently inept, Robert Warzycha cut an enigmatic figure, yet over the personable Pole's potential there could be no dispute. He boasted skill, pace and power aplenty, combining those attributes in a highly individual manner which highlighted both his footballing strengths and weaknesses.

Once in possession, Robert liked to run with the ball, and so determined was he not to lose it that even after stumbling he would continue dribbling, almost on his kness, until it was gone. The down side of that admirable resolution was that, on occasion, he retained possession when a pass to an unmarked colleague would have been infinitely more effective.

However, Robert - his surname was pronounced 'Va-shee-ka', although Gwladys Street wags delighted in the sobriquet 'Wazza' - did enough on Everton's right flank to justify the club's patience in waiting for a work permit and the subsequent £500,000 purchase of the 27-year-old international from Gornik Zabrze in March 1991.

In a number of games, including the goalless Goodison clash with Manchester United at the outset of the following campaign, he ran defences ragged while not getting the luck his enterprise deserved. He carried a fierce shot and would unleash it from any angle, yet his goal tally was minimal.

'Wazza's' tactical awareness had been expected to improve with time, but it never really happened, his English career petering out in 1993/94, after which he returned to Poland.

BORN: Poland, 20.6.63. GAMES: 35 (14). GOALS: 5.
HONOURS: Poland caps.
OTHER CLUBS: Gornik Zabrze, Poland.

1990/91 - 1993/94

STUART BARLOW

Though statistics can be preposterously misleading, in the case of Stuart Barlow's Everton experience they paint a telling picture. The blond striker's senior starts were outnumbered almost two to one by his appearances from the bench, illustrating a frustratingly peripheral contribution spread over half a decade.

That was a shame because Stuart possessed in abundance one of the modern game's most envied attributes, a blistering turn of pace. The problem was, though he was a willing and selfless runner in the team cause, the Merseyside-born marksman failed to apply his gift to consistent effect, all too frequently straying offside or heading in unproductive directions.

Then there was his finishing, which could be devastating for the reserves but sometimes was little more than lamentable in the senior side. It became such a familiar sight for Stuart to work himself cleverly into a dangerous position, only for his shot to carome wildly from his boot. He appeared to lack composure and his luck was repeatedly abominable, an abnormally high percentage of his efforts seeming to scrape the woodwork or flash narrowly wide.

After failing to impose himself despite repeated opportunities, and with a plethora of front-runners jockeying for recognition, he was sold to Oldham for £450,000 in November 1995. Happily, in the less rarified environment of Boundary Park, the amiable Barlow found a more fulfilling niche before heading west to join Wigan.

BORN: Liverpool, 16.7.68. GAMES: 31 (57). GOALS: 13.
OTHER CLUBS: Rotherham United *on loan* 91/2 (1, 0);
Oldham Athletic 95/6-97/8 (93, 31);
Wigan Athletic 97/8- (9, 3).

1990/91 - 1995/96

MATTHEW JACKSON

Matt Jackson was Howard Kendall's find of 1991/92. The slim, blond six-footer arrived from Luton Town to make his Everton debut on his 20th birthday, and by season's end had lain persuasive claim to the Blues' right-back berth.

From the early moments of that first match - at home to his boyhood heroes, Aston Villa, in late October - it was apparent that Matt had class. He moved smoothly, seemed to possess a natural feel for the ball and, even at that stage, read the game with commendable composure. As games went by his aerial work and tackling proved admirably steady, his distribution was measured and he was keen to venture into attack. In addition he could play in central defence, and to top it all, the youngster's temperament seemed perfectly adapted to the big time.

No wonder Luton manager David Pleat had been loth to lose Matt, but the lure of £600,000 - plus a further £300,000 if the Yorkshireman should rise to full England status - for a novice who had made a mere nine First Division appearances proved too good to turn down.

As the Blues' mediocre campaign wore on, there was some consolation, at least, in Matt's progress, which was recognised by an England under-21 call-up. The next two terms brought steady consolidation under Kendall and his replacement, Mike Walker, but the arrival of Joe Royle signalled a change for the worse in the Jackson fortunes. One of Joe's first acts as Everton boss in January 1995 was to sign his former Oldham protege Earl Barrett, who went straight into the side at Matthew's expense.

However, Earl was cup-tied, which safeguarded the younger man's place on the FA Cup road to Wembley, where he performed with his customary poise and helped to set up Paul Rideout's winner against Manchester United.

Thereafter, though, Matt slipped further down the pecking order with the recruitment of Marc Hottiger, and in December 1996 Mike Walker, a man destined to know his owen travails at Goodison Park, took him to Norwich in a £450,000 deal.

BORN: Leeds, 19.10.71. GAMES: 158 (6). GOALS: 6.
HONOURS: FA Cup 94/5. OTHER CLUBS: Luton Town 91/2 (9, 0);
Preston North End *on loan* 90/1 (4, 0); Charlton Athletic *on loan* 95/6 (8, 0);
Queen's Park Rangers *on loan* 96/7 (7, 0); Birmingham City *on loan* 96/7 (10, 0);
Norwich City 96/7- (60, 5).

1991/92 - 1995/96

GARY ABLETT

It hadn't happened much down the years, but now Peter Beardsley had done it, Barry Venison had thought about it, and Ian Rush was rumoured (perhaps wildly, perhaps not) to be considering it; so why shouldn't Gary Ablett swap the red shirt of Liverpool for Everton's blue? In fact, the possible implications of any mass migration across Stanley Park apart, Gary's £750,000 move in January 1992 was hardly a surprise.

Despite winning two League Championship medals, helping to lift the FA Cup and being honoured at England 'B' and under-21 level during five years in the Anfield senior squad, the gaunt, gangly, left-sided utility defender could not count on a regular place as he approached his prime. What better place than Goodison for a player of sound all-round ability and ideal temperament to realise his full potential?

Though a little ponderous on the turn, Gary was a crisp tackler, confident in the air and passed the ball with a smoothness which might be expected of any graduate from the old enemy's footballing academy.

On arrival, he slotted in competently at left-back, though his most impressive performances for Liverpool, and subsequently Everton, tended to be in his preferred role of central defence. Thus, the Ablett presence afforded his new employers high-quality cover in case of injury to Dave Watson and company and freed others, initially Martin Keown, when a sweeper was needed.

Gary's imperturbability and experience served the Blues admirably during their triumphant 1995 FA Cup campaign, and he remained a dependable influence until the continuing development of Andy Hinchcliffe and David Unsworth eased him out of senior contention later that year.

Still with plenty to offer at 30, Gary was borrowed for Sheffield United by Howard Kendall for the last two months of 1995/96, but the expected permanent move failed to materialise. However, that summer a £400,000 deal took him to Birmingham City, where he formed a canny defensive pairing with the former Manchester United hero, Steve Bruce.

BORN: Liverpool, 19.11.65. GAMES: 155. GOALS: 6.
HONOURS: FA Cup 94/5. OTHER CLUBS: Liverpool 86/7-91/2 (109,1); Derby County *on loan* 84/5 (6, 0); Hull City *on loan* 86/7 (5, 0); Sheffield United *on loan* 95/6 (12, 0); Birmingham City 96/7- (78, 1).

1991/92 - 1995/96

PREDRAG RADOSAVLJEVIC

By turns captivating and exasperating, Preki was a left-footed ball charmer who might have created a more lasting impact at Goodison Park in less troubled times.

When Howard Kendall spent £100,000 to pluck the Yugoslavian flankman cum midfielder from the North American Indoor League on the eve of the 1992/93 campaign, he was an unknown quantity to most English fans. However, when offered first-team opportunities in the autumn he furnished glorious, if tantalisingly fitful glimpses of his true pedigree.

Whether operating on his favoured side or, occasionally, coaxing a mazy path inside from the right touchline, Preki demonstrated the impressive mastery of a football which had won him international caps before his emigration to the States. He could pass beautifully and packed a powerful shot, too, but struggled to adapt to the frenetic nature of the English game.

Accordingly, during the two terms before Everton got their money back by selling him to Portsmouth in July 1994, Preki never earned a regular place and proved most effective when used as a substitute to inject new ideas into an ailing attack, an all-too-frequent occurrence. As for that contraction of his name, it was a veritable mercy to commentators and writers alike.

BORN: Belgrade, Yugoslavia, 24.6.63. GAMES: 25 (28). GOALS: 4. HONOURS: Yugoslavia caps; USA caps. OTHER CLUBS: Tacoma Stars, St Louis Storms, both USA; Portsmouth 94/5 (40, 5).

1992/93 - 1993/94

BILLY KENNY JNR

The case of Billy Kenny Jnr is an overwhelmingly sad one. The rough-hewn Scouser, whose father of the same name made a dozen senior appearances for Everton in the early and mid seventies, was a midfielder blessed with every talent needed to succeed at the top level.

To illustrate his limitless potential, as a 19-year-old rookie he bossed proceedings in the Merseyside derby victory at Goodison in December 1992. That day he revealed immaculate passing skills with either foot, instinctive vision and clever positional play, all topped off by the courage and appetite for a full-blooded tackle.

Billy had it all then, but the life of a professional athlete was not for him. Despite having seized the opportunity at club level afforded to him by injury to John Ebbrell, then going on to win England under-21 honours, he fell prey to off-the-pitch distractions and all that massive potential went to waste.

At the instigation of the Professional Footballers' Association he received a second chance at Oldham but that, too, was squandered. Everton coaches, players and fans will remember Billy Kenny rising meteorically through the youth ranks, his gifts being nurtured faithfully by the club, and they will sigh . . .

BORN: Liverpool, 19.9.73. GAMES: 22 (1). GOALS: 1. OTHER CLUBS: Oldham Athletic 94/5 (4, 0).

1992/93

PAUL HOLMES

At the age of 25, Paul Holmes had progressed through Doncaster Rovers and Torquay United to reach the fringe of Birmingham's First Division side and could have been excused for bidding a philosophical farewell to realistic hopes of a top-flight breakthrough. But then up popped Howard Kendall at a City reserve game, the Everton boss was immensely impressed by the smooth competence of the Brummies' right-back and the upshot was a £100,000 move to Everton in March 1993.

Most observers presumed that Paul was bought as cover but he made his Premier League debut that spring and retained his place for the first three months of the following season. The athletic Yorkshireman proved himself an enterprising overlapper, intelligent interceptor and reliable passer whose all-round skills enabled him to double in midfield.

Paul, whose father Albert Holmes was a Chesterfield stalwart in the sixties and seventies, lost the right-back slot to Matthew Jackson in a defensive reshuffle, never to regain it on a regular basis, and he joined West Bromwich Albion for £80,000 in January 1996. However, his Goodison experience had renewed the impetus of his career and he went on to enterprising service with the Throstles.

BORN: Wortley, Yorkshire, 18.2.68. GAMES: 26 (2). GOALS: 0. OTHER CLUBS: Doncaster Rovers 85/6-87/8 (47, 1); Torquay United 88/9-91/2 (138, 4); Birmingham City 92/3 (12, 0); West Bromwich Albion 95/6- (86, 1).

1992/93 - 1995/96

DAVID BURROWS

Though his tackles were as lustily abrasive as in his Anfield heyday, David Burrows made minimal lasting impact as an Evertonian. It was not that he let anyone down during his brief Goodison sojourn, merely that with Messrs Hinchcliffe, Ablett and Unsworth on hand the Blues were well stocked with left-sided defenders, and with the ever-present need of balancing the financial books, manager Joe Royle judged 'Bugsy' surplus to requirements.

He had been signed from West Ham by previous boss Mike Walker in September 1994 as part of the transaction which took Tony Cottee back to Upton Park, and he slotted straight into the side at left-back. A natural competitor endowed with bullish strength and infectious enthusiasm, David displayed his customary vigorous competence though sometimes his eagerness to get forward left alarming spaces behind him.

Nevertheless, such a versatile player - at need he could perform capably as a centre-back or a midfield man-marker - was seen as a valuable acquisition and it was mildly surprising when he was dispatched to Coventry for £1.1 million only six months after his arrival. David Burrows was never going to reach the heights predicted for him during his early days at Liverpool, when he had earned title and FA Cup honours, but he had matured into an admirably solid Premiership professional.

BORN: Dudley, Worcestershire, 25.10.68. GAMES: 23. GOALS: 0. OTHER CLUBS: West Bromwich Albion 85/6-88/9 (46, 1); Liverpool 88/9-93/4 (146, 3); West Ham United 93/4-94/5 (29, 1); Coventry City 94/5- (73, 0).

1994/95

BARRY HORNE

When extra steel, both physical and mental, was needed in the Everton midfield, Howard Kendall turned to Barry Horne. On the face of it, the 30-year-old chemistry graduate was hardly the obvious candidate to fire the imagination of fans crying out for a thoroughbred performer in the mould of Alan Ball or Peter Reid. But Howard, while knowing that the articulate, many-capped Welshman was not in the class of such illustrious predecessors, knew also that he was getting a battle-hardened bargain.

Barry cost £675,000 from Southampton in July 1992 and brought with him the priceless experience of nearly 400 club games, scattered through the divisions. He was an ultra-consistent box-to-box dynamo, a tough, spoiling tackler who would win the ball in all areas of the pitch, then dispense with it safely and thoughtfully.

There was nothing much about a footballing scrap that Barry didn't know, and he was to need all his natural resilience as a sticky start provoked terrace criticism. However, he prevailed and won over the doubters so comprehensively that he was voted the supporters' player of the year for 1994/95. The Horne approach was personified by his man-of-the-match display in the home defeat of Manchester United in February 1995 when he outfought Messrs Keane and Ince, a feat he repeated three months later in the stirring Wembley triumph over the Red Devils.

Though Barry was a beautifully clean striker of the ball, his goals were exceedingly rare, yet one was so important that it will be remembered as long as there is an Everton. It arrived on the last day of 1993/94, with the Blues 2-1 down at home to Wimbledon and needing a win to preserve their Premiership status. Deep in the second half, with the clock racing and belief draining visibly from some of his colleagues, Barry picked up the ball in midfield, strode forward defiantly and dispatched a wickedly dipping 25-yard thunderbolt into the visitors' net. He hadn't scored for 18 months but he had hit the target when it really mattered, creating the vital momentum which led to the yearned-for winner.

Come June 1996, with Barry in his 35th year, he accepted a £250,000 move to Birmingham, yet such was the esteem in which he was held by Joe Royle that when the going got tough in the spring, the doughty old warrior was set to return, only for the manager's resignation to scupper the deal.

BORN: St Asaph, Flintshire, 18.5.62. GAMES: 143 (7). GOALS: 3. HONOURS: FA Cup 94/5; 59 Wales caps (87-). OTHER CLUBS: Wrexham 84/5-86/7 (136, 17); Portsmouth 87/8-88/9 (70, 7); Southampton 88/9-91/2 (112, 6); Birmingham City 96/7 (33, 0); Huddersfield Town 97/8- (30, 0).

1992/93 - 1995/96

PAUL RIDEOUT

There was nothing wrong with Paul Rideout. He was an admirably professional and accomplished striker worthy of his place on the Premiership stage. But as the main marksman for a team with title ambitions? The objective answer has to be: not quite.

In mitigation, it should be stressed that he played with eight different front-running partners and was under constant threat of replacement by incoming stars. Also, he headed the only goal in the 1995 FA Cup Final victory over Manchester United so, whatever the critics' feeling about his overall merit, his name will always provoke joyful memories among Evertonians.

Paul was a former schoolboy prodigy who had fared creditably, if not outstandingly, in both the English and Italian Leagues when he arrived at Goodison as a £500,000 acquisition from Glasgow Rangers in August 1992. During his first campaign as a Blue he was disappointing, struggling to gel with either Peter Beardsley or Tony Cottee, a situation exacerbated by unconstructive criticism from sections of the Goodison crowd and a sequence of niggling injuries.

There were brighter moments during the following season but then, after netting four times in the opening six games of 1994/95, he was axed by Mike Walker and, understandably, began to feel unwanted. It was the manager who departed, though, and that campaign turned into Paul's most productive as a Blue as he finished top scorer with 16 strikes.

At the time, with Everton experiencing a relative revival, his assets were thrown into sharper relief. He worked ceaselessly, controlled and held the ball well and offered both power and subtlety in the air. He was versatile enough to be a target man when deployed with Daniel Amokachi, or to play as a feeder off Duncan Ferguson, and he kept trying even when chances went begging.

That term turned out to be Paul's peak, though he demonstrated notable all-round value in the relegation dogfight of spring 1997, when he excelled for several games in a hitherto unfamiliar central midfield role. That final task completed successfully, Paul departed with honour for a lucrative soccer swansong in China.

BORN: Bournemouth, Hampshire, 14.8.64. GAMES: 110 (29). GOALS: 40. OTHER CLUBS: Swindon Town 80/1-82/3 (95, 38); Aston Villa 83/4-84/5 (54, 19); Bari, Italy, 85/6-87/8 (99, 23); Southampton 88/9-91/2 (75, 19); Swindon Town *on loan* 90/1 (9, 1); Notts County 91/2 (11, 3); Rangers 91/2-92/3 (12, 1); Huan Dao Vanguards, China, 97-.

1992/93 - 1996/97

EARL BARRETT

Earl Barrett is a strong character and he needed every ounce of his undoubted resolution in the months following his £1.7 million move from Aston Villa to Everton in January 1995. Signed by Joe Royle, his mentor from his days at Oldham, the England defender was pitched into an improving Blues side and made an unenviable start when he was sent off for two bookable offences on his debut at Newcastle. Then he became the target for mindless barracking from a tiny but loud section of Goodison 'fans'.

Their apparent gripe was that the popular Matt Jackson was unlucky to lose his right-back slot, which was true enough. Clearly Matt was the more constructive performer and he had done little wrong in the weeks before being axed. Of course, this was none of Earl's doing but he was left to endure the inhospitable welcome.

His situation was made even more frustrating because he was FA Cup-tied, thus missing out on the rousing progress to Wembley, in which Matt played a splendid part. However, the more experienced newcomer showed his mettle by buckling down to League action, not missing a match for the remainder of the campaign and gradually earned his due respect.

Earl's prime attribute was his superb athleticism, most evident during his rampaging sprints down the right flank when he appeared to float over the ground, reminiscent of a West Indian fast bowler in full flight. It was a massive asset at the back, too, where his manoeuvrability and spring-heeled agility was matched by his courage in the tackle. Thus he could slot in effectively at centre-half, and also offered a midfield man-marking service which denied plenty of top-class opponents a kick of the ball. Sadly, his all-round technique did not match his physical prowess, and occasionally his passing could be embarrassingly wayward.

Nevertheless, it was a severe blow to Royle's plans for 1995/96 when Earl's season was ended by a knee injury sustained at home to Feyenoord in October. Typically, the easy-going Lancastrian fought back to figure as arguably the Blues' most reliable defender during 1996/97, seeing off the challenge of new signing Marc Hottiger. After that, though, Earl's opportunities under Howard Kendall proved limited and he was free to join Sheffield Wednesday early in 1998.

BORN: Rochdale, Lancashire, 28.4.67. GAMES: 81 (1). GOALS: 0. 3 England caps (91-93). OTHER CLUBS: Manchester City 85/6-86/7 (3, 0); Chester City *on loan* 85/6 (12, 0); Oldham Athletic 87/8-91/2 (183, 7); Aston Villa 91/2-94/5 (119, 1); Sheffield United *on loan* 97/8 (5, 0); Sheffield Wednesday 97/8- (9, 0).

1994/95 - 1997/98

VINNY SAMWAYS

For a footballer of such subtle creative talent, Vinny Samways under-achieved depressingly during his unexpectedly short stint as an Evertonian. The perky, sharp-eyed prompter cost £2.2 million when Mike Walker took him from Tottenham in August 1994, believing he had captured a play-maker in the traditional Toffees mould who would blossom fully on Merseyside as he had never quite managed in North London.

The first half of his Premiership debut, in the season's opener at home to Aston Villa, bore out his new boss's judgement and Goodison regulars spent the interval purring with approval at the Eastender's fluid distribution and contemplating a 1-0 lead. But the second half, in which the visitors battled back for a point, saw Vinny all but disappear - and that was his Everton career in microcosm. In fairness he was troubled sorely by knee injuries, but the delicate Samways touch never seemed likely to figure in the long-term thinking of Mike Walker's pragmatic successor, Joe Royle, and so it proved.

The 1995/96 campaign, which Vinny began upliftingly by netting the only goal of the Charity Shield victory over Blackburn with a speculative lob, proved to be his last as a Blue. After loan spells with Wolves and Birmingham failed to produce a permanent move, he accepted a £700,000 switch to Las Palmas.

BORN: Bethnal Green, London, 27.10.68. GAMES: 21 (6). GOALS: 3. OTHER CLUBS: Tottenham Hotspur 86/7-93/4 (193, 11); Wolverhampton Wanderers *on loan* 95/6 (3, 0); Birmingham City *on loan* 95/6 (12, 0); Las Palmas, Spain, 96/7-.

1994/95 - 1995/96

BRETT ANGELL

Brett Angell was a towering, endlessly willing centre-forward but, sad to record, he appeared out of his depth in the Premiership. After a brief loan stint at Goodison under Howard Kendall in September 1993 had ended inconclusively following one outing as a substitute, Angell returned on a 'permanent' basis in the January, Mike Walker paying Southend United £500,000 to make the Wiltshireman his first signing as Everton boss.

The idea was that big Brett, who had netted prolifically for the First Division Shrimpers, would prove an ideal foil for little Tony Cottee or the mobile Paul Rideout as the Blues scrapped to move clear of relegation. However, from the outset the newcomer looked leaden, even bewildered at times, as he tried manfully but unsuccessfully to come to terms with top-flight football.

Clearly Brett, who managed only one goal in 16 senior starts but could never be faulted for effort, had no Goodison future following the arrival of Duncan Ferguson and, after recovering from a broken leg suffered while playing for the reserves, he joined Sunderland for £600,000 in March 1995. There was to be no joy at Roker, either, but Brett went on to make a happy return to his first club, Stockport County.

BORN: Marlborough, Wiltshire, 20.8.68. GAMES: 16 (5). GOALS: 1. OTHER CLUBS: Stockport County 88/9-89/90 (70, 28); Southend United 90/1-93/4 (115, 47); Sunderland 94/5-95/6 (10, 0); Sheffield United *on loan* 95/6 (6, 2); West Bromwich Albion *on loan* 95/6 (3, 0); Stockport County 96/7- (78, 33).

1993/94 - 1994/95

DANIEL AMOKACHI

Daniel Amokachi was a deliciously unpredictable, rousingly rumbustious presence on a football pitch, and the fans loved him. However, he was emphatically not the reliable goal-scorer Everton lacked so conspicuously during the mid nineties. Dubbed 'The Buffalo' in his native Nigeria for his rampaging style, he was strong, nimble and skilful, his wildly flailing arms and legs contributing to an aura of furious persistence which characterised his play. Though acquired by Mike Walker as a specialist striker, Daniel proved more effective when running from deep as a counter-attacker, building irresistible momentum for the thunderous shot he could deliver with either foot. When starting farther forward he exuded anxiety in front of goal, his disappointing tally not doing justice to his all-round accomplishment.

Though only 21 when he spurned overtures from Juventus to join the Blues from FC Bruges for £3.2 million in August 1994, Daniel was already an experienced performer, having pocketed a Belgian championship medal, then earned global prominence with a clutch of exciting displays for his country during USA '94.

As the first high-profile black player in Everton history, Daniel attracted enormous attention but appeared unfazed by the publicity, greeting every inquiry with a vast grin. He began encouragingly with several adventurous displays and when Duncan Ferguson signed in October, hopes burgeoned that the two might prove lethal in tandem. But the Nigerian struggled to attain consistency, understandably enough for a fresh face from overseas in an unsettled side, and in early 1995 his Goodison future appeared in doubt when he was unable to break into new manager Joe Royle's team.

A change of fortune, albeit temporary, was imminent. Called on as a substitute for Brett Angell at Queen's Park Rangers in March, Daniel inspired a stirring fightback with his unorthodox approach and was rewarded by further opportunities. He responded by rising from the bench to net twice in the last eight minutes of the 4-1 FA Cup semi-final defeat of Spurs, then five days later scoring both goals in a 2-0 victory over Newcastle.

There followed a Wembley winner's medal after going on against Manchester United as a replacement for Anders Limpar, and the future looked distinctly promising. However, he became increasingly frustrated as barren spells saw him in and out of the side during the 1995/96 campaign, after which he joined Besiktas for £1.75 million. In the final reckoning, Daniel Amokachi represented a sparky gamble which didn't quite come off - but it was well worth a try.

BORN: Groko, Nigeria, 30.12.72. GAMES: 42 (12). GOALS: 14. HONOURS: FA Cup 94/5; Nigeria caps. OTHER CLUBS: Ranchiers Bees, Nigeria; FC Bruges, Belgium; Besiktas, Turkey, 96/7-.

1994/95 - 1995/96

ANDERS LIMPAR

It was easy to concentrate on what was missing from the footballing make-up of Anders Limpar, thus omitting to do justice to luxuriant talents which the mercurial Swede possessed in glorious measure. His brilliance was infuriatingly fitful, his reaction to adversity sometimes petulant and his idea of a hard afternoon's graft did not always accord with that of his managerial taskmasters. But when he seized the moment, improvising enchantingly with the hint of a swagger, he was one of the Premiership's most irresistible performers.

Anders' £1.6 million move from Arsenal in March 1994 rescued him from an unpalatable situation at Highbury, where he had been accused of lacking endeavour and, despite his mammoth contribution to the Gunners' title triumph of 1990/91, he was in danger of becoming a forgotten talent. Though nominally a winger, on arrival the Goodison newcomer was given licence to roam by Mike Walker and did his bit in the melodramatic last-day escape from relegation, notably tumbling to secure a spot-kick after making an earlier mistake which gifted Wimbledon a goal.

During 1994/95 Anders' appearances were limited by injuries, and when he did play he spent such lengthy interludes as an inconsequential onlooker that some fans turned against him and there were frequent hard looks from frustrated colleagues. However, his sumptuous touch, visionary passing and occasionally destructive finishing power underlined his status as the most gifted player on Everton's books, and though he tested the patience of new boss Joe Royle, he added much-needed refinement to a workaday side.

Predictably enough, come the big occasion and the Swede shone. Throughout his 70-minute contribution to the 1995 FA Cup Final, he demanded the ball and used it tellingly, setting up the only goal with a penetrative run through midfield and a well-timed pass to the overlapping Matthew Jackson. But not only did Anders delight with his incisive distribution, also he laboured constantly in the common cause, even finding time to repeatedly rob the ultra-competitive Paul Ince of possession.

This might have signalled a productive new phase of his Blues tenure but, as at Arsenal, triumph was followed by anti-climax and niggling injuries. Season 1995/96, during which it was hoped he would dazzle on the left while Andrei Kanchelskis marauded on the right, brought stop-start progress and a transfer became inevitable. In January 1997 Anders moved to Birmingham for a mere £100,000, a poignantly low-key exit for a flawed but thrilling entertainer.

BORN: Solna, Sweden, 24.9.65. GAMES: 63 (18). GOALS: 6. HONOURS: FA Cup 94/5; Sweden caps. OTHER CLUBS: Brommapojkama, Sweden 81-85 (77, 12); Orgryte, Sweden 86-88 (47, 9); Young Boys, Switzerland 88/9-89/90 (17, 6); Cremonese, Italy 89/90 (24, 3); Arsenal 90/1-93/4 (96, 17); Birmingham City 96/7 (4, 0); Solna, Sweden, 97-.

1993/94 - 1996/97

TONY GRANT

Tony Grant is exactly the sort of footballer Everton purists delight to see flourishing at Goodison Park. An imaginative young play-maker who can spot passing options where others perceive a blank wall and who can deliver the ball with instant and incisive accuracy, he offers a welcome new dimension to a Blues side which has been crying out for midfield subtlety since the golden pomp of Reid and Sheedy.

Certainly, no one connected with the club would dispute the slim Merseysider's creative eminence. Andrei Kanchelskis, without a thought for diplomacy but with revealing honesty, declared that Tony was the only player in the team who supplied him with the service he craved, while irreverent but perceptive colleagues dubbed him Grantona!

If the allusion to Manchester United's departed Frenchman seems fanciful as yet, the underlying message does not. So why has such a rare talent been seen only fleetingly at senior level since his debut back in 1994/95? There is no shortage of reasons, all of them understandable, beginning with the unpalatable truth that Everton have struggled dismally in recent seasons, thus not offering ideal circumstances in which to blood a rookie artist. True, Alex Ferguson has reaped rich dividends from pitching similarly gifted young men into battle but that was against a background of continuing success. Had Tony risen through the ranks at Old Trafford rather than Goodison, then we might now be discussing the merits of a recognised star.

In addition, the slender Grant physique has needed building up through specialist training, and there has been a succession of debilitating injuries, most disruptively during promising spells in 1996/97 (ankle) and 1997/98 (knee). However, lifelong Evertonian Tony is no delicate bloom who needs to be cosseted. Far from it. He whips into tackles, his stamina has improved and he oozes composure and self-confidence, being nothing loth to order more experienced team-mates into position to receive his dispatches.

What the England under-21 international needs more than anything, and what Howard Kendall was endeavouring to give him early in 1998 (fitness permitting), was a settled run in the senior side. A sample of what he can achieve was furnished at home to Chelsea in January when he slid a breathtakingly cunning through-pass on the blind side of several defenders, facilitating Nick Barmby's cross for Gary Speed's equaliser. Thereafter Everton went on to win a game they had hardly been in until Tony's intervention. Ooh Aah Grantona?

BORN: Liverpool, 14.11.74. GAMES: 35 (16). GOALS: 2.
OTHER CLUBS: Swindon Town *on loan* 95/6 (3, 1).

1994/95 -

JOE PARKINSON

Joe Parkinson has been one of the most underrated performers in Everton's recent history and his loss through injury for the whole of 1997/98 delivered a savage blow to the Blues' revival prospects.

Characterised widely as a midfield scuffler, denigrated as one of Joe Royle's 'Dogs of War', the unassuming Lancastrian deserves better. True, he is an implacable ball-winner and a consummate pressuriser whose claustrophobic attentions deny star opponents the time and space in which to parade their more spectacular wares. But Joe's own footballing merits, although invariably subjugated to the side's interests, are anything but negligible.

For example, his passing tends to be of the safe and simple variety, yet he has the ability to encompass a more panoramic range which would become apparent if team circumstances and his own undemonstrative nature allowed him to play a tad more ambitiously. A whiff of adventure might add to his niggardly goal tally, too.

In addition, though it's rarely mentioned, Joe carries an unexpected trick or two in his armoury, which he reveals just occasionally in delicious cameo moments, a sweet body-swerve here and a delicate pull-back there, hinting further at untapped potential.

But let's not get carried away. First and foremost Joe Parkinson is a strong, tireless and unselfish operator who has more than justified Mike Walker's decision to pay Bournemouth some £250,000 (rising to £800,000 after subsequent appearances) for his doughty services.

After arriving at Goodison on the same day in March 1994 as Anders Limpar - what a contrast in style the two newcomers offered - Joe won a senior berth early in 1994/95. He lost lost it briefly before cementing his place with a succession of consistent displays that earned him selection for that season's FA Cup Final against Manchester United at the expense of John Ebbrell, an immense achievement which underlined his worth. He was far from overwhelmed by Wembley, either, excelling alongside Barry Horne in the successful battle for midfield supremacy with Paul Ince and Roy Keane.

Thereafter Joe grew in stature to the extent that his progress was monitored by both the English and Welsh international managers, until his impetus was shattered by chronic knee problems in 1996/97. His full recovery in the near future is crucial to the Everton cause.

BORN: Eccles, Lancashire, 11.6.71. GAMES: 104 (2). GOALS: 4.
HONOURS: FA Cup 94/5. OTHER CLUBS: Wigan Athletic 88/9-92/3 (119, 6); Bournemouth 93/4 (30, 1).

1994/95 -

DAVID UNSWORTH

For several seasons, Evertonians rejoiced in the apparent certainty that, in David Unsworth, their club had unearthed the natural long-term heir to Kevin Ratcliffe. Like the Welshman before him, David was a quick, powerfully efficient, left-sided central defender and when he won a full England call-up at the age of 21, at least one piece in the eternal team-building jigsaw appeared to be in place.

Not so. The bullishly built Lancastrian's form hit a plateau, the side struggled woefully and, to the consternation of many Goodison regulars, in August 1997 David was dispatched to West Ham United, along with £1 million, to facilitate the arrival of midfielder Danny Williamson from Upton Park.

Why? Well, manager Howard Kendall was not short of defenders at the time, he was extremely keen on Williamson, and the Blues' transfer fund was not exactly bulging. Presumably, therefore, the deal represented the only practical method of capturing his quarry. Sometimes, too, an individual needs a change of club to grow as a player and this may be the case with David, who has plenty of time to prove that Everton were wrong to release him.

Certainly, there is no shortage of supporters who believe the decision will prove a costly mistake. They hark back fondly to 1994/95, during which the Unsworth star was in glorious ascendancy as his pace, strength and composure commanded attention. True, there was an occasional tendency to dive in with rash tackles and his distribution could be a little erratic, but his basic technique was sound, he was versatile enough to play at left-back or in midfield at need and he could strike a fearsome penalty.

There was a majestic Merseyside derby performance in November followed by a succession of dominant displays in the FA Cup, culminating with a storming Wembley show in which he muzzled the formidable Mark Hughes of Manchester United. David made his international debut that summer but mysteriously, come 1995/96, he seemed strangely hesitant, his former assertiveness gone. There followed sequences of indifferent form, and though he was usually in the team, and often played well, he did not seem quite the Unsworth of old. So now David, who had already deputised as Everton skipper and had seemed a prime candidate eventually to inherit the armband on a permanent basis, is a Hammer. From Merseyside, it need hardly be said, his progress down south will be monitored minutely.

BORN: Preston, Lancashire, 16.10.73. GAMES: 123 (10). GOALS: 12. HONOURS: FA Cup 94/5. 1 England cap (95). OTHER CLUBS: West Ham United 97/8- (31, 2).

1991/92 - 1996/97

ANDY HINCHCLIFFE

Andy Hinchcliffe is a man with a golden gift. The quiet Mancunian is a wickedly fine crosser of the ball, as devilish a deliverer as any in the English game, on a par in this one area of speciality with Manchester United's David Beckham or Jason McAteer of Liverpool.

Indeed, when his left foot is in the groove, Andy is a set-piece master against whom it is impossible to defend with any certainty. From the left flank, his low-trajectory missiles home in unerringly on the six-yard box, only to bend away tantalisingly at the last instant, creating absolute havoc for defenders. From the right, usually from the corner quadrant, they veer inwards with destructive accuracy, luring the 'keeper to commit himself but inviting decisive intervention from an attacker's head. Then there are his variations on a theme, the floaters, the dippers, the raking bullets that can shred the confidence of the sturdiest rearguard, opening the way for colleagues to employ other options.

Clearly, if the rest of Andy's game was as accomplished as his crossing, he would be a fixture in every manager's World XI. It isn't, but that is less a criticism of his all-round attributes than a tribute to that one glorious knack. In other respects he is a solidly competent Premiership defender, quick, strong and a fine passer, though sometimes lacking the vision to go with that last-mentioned ability. His tackling is generally crisp and resolute, though if he is beaten there is a rather disturbing tendency to stand and stare for what can be a vitally important moment.

Andy's best position? Undoubtedly left-wing-back, a role which allows him to roam forward without worrying too much about the gap behind him, though he is also capable in both central defence and midfield.

His Everton contribution, which began in July 1990 when he was signed from Manchester City in exchange for Neil Pointon and £200,000, was hindered by various injuries and was hardly enhanced by his apparently uneasy relationship with Howard Kendall - the man who had sent him on his way from Maine Road! Also there remains a nagging impression that the Hinchcliffe-Ferguson dream ticket, that ideal combination of dispatcher and finisher, never attained its full potential. However, there is no doubt that when the England international departed to Sheffield Wednesday for £2.75 million in January 1998, thus ending an excruciatingly tedious transfer saga, the Blues had lost a unique if distinctly enigmatic performer.

BORN: Manchester, 5.2.69. GAMES: 206 (16). GOALS: 9. HONOURS: FA Cup 94/5. 5 England caps (96-).
OTHER CLUBS: Manchester City 87/8-89/90 (112, 8); Sheffield Wednesday (14, 1).

1990/91 - 1997/98

DUNCAN FERGUSON

When Duncan Ferguson is climbing his own invisible ladder, soaring into that personal space above the crowd that is inviolate to even the most spring-heeled defender, he is awesome. Indeed, in the air, if his timing is right, the man is unstoppable. And yet, maddeningly, the tempestuous Scot remains a towering talent who has never been harnessed consistently and efficiently to his team's cause. The bottom line is that Duncan has neither scored nor created enough goals, his 37 in 116 outings since heading south to Goodison a niggardly return for a spearhead of such vast potential. Always, though, there is the tantalising thought that the full flowering of Duncan Ferguson is just around the next corner, and if that comes to pass during his days as a Blue - and there were encouraging signs in the spring of 1998 - then Everton will have on their hands a hero to rival Dixie Dean.

The Stirling-born giant, all 6ft 4ins and 14 stone of him, hit professional football like a runaway juggernaut when he surfaced with Dundee United in 1990. Unfortunately he found it difficult to deal with his early success, he was easily provoked and a bad-boy reputation was born. His notoriety gathered momentum at Rangers - culminating in a 44-day jail term for butting a Raith Rover, a sentence actually served after joining Everton - and many observers interpreted his crossing the border as a desperate bid for salvation.

The process began in October 1994, when an increasingly beleaguered Mike Walker took the controversial international on loan from Ibrox. Duncan displayed admirable commitment from the off, but it was not until the Joe Royle reign commenced in November that he revealed his true potential. He greeted his new boss in the best possible manner, with a headed goal in a victorious Merseyside derby, and did plenty to suggest that his future lay at Goodison. Accordingly, in December, a £4.3 million deal was concluded and Duncan proved a key element in the Blues' steady rise from the foot of the table. There was an FA Cup winner's medal, too, though he managed only a second-half Wembley appearance against Manchester United as he was labouring with a groin problem which had severely curtailed his season.

Come 1995/96 and Evertonians' expectations of their new talisman were gigantic, but frustration was in store. Duncan's interlude behind bars at Barlinnie was hardly conducive to progress, but he suffered from recurring injuries, too, making only 16 Premiership starts, and his longed-for link with winger Andrei Kanchelskis could not fairly be judged.

Over the next two terms Duncan was not helped by playing in a side which, under Royle, became tactically arid and over-reliant on his aerial power and under Howard Kendall was struggling perpetually. However, his sunlight-and-shadow sojourn at Goodison to date has provided a fund of joyous beacons which offer genuine hope, one gratifying example being the all-headed hat-trick against relegation rivals Bolton in December 1997.

In fairness, there is more to Ferguson than aerial omnipotence. With a single deft touch he can control a ball plummeting from the sky; he is quick for a fellow of his size; he can deliver a cute pass, though it must be admitted that his distribution can appear lackadaisical; he is a canny reader of play and he is not afraid of work; and, of course, when Duncan Ferguson goes to war he cuts an imposing, unnerving figure.

Everything seems to be in place but, perhaps, somewhere in the psyche of this avid pigeon-fancier, this 'pleasant young man' as Joe Royle described him, lies a deep-seated insecurity and lack of self-belief. Why else would he announce his international retirement, having failed to score in any of his seven appearances for Scotland, at the age of 26?

Perhaps the Blues captaincy, bestowed on Duncan following the departure of Gary Speed in February 1998, will be the making of him. Certainly early indications were favourable, his all-round contribution growing significantly both on and off the pitch. And if he still needs a boost, he could do worse than recall a goal which was meaningless in terms of the match it graced, but stands out vividly in the memory as definitive Ferguson. During the dying embers of a League clash at Highbury in January 1997, with Arsenal already three goals to the good, Everton's enigma rose so majestically, with such utter certainty, to crash home a header that Messrs Bould and Adams might as well have been back in the dressing room with their feet up. Ability like that is rare and precious, but it needs application, desire and concentration to allow it to flourish. It's down to you, Duncan . . .

BORN: Stirling, 27.12.71. GAMES: 109 (7). GOALS: 37. HONOURS: FA Cup 94/5. 7 Scotland caps (92-). OTHER CLUBS: Dundee United 90/1-92/3 (77, 27); Rangers 93/4-94/5 (14, 2).

1994/95 -

MARC HOTTIGER

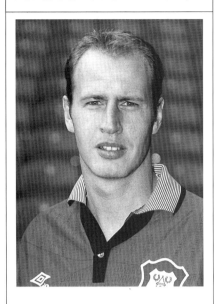

After attracting rave notices for Switzerland during the 1994 World Cup Finals, stylish right-back Marc Hottiger failed to make a success of his subsequent career in England. Immediately after the tournament he joined Newcastle and enjoyed a satisfactory first campaign, but then lost his place to the expensive Warren Barton. Unhappy to be sidelined, Marc accepted a £700,000 transfer to Everton in March 1996.

For the remainder of that term he impressed with his athletic attacking enterprise, revealing quick feet for a defender and an invaluable capacity to deliver accurate raking crosses. A delightful striker of the ball, he contributed a goal with an 18-yard drive at home to Bolton in April and his future as a Blue seemed to be in no doubt.

But the return from injury of Earl Barrett saw Marc ousted at the outset of 1996/97 and his subsequent rare outings hinted at a defensive fraility which was highlighted vividly in a severe chasing by Blackburn's Jason Wilcox on New Year's Day. Thereafter the pacy Swiss's absence from first-team duty raised questions about the validity of his work permit and in the summer Marc joined his hometown club, Lausanne.

BORN: Lausanne, Switzerland, 7.11.67. GAMES: 14 (4). GOALS: 1. HONOURS: Switzerland caps. OTHER CLUBS: Lausanne 88/9-91/2 (123, 5); Sion 92/3-93/4 (67, 13), both, Switzerland; Newcastle United 94/5-95/6 (39, 1); Lausanne 97/8.

1995/96 - 1996/97

TERRY PHELAN

The most enduring image of Terry Phelan is of this feisty little fellow scampering at high velocity down Everton's left flank. Though he's a left-back, the Republic of Ireland international attacks like a specialist winger, though his waspish tackle leaves little doubt about his defensive credentials.

He was drafted in as an £850,000 emergency recruit from Chelsea in January 1997 following injury to Andy Hinchcliffe. Terry didn't see himself as a stopgap, however, and supporters who had been worried by his fitness record at Stamford Bridge soon had their fears allayed by a series of spirited springtime displays.

The combative Mancunian is a fist-waving graduate of the Plough Lane academy who helped Wimbledon lift the FA Cup in 1988 and became the costliest left-back in British football history when he joined Manchester City for £2.5 million. He began the 1997/98 campaign in Everton's senior side, only for a cartilage operation to halt his progress. By May, with the classy young Michael Ball looking ever more comfortable in the left-back berth, 31-year-old Terry's Goodison future seemed to be limited.

BORN: Manchester, 16.3.67. GAMES: 24 (2). GOALS: 0. HONOURS: 37 Republic of Ireland caps (91-). OTHER CLUBS: Leeds United 85/6 (14, 0); Swansea City 86/7 (45, 0); Wimbledon 87/8-92/3 (159, 1); Manchester City 92/3-95/6 (103, 2); Chelsea 95/6-96/7 (15, 0).

1996/97 -

PAUL GERRARD

Unforeseen circumstances may yet result in Paul Gerrard enjoying a golden career as Everton's goalkeeper, but that prospect appeared to recede during the two years following his £1 million acquisition from Oldham Athletic in July 1996.

On arrival Paul had legitimate expect-ations of becoming the long-term successor to the veteran Neville Southall. After all, the newcomer had a fine record as England's under-21 custodian - 12 clean sheets in 18 appearances - and was working for his former boss at Boundary Park, Joe Royle.

But by the spring of 1998 the position had been transformed. Paul had been given opportunities to supplant Neville but had been unable to cement his claim, and Joe was gone.

Most worrying of all for the personable Lancastrian, new manager Howard Kendall had signed a young Norwegian, Thomas Myhre, whose brilliant early form had won him instant and prolonged promotion to the senior side.

Paul is an able 'keeper technically, but his cause has been hindered both by niggling injuries and mistakes in a high-profile encounter with Manchester United in March 1997, when he conceded two soft goals. Clearly, he faces a challenge of the most momentous order.

BORN: Heywood, Lancashire, 22.1.73. GAMES: 10 (1). GOALS: 0. OTHER CLUBS: Oldham Athletic 92/3-95/6 (119, 0).

1996/97 -

CLAUS THOMSEN

Claus Thomsen arrived at Goodison as an unknown quantity, failed to capture the fans' affection, and was unlamented when he departed some 14 months later. That's a stark and accurate summation of the Danish international's Everton experience, but it must be added that it in no way reflects his considerable footballing ability.

Circumstances were against him from the start. Recruited from Ipswich for £900,000 in January 1997 during the dying embers of Joe Royle's reign, the lanky midfielder cum defender was a competent all-rounder with a sound technique, but exciting he was not. Thus, at a time of general discontent, he was damned, with precipitate and sweeping unfairness, as being typical of the manager's perceived dourness.

Throughout an anxious springtime, Claus occupied central midfield, but Royle's resignation appeared to leave him isolated. Sure enough, after only a handful of senior opportunities under Howard Kendall - he performed impressively in front of the back line during the Merseyside derby at Anfield in February 1998 - he headed home to Denmark, joining AB Copenhagen in March for £500,000.

BORN: Aarhus, Denmark, 31.5.70. GAMES: 18 (7). GOALS: 1. HONOURS: Denmark caps. OTHER CLUBS: Aarhus, Denmark; Ipswich Town 94/5-96/7 (81, 7); AB Copenhagen, Denmark, 97/8-.

1996/97 - 1997/98

MITCH WARD

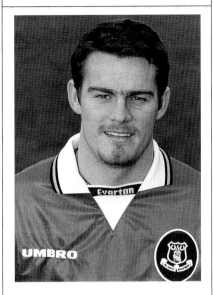

There were no fanfares of welcoming trumpets when Mitch Ward arrived at Goodison in November 1997, along with Carl Tiler in the deal which took Graham Stuart to Sheffield United. Indeed, the most noticeable sounds emanating from anxious supporters were snorts of dissatisfaction that Everton had, once again, dipped into the non-stellar end of the transfer market.

However, in this instance, they were doing less than justice to a experienced and versatile performer who is equally at home at full-back, wing-back or in midfield. Sadly, after he had made only a handful of appearances on the Blues' defensive right flank, an ankle injury scuppered Mitch's season, but not before he had demonstrated his power, commitment and ability to strike a telling cross.

Howard Kendall had rescued the solidly-built Yorkshireman from the transfer list at Bramall Lane and when he needed a man he could trust at Goodison, he looked no further. Fitness permitting, Mitch Ward may yet prove to be a shrewd investment in the seasons ahead.

BORN: Sheffield, 19.6.71. GAMES: 8. GOALS: 0. OTHER CLUBS: Sheffield United 90/1-97/8 (154, 11); Crewe Alexandra *on loan* 90/1 (4, 1).

1997/98 -

TONY THOMAS

Tony Thomas can do what a lot of so-called stars can't. The marauding right-back crosses a ball with intelligence and precision, a priceless knack which created goals galore for John Aldridge at Tranmere and on which Duncan Ferguson was quick to capitalise after the Merseysider's August 1997 switch to Goodison.

Indeed, two-thirds of the Scot's hat-trick against Bolton in December and his majestic header at Crystal Palace in January emanated from accurate Thomas dispatches and a prosperous partnership seemed in prospect. However, the newcomer's opportunities have been severely limited by injuries following his £400,000 move - rising to £650,000 if he makes enough appearances - and that potent attacking link spent most of the campaign on hold.

It should be stressed that Tony is no one-dimensional performer. Quick and a fierce tackler, he uses the ball constructively and during his lengthy tenure at Prenton Park he attracted interest from several leading clubs. In 1996 he almost joined Tottenham, after which he remained on a week-to-week contract with Tranmere until Howard Kendall made the boyhood Evertonian's dearest wish come true.

BORN: Liverpool, 12.7.71. GAMES: 8 (1). GOALS: 0. OTHER CLUBS: Tranmere Rovers 88/9-96/7 (257, 12).

1997/98 -

NICK BARMBY

One of the saddest sights in football is an outstanding player under-achieving, and that was Nick Barmby during his forlorn first year at Everton. He was dropped by successive managers and there was even talk of a move, but the Blues' record signing dug in and battled manfully for his Goodison future. Duly, as autumn turned to winter in 1997, the clouds rolled away and doubting fans began to understand why the unassuming Humbersider was once dubbed 'the new Peter Beardsley'.

After joining Tottenham as the most sought-after schoolboy talent in the country, Nick matured rapidly into a star performer and overcame debilitating injury problems to make impressive early strides on the international stage. A switch to Middlesbrough surprised some observers, but when he arrived on Merseyside for £5.75 million in November 1996 it seemed that the 22-year-old's career was poised for lift-off.

Nick's potential was, and remains, truly awesome. Though he is capable of playing up front or in midfield, nowhere is he more compelling than in the so-called 'hole' between the two. Both sumptuously skilful and chunkily dogged, he is an endlessly inventive link-man, his awareness and quick intelligence adding variety and unexpected angles to attacking movements, and he scores goals, too.

Accordingly, many pundits saw Nick as an ideal prompter for Duncan Ferguson, some even predicting that he might prove a creative catalyst in the same way that Eric Cantona had done for Manchester United. However, after a sprightly start - he scored one and made three in his second outing, the 7-1 home rout of Southampton - Nick degenerated into a pale, enigmatic presence who gave his all but contributed little to a struggling team.

Everton's general turmoil was hardly a help, and nor was the side's reliance on hoofing the ball monotously in the direction of Ferguson's head. Nick endured some rotten luck, too, netting only twice in the League during 1997, yet having three apparently good goals ruled out for offside.

It was a rare test of a young man's mettle, but his work-rate never flagged and by early 1998 his confidence and footballing fluency had returned so completely that he was recalled to the national squad. Now England, and Everton, can expect realisitically to see the best of Nick Barmby.

BORN: Hull, 11.2.74. GAMES: 52 (8). GOALS: 9. HONOURS: 10 England caps (95-).
OTHER CLUBS: Tottenham Hotspur 92/3-94/5 (87, 20); Middlesbrough 95/6-96/7 (42, 8).

1996/97 -

ANDREI KANCHELSKIS

Evertonians are a justifiably proud bunch and they don't seek sympathy. However, in the case of Andrei Kanchelskis, heartfelt commiserations must be in order. Just consider. After irreconcilable differences between the mercurial Ukrainian flankman and Alex Ferguson had terminated his sumptuously successful tenure at Old Trafford, he joined the Blues in August 1995, following one of the most tedious on-off transfer sagas of recent years. Such was the euphoria around Goodison at the £5.5 million capture of a world-class performer that, even before he had kicked a ball in anger, the FA Cup holders had sold thousands of shirts with his name emblazoned on the back. Ecstatic fans drooled at the prospects of what an attack containing Messrs Kanchelskis, Ferguson and Limpar might achieve.

True, there was a temporary setback when Andrei picked up a shoulder injury, ironically in an accidental collision with former Manchester United team-mate Lee Sharpe, which cost him a five-week autumn absence. But for the remainder of that campaign, the explosively gifted newcomer's personal form, if not that of his two talented colleagues, lived up to every expectation.

Andrei's first two goals for Everton, a cute glancing header and a typical near-post power drive, arrived in front of the Kop and secured a 2-1 victory in the Merseyside derby. Thereafter, his confidence bubbling, he treated his new supporters to six months of bliss. With his ungovernable sprints and penetrating dribbles he could make defenders look like traffic cones in a training exercise and his shoot-on-sight policy brought an avalanche of goals. Andrei's input was encapsulated in a 5-2 win at Sheffield United in April, to which he contributed a hat-trick and two 'assists', also rapping the woodwork and seeing another strike disallowed for offside.

Presumably, went the theory, having bedded in he would be even better in 1996/97, but now the script went horribly awry. His never-ending runs became ever more blinkered - supremely frustrating for colleagues screaming for a pass - and his greed in front of goal became irksome as ball found net with decreasing frequency. Meanwhile his willingness to tackle back was, shall we say, negligible.

Eventually Andrei appeared listless, a mood ominously reminiscent of his latter days in Manchester; rumours circulated of personal problems and that he coveted a move to Italy. Sure enough, in January 1997, an £8 million fee secured his services for Fiorentina. It was a lot of cash, but then, a lot of shirts had to be ditched by distraught fans. Andrei Kanchelskis left some rousing memories, but what might have been? It doesn't bear thinking about.

BORN: Kirovograd, Ukraine, 23.1.69. GAMES: 60. GOALS: 23. HONOURS: USSR, CIS and Russia caps. OTHER CLUBS: Dynamo Kiev 88-89 (22, 1); Shakhtyor Donetsk 90-91 (21, 3), both USSR; Manchester United 90/1-94/5 (123, 28); Fiorentina, Italy 96/7.

1995/96 - 1996/97

GRAHAM STUART

If ever a fellow lived up to a nickname it was Graham Stuart. Dubbed 'Diamond' because he was, in the chirpy parlance of his hometown, a 'diamond geezer', the affable Londoner displayed talent and spirit in equal measure. Despite being singled out unfairly as the crowd's whipping boy on occasions, the versatile midfielder cum striker never shirked in bad times or good, rolling up his sleeves through several relegation dogfights as well as contributing mightily to Everton's one moment of true glory during his Goodison sojourn.

Indeed, Graham was at the heart of the two most compellingly dramatic sequences of action the Blues have experienced in recent seasons. At home to Wimbledon in May 1994, desperately needing victory to avoid demotion and finding themselves two goals down, Everton needed a miracle. Enter 'Diamond' to convert a penalty and then, after Barry Horne had equalised, to scuff home a late 12-yarder which saved the day. In more welcome circumstances a year later, it was Graham who drove a shot against Manchester United's crossbar at Wembley, enabling Paul Rideout to net the FA Cup winner on the rebound, and that after starring in the semi-final against Spurs.

But the England under-21 international, signed from Chelsea for £850,000 in August 1993, was not just a man for the big occasion. Whether in his most effective role on the right of midfield, or as a striker, or as a wing-back, or in the 'hole' behind the front men, Graham supplied consistent application. Quick, brave and a gifted dribbler when given free rein, he possessed smart control, ran intelligently and could finish emphatically.

Admittedly, sometimes he seemed anonymous and had his game contained more of a strut then he might not have been targeted for criticism. Probably he suffered for his own adaptability, never knowing what job he might be asked to do next, and even Joe Royle wondered publicly whether he had been fair to the player. Certainly when Graham was allowed to specialise he responded positively, scoring 14 times when deployed up front for much of 1995/96. Others might have complained but that was not his way and he beavered faithfully until he left for Sheffield United in the deal that took Carl Tiler and Mitch Ward to Goodison in November 1997. If there is any justice, when Graham Stuart is recalled in years to come, it will be as a genuine sparkler.

BORN: Tooting, London, 24.10.70. GAMES: 138 (24). GOALS: 31. HONOURS: FA Cup 94/5.
OTHER CLUBS: Chelsea 89/90-92/3 (87, 14); Sheffield United 97/8- (28, 5).

1993/94 - 1997/98

CRAIG SHORT

Craig Short resembles an Identikit picture of the ideal centre-half. Tall and imposing, quick and courageous, he is a fearsome challenger in the air and on the ground, and has become increasingly capable of carrying the ball forward with assurance. And yet, somehow, the square-jawed Yorkshireman has not proved consistently convincing since his move to Everton from Derby in the summer of 1995.

It was a transaction on which Goodison boss Joe Royle was exceedingly keen, pursuing his quarry from March until July before clinching the signature in exchange for £2.75 million and the services of young defender Gary Rowett. It was the second big deal in which Craig had been involved - for a while he had been Britain's costliest defender after switching from Notts County to the Baseball Ground - and the feeling was that the Blues were acquiring the finished article.

Having served as Derby's skipper afforded extra stature and Craig was touted widely as the long-term replacement for Dave Watson, which may yet turn out to be the case. However, the transition from Derby's back-four system to a three-man central defence proved hugely testing, appearing sometimes to disorientate the newcomer, who was hindered initially by injuries and the fine form of Unsworth and Watson.

Though Craig's physical presence has been impressive, and his effort exemplary, there has been scope for improvement in both his positional play and his distribution. As a result, he has been discarded periodically when the manager has opted for the dual-stopper method, and his confidence must have suffered accordingly.

But Craig is a feisty character who has worked assiduously and season 1997/98 brought a new dimension to his game. Now he appeared far happier in possession, and in October he capped a towering all-round display in the Goodison victory over Liverpool by running with the ball from deep inside his own half to the Reds' penalty area, before delivering a lovely pass to Danny Cadamarteri. One writer evoked the name of Beckenbauer, which was a tad rich, but readers got the idea! With fierce competition from the likes of Bilic, Tiler, Dunne and the faithful Watson, Craig Short faces a challenging Goodison future, but it is not inconceivable that he will rise to it majestically.

BORN: Bridlington, Yorkshire, 25.6.68. GAMES: 79 (9). GOALS: 4. OTHER CLUBS: Scarborough 87/8-88/9 (63, 7); Notts County 89/90-92/3 (128, 6); Derby County 92/3-94/5 (118, 9).

1995/96 -

SLAVEN BILIC

Cultured Croat or Barmy Balkan? As Everton scrapped desperately for Premiership survival in 1997/98, there was no shortage of Goodison regulars who could not make up their minds about Slaven Bilic.

On the one hand, there was no doubting the sheer quality of the big, stylish central defender. Terrific in the air, a destructive tackler and an intelligent interceptor, he was equally effective when carrying the ball out of defence and delivering perceptive passes to gladden the hearts of those who delight in the Blues' somewhat tarnished tradition as the School of Soccer Science.

Courtesy of a comprehensive range of skills, Slaven was equipped to double in midfield on the rare occasions when he could be spared from rearguard duty and, to complete the picture, he was a gifted organiser and natural leader who could lift the spirits of those around him.

On the other hand? Discipline, or rather the lack of it, was all that stood between the multi-lingual law graduate and unreserved acceptance as a truly outstanding Evertonian. The inescapable truth was that a trio of sendings-off, a succession of bookings and spats with the manager were hardly what was needed at a club embroiled in a long battle against demotion. His third dismissal, against Southampton at the Dell, arguably cost the Blues at least a point, and his suspensions caused disruption at a time when stability was at a premium. In the circumstances, his attempts to justify his misdemeanours as professional fouls carried a rather hollow ring.

Slaven, a national hero back home in Croatia, had also become a massively popular figure at his first English club, West Ham, whose supporters were mortified when he agreed to join Everton in March 1997. However, with the Hammers in relegation trouble at the time, he agreed to defer his £4.5 million move until the summer.

Ironically, the reason Slaven gave for heading north was to have a better chance of winning trophies and the relative fortunes of his former and current employers during 1997/98 must have given him pause for thought. As the season ended he expressed dissatisfaction with the club's transfer policy and speculation about his own future began to mount.

BORN: Croatia, 11.9.68. GAMES: 25 (2). GOALS: 0. HONOURS: Croatia caps. OTHER CLUBS: Hajduk Split, Yugoslavia, 88/9-92/3 (109, 13); Karlsruhe, Germany, 93/4-94/5 (54, 5); West Ham United 95/6-96/7 (48, 2).

1997/98 -

GARY SPEED

It all started so idyllically. When lifelong Evertonian Gary Speed joined the Toffees, it offered the club's long-suffering supporters the reasonable expectation that, at 26, he would devote the best years of his career to the Goodison cause. After a steady first season on the left of midfield, he was appointed captain and, from the outside, it seemed that the Welshman was living out a childhood dream. But, as the Blues began to labour, perplexing rumours began to circulate that he was unhappy and by late 1997 the fans, who had taken Gary to their heart as one of their own, were dumbfounded by the revelation that he wanted a move. In February he departed amidst a hail of rancorous recriminations from disillusioned erstwhile admirers, who were left to ponder one simple question: why?

That sad scenario contrasted starkly with the optimism surrounding Gary's £3.5 million signing in July 1996 from Leeds, with whom he had gone perplexingly stale after excelling in their title triumph of 1991/92. He scored coolly on his Everton debut at home to Newcastle and bedded in promisingly if rather inconsistently, a highlight being a fine hat-trick - two headers and a 20-yard drive - in the 7-1 annihilation of Southampton in November.

Come the spring, Gary was improving steadily and looking set to emerge as a major influence, the powerful goal-scoring midfielder the side needed so urgently. His left-foot control, passing and shooting were of the highest quality, while his right-sided work was competent enough, and he could not be faulted for strength or stamina, industry or courage. But the most compelling weapon in the Speed armoury was his knack of timing late runs into the penalty box which, given his spring-heeled aerial excellence, offered a thrillingly potent threat.

At the outset of 1997/98, sensing that Gary had even more to give, Howard Kendall followed the example of Wales manager Bobby Gould and made him skipper. The new Goodison boss was rewarded throughout the autumn by a series of impressively mature personal displays which, unfortunately, were set against a background of team travail. At some point thereafter, for reasons never disclosed publicly, Gary decided that he must leave the club he loved and, following a particularly acrimonious transfer saga, he accepted a £6 million switch to Newcastle. The venom which poured from the stands on his subsequent return to Goodison in a black-and-white shirt was disagreeable, but hardly surprising.

BORN: Mancot, Flintshire, 8.9.69. GAMES: 65. GOALS: 18. HONOURS: 44 Wales caps (90-).
OTHER CLUBS: Leeds United 88/9-95/6 (248, 39); Newcastle United 97/8- (13, 1)

1996/97 - 1997/98

MICHAEL BALL

The steady march towards excellence of Michael Ball was Everton's quiet success story of 1997/98. The merits of Messrs Cadamarteri and Myhre, for instance, may have attracted considerably more media attention, but the blond Merseysider's less trumpeted but hugely significant progress during a trying campaign produced equal satisfaction among Goodison insiders.

Indeed, so sanguine was manager Howard Kendall about Michael's burgeoning capabilities as a left-sided wing-back, who could also perform in central defence or midfield, that he sold England's Andy Hinchcliffe in mid season.

It was as a 17-year-old that Michael made his senior debut, rising from the bench as a first-half substitute for the injured Terry Phelan in a tense, bottom-of-the-table tussle at home to Tottenham in April 1997. He let no one down as a crucial 1-0 victory was clinched, then underlined his quality as a substitute in the Merseyside derby four days later and made his first senior start in the next match, at West Ham.

Throughout that taxing sequence, Michael showed commendable maturity and composure, and when the chance of a regular berth materialised during the following term he claimed it with alacrity.

At this early stage in his career, the Ball game lacks little that experience cannot be expected to furnish. He has, as they say, 'good feet', being able to control a football with assurance and pass it accurately over distances short and long; he tackles briskly and is splendid in the air; he is an increasingly expert crosser and a long-throw specialist, an enormous boon to a wing-back.

In general, too, Michael is a good decision-maker, knowing instinctively when to challenge and when to stand off, when to surge forward and when to cover for others, and while there is an occasional tendency to be caught out of position by balls played in behind him - something of an occupational hazard in his up-and-back role - he is blessed with the speed and stamina to effect a recovery in all but the direst of circumstances.

A graduate from the FA National School, a regular in the reserves at 16, in the first team a year later, an under-21 international - is Michael Ball an England star of the future? He's still got oceans of work to do and, even then, it's impossible to be sure. But don't bet against it.

BORN: Liverpool, 2.10.79. GAMES: 25 (8), GOALS: 1.

1996/97 -

DANNY CADAMARTERI

Like a sudden shaft of dancing light, Danny Cadamarteri pierced the gloom that gathered over Goodison during the dog days of 1997/98. By his sheer verve and audacity as much as by his exhilarating attacking skills, the daring young Yorkshireman stirred joy and hope in the breasts of downcast Everton supporters who had well-nigh forgotten that such emotions were possible.

Danny is a confident lad, seemingly nerveless, and that carefree outlook is reflected in his football as he demonstrated upliftingly in one of his earliest senior outings, at home to Arsenal in September. When a loose ball fell to him some 15 yards from goal, he was surrounded by a posse of the Premiership's most forbidding defenders. Did he freeze? Not a bit of it. Danny feinted one way, then darted the other before dispatching a wickedly swerving right-foot drive over David Seaman's shoulder from 15 yards.

It was a manoeuvre which summed up the Cadamarteri ethos, and there followed an interlude of frantic euphoria during which the dreadlocked rookie could do no wrong. He scored five times in six starts, an exuberant sequence capped by a brilliant individual effort to kill off Liverpool at Goodison in October, just a few days after his 18th birthday.

Danny's attributes are legion, but extreme pace, immense body strength and boundless enthusiasm share top billing. If he gets away from a defender he will not be caught, he is extremely difficult to dislodge from possession, and he chases so relentlessly that he can occupy an opposing back line on his own. Since earlier days, when he couldn't get into his school team because of technical shortcomings, Danny has worked wonders with his control, and his abrupt changes of direction can befuddle the tightest of markers.

Naturally enough, after a while it became apparent that there is much for the boy to learn. His distribution demands extra care, he needs to improve his overall awareness and, without losing the impetuosity that makes him special, he could do with more composure. Sensibly in the circumstances, the arrival of Mickael Madar in January cost him his regular place. His 1997/98 campaign - during which he opted to pursue international ambitions with England ahead of five other nations for which he was qualified - was all about freshness and enjoyment. The big test of consolidation lies ahead, and it would be a sad surprise if Danny Cadamarteri did not pass it with flying colours.

BORN: Bradford, Yorkshire, 12.10.79. GAMES: 17 (14). GOALS: 5.

1996/97 -

MICHAEL BRANCH

Michael Branch plays his football like a whippet on hot bricks. The precociously gifted young striker makes lightning runs, often too quick for colleagues to perceive, so they lump the ball in the direction of big Ferguson instead. That leaves Michael, who looks to be an intense fellow utterly consumed with the desire to score goals, sorely frustrated and seemingly burdened by the huge weight of expectation created by earlier successes.

About his ability there is no question. So pacy that, as one wag put it, he makes Robbie Fowler look like Brett Angell, the England under-21 international is blessed with control, aggression and an instinctive eye for an opening. He is adept at electrifying off-the-ball excursions, darting nimbly away from defenders and bewildering them by constant movement. What he lacks, presently, is the penalty-area composure to make the most of his talent.

In fairness he has endured awful luck with injuries since making his senior debut as a 17-year-old at Old Trafford in February 1996, a broken ankle in mid 1997/98 being the most recent setback. Also, his slim physique needs strengthening.

Nevertheless, three goals from 16 starts and 20 substitute outings to date is a disappointing record and there is a danger of being leapfrogged by rivals. But Michael is still young and, if he can relax just a little, success should surely be his.

BORN: Liverpool, 18.10.78.
GAMES: 16 (20). GOALS: 3.

1995/96 -

JOHN OSTER

John Oster doesn't hang around. The baby-faced ball artist was a Welsh under-21 international before playing his first League game for Grimsby and he won full caps during his debut campaign at Goodison Park.

Yet most Everton fans had never heard of the bounteously talented 18-year-old when Howard Kendall paid the Mariners £1.6 million for his precocious services in July 1997. Alex Ferguson had, though, and was so impressed with the Oster potential that he wanted to take the flankman cum midfielder on Manchester United's pre-season tour of the Far East. But John chose the Blues and early indications are that the Merseysiders will bless the day they signed him.

So instant was his impact that he went straight into the Premiership side and held his place for much of the season. Right-footed but preferring to operate on the left so that he can cut inside to devastating effect, John is extravagantly skilful and brilliantly balanced. He can pass defenders on either side and, though he's no specialist speed merchant, he surprises markers by sudden changes of gear and direction. In addition, he is tougher than he looks and ultra-confident, and when experience brings heightened all-round awareness, John Oster should be some player.

BORN: Boston, Lincolnshire, 8.12.78. GAMES: 19 (15).
GOALS: 3. HONOURS: 2 Wales caps (98-).
OTHER CLUBS: Grimsby Town 96/7 (24, 3).

1997/98 -

GARETH FARRELLY

When Howard Kendall paid Aston Villa £700,000 to make Gareth Farrelly his first signing, only days after beginning his third spell as Everton boss in June 1997, he declared that the Irish international schemer had the ability to become a household name. Howard didn't offer a time-scale and, on the evidence of Gareth's first Goodison season, the young man has a way to go. But there is no denying that the sweet-passing, left-sided midfielder has the potential, at least, to become a major Premiership force.

Gareth had been expected to achieve much at Villa in 1996/97, only to be frustrated by the consistency of Andy Townsend. With his career standing still he opted for a new start and, being a lifelong Evertonian, had little hesitation in choosing the Blues ahead of Celtic, Derby and others. A knee injury marred his start, but he enjoyed a settled spell in the side from November to March, impressing with his vision, skill and energy but appearing sometimes to try a bit too hard, perhaps attempting one pass too many.

However, Gareth finished the campaign on an uplifting note. His 25-yard half-volley against Coventry, struck perfectly with his unfavoured right foot, opened his Premiership account for the club and, more importantly, ensured that Goodison will continue to play host to top-flight football in 1998/99.

BORN: Dublin, 28.8.75. GAMES: 20 (8). GOALS: 2. HONOURS: 4 Republic of Ireland caps (96-). OTHER CLUBS: Aston Villa 95/6-96/7 (8, 0); Rotherham United *on loan* 94/5 (10, 2).

1997/98 -

DANNY WILLIAMSON

The jury was out on the claims of Danny Williamson to earn a regular place in the Everton midfield after injury sabotaged his opening campaign at Goodison Park.

Despite half a decade of intermittent service to West Ham, comparatively little was known of the energetic Eastender when he moved north in August 1997, although the scale of his fee - £1 million plus the highly-rated David Unsworth - indicated that manager Howard Kendall was confident that he had captured a major talent.

As the Blues endured a troubled first half of the season, Danny emerged as a tidy all-round craftsman, passing deftly, intercepting perceptively and tackling firmly. His presence tended to be unobtrusive but efficient, never hiding from the ball when the team plan was going awry, which happened all too frequently at that juncture, but not seizing centre stage either. Though he scored no goals he had a hand in a few and it says much for Danny's contribution that he retained his place in the face of brisk competition until sidelined by a serious knee injury in December.

Many West Ham fans regretted the departure of a promising performer who could sit in front of the back line or operate further forward. Whether he can win similar approbation on Merseyside remains to be seen.

BORN: West Ham, London, 5.12.73. GAMES: 17. GOALS: 0. OTHER CLUBS: West Ham United 93/4-96/7 (51, 5); Doncaster Rovers *on loan* 93/4 (13, 1).

1997/98 -

CARL TILER

As a young centre-half in the late 1980s and early 1990s, Carl Tiler was tipped for the game's highest honours. But somehow, although he earned England under-21 recognition, a combination of injuries and fierce competition for places at a succession of clubs combined to prevent the 6ft 4in Yorkshireman from realising his full potential.

Yet all is not lost. After he moved from Sheffield United to Everton in November 1997 - in a package deal which also took Mitch Ward to Goodison, with Graham Stuart and £500,000 travelling in the opposite direction - left-sided Carl has enjoyed arguably the finest form of his career to date.

Stepping into a leaky rearguard, he tightened it immeasurably, barely putting a foot or a head wrong as the Blues' fortunes began to improve during December and January. At first he had to battle to win over the fans, who were hungry for star signings, but soon they warmed to his composed, classy and dominant contribution. Still only 28 at the outset of 1998/99, Carl Tiler may be approaching his footballing zenith at last.

BORN: Sheffield, 11.2.70. GAMES: 20. GOALS: 1. OTHER CLUBS: Barnsley 87/8-90/1 (71, 3); Nottingham Forest 91/2-94/5 (69, 1); Swindon Town *on loan* 94/5 (2, 0); Aston Villa 95/6-96/7 (12, 1); Sheffield United 96/7-97/8 (23, 2).

1997/98 -

RICHARD DUNNE

Jimmy Gabriel called him 'a marvellous big laddie' and the former Everton hero was not wrong. Richard Dunne is a vastly promising young central defender with the raw ability to become a cornerstone of the Blues' rearguard for the foreseeable future, maybe even into the second decade of the 21st century.

The equable Dubliner, whose all-round expertise has been likened to that of his eminent countryman Paul McGrath, cuts a commanding figure, as befits a lad who tipped the scales at 15 stone before his 16th birthday. However, big Richard is no lumbering giant whose usefulness is limited to aerial combat. Indeed, he is a nimble operator both physically and mentally, reading the game with commendable astuteness for one so inexperienced, and passing the ball with admirable composure and accuracy.

At the age of 17 years and 106 days in January 1996, Richard became Everton's youngest Goodison debutant when he faced Swindon in the FA Cup. He did well and three months later the favourable impression was confirmed with a characteristically cool display at home to Liverpool. Competition for Everton's central defensive berths is brisk, to say the least, but it seems only a matter of time before one of them becomes the long-term property of Richard Dunne.

BORN: Dublin, 21.9.78. GAMES: 10 (2). GOALS: 0.

1996/97 -

MICKAEL MADAR

Mickael Madar scored a clutch of important goals for Everton following his arrival on a free transfer from Spain in December 1997, but nothing summed up his audacious presence more aptly than a spectacular near-miss in the Merseyside derby at Anfield in February. The pony-tailed Parisian had roamed to the left flank where he allowed a long pass from Claus Thomsen to bounce once and then, with the Liverpool defence expecting a cross, he dispatched a sudden, swirling 30-yard volley which came perilously close to beating astonished 'keeper David James.

The Madar repertoire of unorthodoxy is graced, also, with outrageous backheels, delightful cushioned lay-offs and unexpectedly cute passes and, despite some alarming miscues in front of goal, the Blues' darkly menacing stranger lacks none of a striker's traditional attributes, either. Big and combative, he offers a potent aerial threat and though his pace is limited, he compensates by assessing situations quickly.

Before his move Mickael had been out for nearly a year with a broken leg and, consequently, took time to adjust to the Premiership tempo. If his stamina and workrate eventually match his imagination, then he should prosper at Goodison.

BORN: Paris, France, 8.5.68. GAMES: 15 (2). GOALS: 6. HONOURS: 3 France caps. OTHER CLUBS: Sochaux 86/7-88/9 (32, 8); Laval 89/90 (29, 9); Sochaux 90/1-91/2 (39, 6); Cannes 92/3-93/4 (54, 26); Monaco 94/5-95/6 (52, 14), all France; Deportivo La Coruna, Spain, 96/7-97/8 (28, 7).

1997/98 -

DON HUTCHISON

Howard Kendall might have struck a stupendous bargain when he signed Don Hutchison for £1.5 million from Sheffield United in February 1998. Then again, it might all end in tears. But such is the all-round quality of the former Liverpool midfielder that few would deny that the risk was worth it.

Don arrived with the baggage of misdemeanours aplenty in his past, but insisting that his so-called bad-boy days were behind him. He stepped into an Everton midfield sorely in need of his perceptive distribution and steely physical presence, and did enough to raise hopes that he might, at last, be on the verge of fulfilling his massive potential.

For example, the Scotland 'B' international exerted a splendidly creative influence during the home triumph over Blackburn in March. Undeterred by the robust attentions of Tim Sherwood, he showed outstanding craft and control, moving one shrewd observer to compare him to Gary McCallister. Meanwhile his height and eye for goal offered an added dimension and it should not be forgotten that he can double as a striker.

Don was still only 27 as 1998/99 commenced and there was no footballing reason why his prime should not lie ahead of him. Fingers crossed . . .

BORN: Gateshead, County Durham, 9.5.71. GAMES: 11. GOALS: 1. OTHER CLUBS: Hartlepool United 89/90-90/1 (24, 2); Liverpool 91/2-93/4 (45, 7); West Ham United 94/5-95/6 (35, 11); Sheffield United 95/6-97/8 (78, 4).

1997/98 -

JOHN O'KANE

It speaks volumes for John O'Kane that Howard Kendall took him on a week's trial and saw enough to sign him for Everton within two days. Such enthusiasm surprised no-one at Old Trafford, where the versatile Midlander had been schooled comprehensively in the immaculate pass-and-move technique which has underpinned Manchester United's modern success.

John, who prefers right-back but can operate with equal facility on the left or in midfield, settled quickly at Goodison, relishing the chance of Premiership football and taking to it impressively. Having spent some seven seasons in United's reserves, the 23-year-old was in danger of stagnating, so his £400,000 transfer in January 1998 was timely.

But for the presence of Denis Irwin and the Nevilles, John might have covered himself with glory as a Red Devil, but had to be content with an FA Youth Cup winner's medal in 1992 and a Second Division title gong gained while on loan at Bury in 1997. Evertonians will hope that John O'Kane's collection of honours is only just beginning . . .

BORN: Nottingham, 15.11.74.
GAMES: 12. GOALS: 0.
OTHER CLUBS: Manchester United 94/5-96/7 (2, 0); Bury *on loan* 96/7 (13, 3); Bradford City *on loan* 97/8 (7, 0).

1997/98 -

JOHN SPENCER

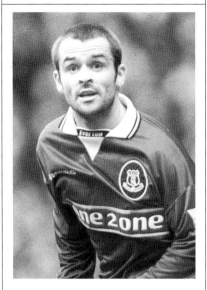

In this era of ludicrously inflated prices, where could a manager find a 27-year-old international striker with a proven Premiership goalscoring pedigree for a mere £1.5 million? The answer, as Howard Kendall discovered in March 1998, was Queen's Park Rangers, from whom he acquired the services of John Spencer.

After excelling at Chelsea until being supplanted by star Italians, the sparky little Glaswegian shone briefly at Loftus Road, then fell out of favour. Enter Everton's beleaguered manager, in desperate need of nippy support for his big lads, Duncan Ferguson and Mickael Madar. Thus John joined the Blues, initially on loan but eventually, after worrying confusion about a suspected heart murmur had been cleared up, on a three-year contract.

It could be an inspired piece of business. Hugely confident, endlessly enthusiastic and endowed with neat control, a savage shot and a knack of turning past defenders with the ball in confined areas, he contributed gutsily to the fight against relegation and can be expected to flourish in less desperate circumstances.

BORN: Glasgow, 11.9.70. GAMES: 3 (3). GOALS: 0. HONOURS: 14 Scotland caps (94-). OTHER CLUBS: Glasgow Rangers 86/7-91/2 (13, 2); Morton on loan 88/9 (4, 1); Chelsea 92/3-96/7 (103, 36); Queen's Park Rangers 96/7-97/8 (48, 22).

1997/98 -

GAVIN McCANN

Gavin McCann showed sufficient promise towards the end of Everton's generally wretched 1997/98 campaign to suggest that the young central midfielder might have a significant contribution to make in happier times.

Keeping several more experienced operators on the sidelines at one point of the desperate late push for safety, the tall Lancastrian impressed with the range of his distribution, resolution in the tackle and busy work-rate. With a satisfyingly well-rounded game underpinned by natural athleticism, it seemed that all Gavin needed to make further progress was the extra assertiveness which can be expected to come with experience.

After earning plaudits during pre-season friendlies, he made his senior debut as a substitute at Newcastle in September, only for a cracked ankle to sideline him throughout mid-season. However, the heart and craft he displayed after rising from the bench to make his return in the Merseyside derby at Anfield in February set him up for a series of starts which marked Gavin McCann as a name to watch.

BORN: Blackpool, Lancashire, 10.1.78.
GAMES: 5 (6). GOALS: 0.

1997/98 -

THOMAS MYHRE

The exit of a hero can be traumatic for supporters, especially if their team is enduring turbulent times. But sorrow over the inevitable termination of Neville Southall's magnificent reign between Everton's posts was lightened immeasurably during 1997/98 by the emergence of Thomas Myhre as prime candiidate to become the Welshman's long-term successor.

Recruited from Viking Stavanger for £800,000 after protracted negotiations in November 1997, the phlegmatic Norwegian under-21 international made such an impressive instant impact in training that he was pitchforked straight into the Premiership relegation struggle.

Thomas responded by keeping three successive clean sheets, radiating authority and composure as well as earning widespread plaudits for his athleticism, reflexes and safe handling. Standing 6ft 3ins tall and with shovel-like hands at the end of long, muscular arms, he presented a formidable barrier and his debut at Leeds was especially eye-catching, notably two splendid diving saves from Harry Kewell and a triumphant one-on-one confrontation with Rod Wallace.

He earned corny headlines for his 'Myhre-cle' save to deny Nathan Blake a late equaliser in the December 'six-pointer' against Bolton at Goodison and yet, ironically, it was that match which furnished evidence that the 24-year-old was not yet the finished article. His positioning was at fault for one of the Trotters' goals, and that is an area of his game which will need specific scrutiny from Blues' goalkeeping coach, Mervyn Day.

However, that is but a quibble and Thomas, a highly motivated self-improver, demonstrated with his sterling form over the remainder of the campaign that he has all the makings of a top-quality custodian. Importantly, too, with Neville having departed, the newcomer can develop his game without the pressure of having a club legend waiting to make a comeback from the bench.

The fans, recognising quality when it's leaping about in front of them, took to him immediately, though it was not only his professional excellence that appealed to them. While he's a down-to-earth fellow, Thomas loves an extravagant goal celebration, and his obvious enthusiasm for the cause was endearing.

Beyond doubt, the Norwegian's arrival at Goodison was a key factor in the team's immediate defensive improvement. Project that effect over a few seasons and the prospects for Thomas Myhre and Everton prospering together in the new century are bright, indeed.

BORN: Sarpsborg, Norway, 16.10.73. GAMES: 23. GOALS: 0.
OTHER CLUBS: Viking Stavanger, Norway.

1997/98 -

WARREN ASPINALL   1985/86 - 1986/87

Forward. BORN: Wigan, Lancashire, 13.9.67. GAMES: 0 (8). GOALS: 0.
OTHER CLUBS: Wigan Athletic 84/5-85/6 (51, 22); Aston Villa 86/7-
87/8 (44, 14); Portsmouth 88/9-93/4 (132, 21); Swansea City *on loan* 93/4
(5, 0); Bournemouth 93/4-94/5 (33, 9); Carlisle United 94/5-97/8
(107, 12); Brentford 97/8- (23, 3).

PHIL JONES   1987/88

Defender. BORN: Liverpool, 1.12.69. GAMES: 0 (1). GOALS: 0.
OTHER CLUBS: Blackpool *on loan* 89/90 (6, 0);
Wigan Athletic 90/1-92/3 (88, 1); Bury 93/4 (4, 0).

STEFAN REHN   1989/90

Midfielder. BORN: Stockholm, Sweden, 22.9.66.
GAMES: 2 (4). GOALS: 0.
OTHER CLUBS: Djurgaarden, Sweden; Gothenburg, Sweden.

MARK WRIGHT   1989/90 -

Defender. BORN: Manchester, 29.1.70. GAMES: 1. GOALS: 0. OTHER
CLUBS: Blackpool *on loan* 90/1 (3, 0); Huddersfield Town 90/1-92/3
(32, 1); Wigan Athletic 93/4-94/5 (30, 1).

EDDIE YOUDS   1990/91 - 1991/92

Defender. BORN: Liverpool, 3.5.70. GAMES: 5 (4). GOALS: 0.
OTHER CLUBS: Cardiff City *on loan* 89/90 (1, 0);
Wrexham *on loan* 89/90 (20, 2); Ipswich Town 91/2-94/5 (50, 1);
Bradford City 94/5-97/8 (85, 8); Charlton Athletic 97/8- (8, 0).

IAIN JENKINS   1990/91 - 1992/93

Defender. BORN: Prescot, Liverpool, 24.11.72. GAMES: 3 (3). GOALS:
0. HONOURS: 4 Northern Ireland caps (97-). OTHER CLUBS:
Bradford City *on loan* 92/3 (6, 0); Chester City 93/4-97/8 (160, 0);
Dundee United 97/8- (6, 0).

IAIN DURRANT   1994/95

Midfielder. BORN: Glasgow, 29.10.66. GAMES: 4 (1) on loan from
Rangers. GOALS: 0. HONOURS: 11 Scotland caps (87-93). OTHER
CLUBS: Rangers 84/5- (246, 26).

PHIL JONES

MARK WRIGHT

IAIN JENKINS

IAIN DURRANT

WARREN ASPINALL

STEFAN REHN

EDDIE YOUDS

GRAHAM ALLEN   1996/97 -

Defender. BORN: Bolton, Lancashire, 8.4.77. GAMES: 2 (4). GOALS: 0.

JOHN HILLS   1996/97

Defender. BORN: St Annes-on-Sea, Lancashire, 21.4.78. GAMES: 1 (2).
GOALS: 0. OTHER CLUBS: Swansea City *on loan* 96/7-97/8 (18, 0);
Blackpool 97/8- (19, 1).

NEIL MOORE   1992/93 - 1993/94

Defender. BORN: Liverpool, 21.9.72. GAMES: 4 (2). GOALS: 0.
OTHER CLUBS: Blackpool *on loan* 94/5 (7, 0); Oldham Athletic *on loan*
94/5 (5, 0); Carlisle United *on loan* 95/6 (13, 0); Rotherham United *on loan*
95/6 (11, 0); Norwich City 96/7 (2, 0); Burnley 97/8- (40, 3).

JON O'CONNOR   1995/96 - 1997/98

Defender. BORN: Darlington, County Durham, 29.10.76. GAMES: 3 (2).
GOALS: 0. OTHER CLUBS: Sheffield United 97/8- (2, 0).

GARY ROWETT   1993/94 - 1994/95

Defender. BORN: Bromsgrove, Worcestershire, 6.3.74. GAMES: 2 (2).
GOALS: 0. OTHER CLUBS: Cambridge United 91/2-93/4 (63, 9);
Blackpool *on loan* 94/5 (17, 0); Derby County 95/6- (105, 3).

KENNY SANSOM   1992/93

Left-back. BORN: Camberwell, London, 26.9.58. GAMES: 6 (1).
GOALS: 1. HONOURS: 86 England caps (79-88). OTHER CLUBS:
Crystal Palace 74/5-79/80 (172, 3); Arsenal 80/1-87/8 (314, 6); Newcastle
United 88/9 (20, 0); Queen's Park Rangers 89/90-90/1 (36, 0); Coventry
City 90/1-92/3 (51, 0); Brentford 92/3 (8, 0); Watford 94/5 (1, 0).

FRANCIS JEFFERS   1997/98 -

Forward. BORN: Liverpool, 25.1.81. GAMES: 0 (1). GOALS: 0.

JASON KEARTON   1992/93 - 1994/95

Goalkeeper. BORN: Ipswich, Australia, 9.7.69. GAMES: 5 (3). GOALS:
0. OTHER CLUBS: Brisbane Lions, Australia; Stoke City *on loan* 91/2
(16, 0); Blackpool *on loan* 91/2 (14, 0); Notts County *on loan* 94/5 (10, 0);
Crewe Alexandra 96/7- (73, 0).

GRAHAM ALLEN

NEIL MOORE

GARY ROWETT

FRANCIS JEFFERS

JOHN HILLS

JON O'CONNOR

JASON KEARTON

KENNY SANSOM

JOHNNY CAREY - MANAGER
OCTOBER 1958 TO MAY 1961

Johnny Carey was a footballing idealist whose style was judged to lack the cutting edge needed to forge success at Everton. A calm Dubliner who had captained Manchester United's fine post-war side, he built an attractive team in his first management job at Blackburn, and when offered the chance to take over at Goodison from coach Ian Buchan in October 1958, he seemed an ideal choice. A sincere man of huge integrity, Johnny was a shrewd judge of soccer talent, and on reviewing his new resources he realised that sweeping changes had to be made. Though the Blues occupied lowly League positions in each of his first two seasons, he fashioned the nucleus of an exciting side, buying the likes of Young, Vernon, Gabriel and Parker. In 1960/61 Everton finished fifth and, though there were mutterings that Johnny was not a firm disciplinarian, there were genuine grounds for optimism. However, new chairman John Moores - who had done much to finance recent transfer deals - wanted fresh blood, and sacked the Irishman as the two men sat in the back of a taxi. Johnny went on to manage Leyton Orient, Nottingham Forest and Blackburn again, ever faithful to his belief in flowing football and his motto: 'Only the 'keeper stops the ball.'

BILLY BINGHAM - MANAGER
MAY 1973 TO JANUARY 1977

Billy Bingham was the first, but not the last, manager to commit the one crime that is unforgiveable in the eyes of all Evertonians: he put out a team that was palpably and consistently second best to Liverpool. The Ulsterman - who had previously bossed Southport, Plymouth Argyle and the national sides of Northern Ireland and Greece - took over in May 1973 when the Blues were at a low ebb. He started solidly, lifting them from the lower reaches to a seventh-place finish in his first season before spending heavily on stars such as Latchford and Dobson. They helped Everton top the table for much of 1974/75, but it proved to be a false dawn and after that campaign concluded with an anti-climactic fourth place, Billy found himself under increasing pressure. Outsiders were misled by his genial character into believing he was a soft touch, but, in fact, he worked his players hard. Sometimes they produced entertaining fare, but although he continued to buy, Billy could not find the right blend. The Blues became a mid-table fixture, there was no cup glory throughout the mid seventies and, accordingly, in January 1977 his time ran out. He went on to manage Salonika in Greece and then Mansfield Town, before becoming long-term boss of Northern Ireland.

HARRY CATTERICK - MANAGER
JULY 1961 TO APRIL 1973

To make sense of Carey's sacking, Everton needed a manager from the very top drawer, a man who could compete successfully with such eminent foes as Matt Busby, Bill Shankly and Bill Nicholson - and they found him in Harry Catterick. Undeniably, he lacked the charisma of his two northern rivals - indeed, he was not one to court publicity - but his two title-winning teams were remarkably eloquent on his behalf. Harry, a single-minded north-easterner, served the Blues as an abrasive centre-forward after the war before going on to manage Crewe, Rochdale and Sheffield Wednesday. He switched from Hillsborough to Goodison in the summer of 1961 and inherited a talented collection of players. Strict but straight, he moulded them into a formidable combination, improving the mix by adding West, Morrissey and Scott and winning the League in only his second term. Everton remained a major force throughout the sixties, lifting the FA Cup in 1966, and by the end of the decade Harry had moulded another Championship team around his midfield trio of Harvey, Ball and Kendall. He was held in awe rather than affection, a remote and powerful presence behind the Venetian blinds of his office, sometimes causing even such an independent spirit as Alan Ball to quail. As the Blues slumped in the early seventies, he was criticised for breaking up his splendid side too soon, but his health was failing and he suffered a heart attack in 1972. A year later he moved to an executive position 'upstairs', later spending two seasons in charge of Preston North End. Harry collapsed and died after watching Everton draw a 1985 cup-tie against Ipswich at Goodison, where he had achieved more than any manager before him.

HOWARD KENDALL   MANAGER MAY 1981 TO JUNE 1987; NOVEMBER 1990 TO DECEMBER 1993; JUNE 1997 TO . . .

Once, twice, three times the manager of Everton, Howard Kendall is synonymous with the club and deserves to be remembered for the great times as well as the dismal. After all, during his first stint at Goodison in the early and mid eighties, he was the man who gave Evertonians back their pride. Following almost a decade and a half of non-achievement, the Blues lifted two League titles, the FA Cup and the European Cup Winners' Cup under the personable north-easterner, all within the space of three years; in addition, they could and should have won the League/FA Cup double that ended up at Anfield in 1985/86. Make no bones about it, even though Liverpool stole that season's thunder, the team that Howard built was the best in the land between 1984 and 1987. What a transformation from the sorry situation he inherited in 1981 and from the even direr crisis of 1984, when a concerted 'Kendall Out' campaign raged around him. Thereafter, with Colin Harvey increasingly influential as first-team coach, the tide turned in spectacular fashion and a procession of trophies ensued. Consequently the fans were stunned when Howard joined Athletic Bilbao in 1987, then watched enviously as he did much to revive struggling Manchester City and eventually were delighted to welcome him back to Goodison in November 1990 to take charge of a side on the skids. That season he arrested the decline, but the expected steady improvement failed to materialise over the next two and a half campaigns and Howard resigned in December 1993, disillusioned over the boards transfer policy. Dogged for a time by personal problems, he went on to a short unhappy spell in charge of Notts County and a longer successful one with Sheffield United before taking Everton's reins for the third time in June 1997. Howard wasn't first choice - far from it - but that didn't faze him as he set about the titanic task of restoring the Blues to a place among the footballing elite. Characteristically he attempted to create an attractive passing side, promoting some of the club's promising rookies to the first team and dabbling frequently in the transfer market. However, it transpired that top-quality targets did not find Goodison an attractive proposition and the increasingly harassed manager, lacking the financial clout to compete for the best, had to make do with something less. Clearly he needed time and the fans remained patient with him, if not with chairman Peter Johnson. By mid season it seemed that Howard was winning the battle and, after he was voted manager of the month for January, Everton appeared to be set for mid-table respctability. But progress was not maintained, most of the cash from the sales of Gary Speed and Andy Hinchcliffe was not reinvested in the team and the Blues slumped anew. The result was a torrid struggle against relegation, which was not won until the last game. Clearly traumatised by the experience, Howard pledged immediate improvement, though that appeared to depend on the resources placed at his disposal.

COLIN HARVEY - MANAGER JUNE 1987 TO NOVEMBER 1990

Colin Harvey is a magnificent coach who can take much of the credit for Everton's huge success in the mid eighties, but he was not cut out to be a manager. Indeed, when he succeeded his friend, Howard Kendall, in June 1987, he seemed almost reluctant to do so, perhaps knowing deep down that it was not the right role for him. Modest, hard-working and as staunch an Evertonian as ever lived, Colin perhaps lacked the administrative and business acumen of his predecessor; certainly, he never enjoyed much luck, his reign being plagued by injuries to key players. Poor results and the consequent pressure bred dressing-room disquiet that manifested itself in Southall's infamous half-time sit-in and a much-publicised tiff between Keown and Sheedy. Colin's major buys, such as Cottee and Newell, were not

unequivocal successes, and as the travail continued, the boss's burden became heavier. If the Blues could have beaten Liverpool in the 1989 FA Cup Final it might have made all the difference, but they were denied and thereafter there was little to cheer. Colin was liked and respected at Goodison, and though there was much sadness at his sacking, there was even greater joy at his return as Kendall's lieutenant in November 1990. When that arrangement ended unfulfillingly, Colin was content to coach elsewhere, away from the limelight.

GORDON LEE - MANAGER JANUARY 1977 TO MAY 1981

Never has a manager been more passionately committed to the Everton cause than Gordon Lee; sadly, his Goodison tenure was to end in abject failure. Yet Gordon, a decent, rather dour man who served Aston Villa as a defender before forging an enviable managerial reputation at

Port Vale, Blackburn and Newcastle, could hardly have wished for a more sprightly beginning. A workaholic who abhorred cheats, he accepted the job with the Blues near the foot of the table, though in the League Cup semi-final; by season's end they had risen to ninth spot, reached the FA Cup semi-final and lost the League Cup Final only after two replays. In his first full term, gelling effectively with imaginative coach Steve Burtenshaw, Gordon led a free-scoring side to third place in the League. There followed a fourth position in 1978/79 and, at last, the club seemed capable of emerging from the Reds' giant shadow. Depressingly, it was not to be. By now Steve had departed, and Gordon struggled. Frequent forays into the transfer market failed to prevent a miserable slump; performances were dreary and attendances fell as the fans grew disillusioned with perplexing team permutations. Gordon's dismissal followed, inevitably, in May 1981, after which he went into coaching, most notably with Leicester.

JIMMY GABRIEL CARETAKER MANAGER NOVEMBER 1990 AND DECEMBER 1993 - JANUARY 1994

Jimmy Gabriel never coveted the responsibility of management yet twice he stepped forward selflessly to help his beloved Everton. On the first occasion, in the brief interregnum between Colin Harvey and Howard Kendall, he presided over one match, a victory over QPR. When called on again, he faced a much more stressful tenure, twixt Kendall and Mike Walker, taking charge of a dispirited team. Jimmy, who coached the reserves both before and after this traumatic experience, guided the Blues through seven games, during which they took one point and scored two goals. A likeable man in an unenviable position, he was blameless for that dire record.

MIKE WALKER MANAGER JANUARY TO NOVEMBER 1994

Mike Walker's managerial reign was the shortest in Everton history - and surely the most hapless. Throughout his 11 months at the Goodison helm, the silver-haired Welshman seemed under siege, beleaguered both by misadventures on the field and shadowy events taking place above his head at boardroom level.

After his unseemly and acrimonious departure from Norwich, where he had built a lovely footballing side, Mike faced the stark reality that he had inherited a very poor one. Relegation was escaped, but only with nine minutes to spare, and the Blues' new boss had the grace to look embarrassed by the hysterical celebrations which climaxed a season of mundanity.

Now money became available but his purchases tended to be of the gifted but fitful variety - the likes of Amokachi, Limpar and Samways - and 1994/95 began abysmally. After an autumn of tumultuous discontent during which the manager's belief in an attractive passing game never faltered, Everton had picked up eight points from a possible 42 and Mike was sacked, ironically after a three-game unbeaten run.

He could argue that he needed more time, that the corner was being turned, and he was right on the first count, perhaps even on the second. But his transfer policy brought to mind the over-excitement of a small boy let loose in a sweetshop, his results were dire, and the outcome was inevitable. The fans never turned against him, always feeling he was a pawn in a game of club politics and that he'd had a raw deal. Maybe. But maybe, too, Mike Walker was in the right place when he returned to Norwich.

JOE ROYLE MANAGER NOVEMBER 1994 TO MARCH 1997

Home was the hero, or at least that was the idea. But after the best conceivable start, Joe Royle's Goodison return did not quite work out like that.

He arrived from Oldham, where he had built an admirable reputation during 12 years of doughty service, to take charge of a team on Premiership death row, with only a solitary League victory to their credit all season.

Joe kicked off with a stirring win in the Merseyside derby, then instilled determination, discipline and confidence to such a degree that the Blues pulled comfortably away from the relegation zone. More remarkable still, they lifted the FA Cup, giving rise to massive expectations for the future.

When 1995/96 began with the capture of Manchester United star Andrei Kanchelskis, hopes leapt even higher, and a sixth-place League finish appeared to emphasise the solidity of Royle's foundations.

Alas, as dawns go it could scarcely have proved more false. The squad proved inadequate to cope with a chronic injury crisis during the following campaign, Kanchelskis became disenchanted and Everton were reduced, with monotonous regularity, to the tactical bankruptcy of aiming long balls at Duncan Ferguson.

The manager's so-called dogs-of-war approach - actually an unfair tag as he employed plenty of gifted players - was revealed as adequate for scrapping clear of the lower reaches but not for long-term progress. School of Science? In the grim days of 1996/97 it more closely resembled Borstal.

As the distressing drift into mediocrity continued, boardroom discontent simmered and the pressure mounted. Understandably, the erstwhile sunny Joe took on a sourer public aspect. The press were banned from Bellefield and there was a depressing feeling that better days were not just around the corner.

Eventually, when his attempts to buy two Norwegians and re-sign Barry Horne were blocked by the board, Royle resigned. His decision was not unexpected but, with a probable relegation battle looming, his timing was terrible. For that alone, many Evertonians will never forgive him.

DAVE WATSON CARETAKER MANAGER APRIL TO JUNE 1997

Just as the players looked to Dave Watson when there was a crisis on the field, so did the Everton directors when Joe Royle resigned in March 1997. The Blues were deep in the relegation mire and Dave, still a crucial part of the team, was left with seven games to ensure that the worst didn't happen. He brought his customary passion and level-headed commitment to the work and a win and three draws proved enough - just. Afterwards, not yet ready for full-time management, the faithful Watson played on under the returned Howard Kendall.

PLAYERS' STATISTICS

Player	Seas	LEAGUE			FA CUP			L CUP			EUROPE			TOTAL		
		Ap	Sb	Gl	Ap	Sb	Gl	Ap	Sb	Gl	Ap	Sb	Gl	Ap	Sb	Gl
Ablett G	91-95	128	(0)	5	12	(0)	1	12	(0)	0	3	(0)	0	155	(0)	6
Adams N	86-87	17	(3)	0	0	(0)	0	4	(0)	1	0	(0)	0	21	(3)	1
Ainscow A	81-82	24	(4)	3	0	(0)	0	1	(1)	0	0	(0)	0	25	(5)	3
Allen G	96-	2	(4)	0	0	(0)	0	0	(0)	0	0	(0)	0	2	(4)	0
Amokachi D	94-95	34	(9)	10	2	(3)	2	3	(0)	0	3	(0)	1	42	(12)	13
Angell B	93-94	16	(4)	1	0	(0)	0	0	(1)	0	0	(0)	0	16	(5)	1
Arnold J	81-83	48	(0)	0	5	(0)	0	6	(0)	0	0	(0)	0	59	(0)	0
Ashworth A	57-59	12	(0)	3	0	(0)	.0	0	(0)	0	0	(0)	0	12	(0)	3
Aspinall W	85-86	0	(7)	0	0	(0)	0	0	(1)	0	0	(0)	0	0	(8)	0
Atkins I	84-85	6	(1)	1	0	(1)	0	0	(0)	0	0	(1)	0	6	(3)	1
Atteveld R	89-91	41	(10)	1	6	(1)	0	6	(1)	1	0	(0)	0	53	(12)	2
Bailey J	79-85	171	(0)	3	22	(0)	0	20	(1)	0	6	(0)	0	219	(1)	3
Ball A	66-71	208	(0)	66	21	(0)	5	10	(0)	3	10	(0)	4	249	(0)	78
Ball M	96-	23	(7)	1	1	(0)	0	1	(1)	0	0	(0)	0	25	(8)	1
Barlow S	90-95	24	(47)	10	4	(3)	2	3	(5)	1	0	(2)	0	31	(57)	13
Barmby N	96-	48	(7)	6	3	(0)	1	1	(1)	2	0	(0)	0	52	(8)	9
Barnett G	65-67	10	(0)	0	0	(0)	0	0	(0)	0	0	(0)	0	10	(0)	0
Barrett E	94-97	73	(1)	0	2	(0)	0	4	(0)	0	2	(0)	0	81	(1)	0
Barton J	78-80	18	(2)	0	0	(0)	0	3	(0)	0	2	(0)	0	23	(2)	0
Beagrie P	89-93 & 97-	92	(28)	11	7	(0)	2	7	(2)	3	0	(0)	0	106	(30)	16
Beardsley P	91-92	81	(0)	25	4	(0)	1	8	(0)	5	0	(0)	0	93	(0)	31
Belfitt R	1972	14	(2)	2	2	(0)	1	0	(0)	0	0	(0)	0	16	(2)	3
Bennett H	1967	2	(1)	0	0	(0)	0	1	(0)	0	0	(0)	0	3	(1)	0
Bentley J	1960	1	(0)	0	0	(0)	0	0	(0)	0	0	(0)	0	1	(0)	0
Bernard M	72-76	139	(8)	8	9	(1)	0	11	(1)	0	2	(0)	0	161	(10)	8
Biley A	1981	16	(3)	3	0	(0)	0	2	(0)	0	0	(0)	0	18	(3)	3
Bilic S	97-	22	(2)	0	0	(0)	0	3	(0)	0	0	(0)	0	25	(2)	0
Billing P	1985	1	(0)	0	0	(0)	0	0	(0)	0	0	(0)	0	1	(0)	0
Bingham W	60-62	86	(0)	23	7	(0)	2	3	(0)	1	2	(0)	0	98	(0)	26
Bishop I	1983	0	(1)	0	0	(0)	0	0	(1)	0	0	(0)	0	0	(2)	0
Borrows B	81-82	27	(0)	0	0	(0)	0	2	(0)	0	0	(0)	0	29	(0)	0
Bracewell P	84-88	95	(0)	7	19	(2)	0	10	(0)	2	8	(0)	1	132	(2)	10
Bramwell J	58-59	52	(0)	0	4	(0)	0	0	(0)	0	0	(0)	0	56	(0)	0
Branch M	95-	15	(19)	3	1	(0)	0	0	(1)	0	0	(0)	0	16	(20)	3
Brand D	75-76	2	(0)	0	0	(0)	0	0	(0)	0	0	(0)	0	2	(0)	0
Brindle W	1967	1	(0)	0	0	(0)	0	1	(0)	0	0	(0)	0	2	(0)	0
Brown A	63-70	176	(33)	9	16	(8)	0	10	(0)	1	6	(2)	1	208	(43)	11
Buckley M	71-77	128	(7)	10	7	(0)	1	12	(0)	1	2	(0)	0	149	(7)	12
Burrows D	1994	19	(0)	0	2	(0)	0	2	(0)	0	0	(0)	0	23	(0)	0
Cadamarteri D	96-	15	(12)	4	1	(0)	0	1	(2)	1	0	(0)	0	17	(14)	5
Clarke W	86-88	46	(11)	18	1	(8)	0	3	(3)	1	0	(0)	0	50	(22)	19
Clements D	73-75	81	(2)	6	6	(0)	2	8	(0)	0	0	(1)	0	95	(3)	8
Collins R	58-61	133	(0)	42	9	(0)	5	5	(0)	1	0	(0)	0	147	(0)	48
Connolly J	71-75	105	(3)	16	3	(1)	0	4	(0)	0	0	(0)	0	112	(4)	16
Cottee A	88-94	161	(23)	72	15	(6)	4	19	(4)	11	0	(0)	0	195	(33)	87
Curran T	82-84	19	(4)	1	1	(0)	0	0	(0)	0	3	(1)	0	23	(5)	1
Danskin J	1984	1	(0)	0	0	(0)	0	0	(0)	0	0	(0)	0	1	(0)	0
D'Arcy F	65-70	8	(8)	0	0	(1)	0	0	(0)	0	0	(0)	0	8	(9)	0
Darracott T	67-78	138	(10)	0	12	(0)	0	12	(0)	0	4	(0)	0	166	(10)	0
Davies D	70-76	82	(0)	0	5	(0)	0	6	(0)	0	1	(0)	0	94	(0)	0
Dobson M	74-78	190	(0)	29	13	(0)	2	22	(0)	8	5	(0)	1	230	(0)	40
Dunlop A	56-62	211	(0)	0	15	(0)	0	5	(0)	0	0	(0)	0	231	(0)	0
Dunne R	96-	8	(2)	0	2	(0)	0	0	(0)	0	0	(0)	0	10	(2)	0
Durrant I	1994	4	(1)	0	0	(0)	0	0	(0)	0	0	(0)	0	4	(1)	0
Eastoe P	78-81	88	(7)	26	12	(0)	6	6	(0)	1	2	(0)	0	108	(7)	33
Ebbrell J	88-96	207	(10)	13	20	(0)	3	17	(0)	1	3	(0)	1	247	(10)	18
Farrelly G	97-	18	(8)	1	1	(0)	0	1	(0)	1	0	(0)	0	20	(8)	2
Fell J	60-61	27	(0)	4	1	(0)	1	0	(0)	0	0	(0)	0	28	(0)	5
Ferguson D	94-	97	(6)	33	8	(1)	4	4	(0)	0	0	(0)	0	109	(7)	37
Ferguson M	1981	7	(1)	4	0	(0)	0	3	(1)	2	0	(0)	0	10	(2)	6
Fielding W	45-58	380	(0)	49	30	(0)	5	0	(0)	0	0	(0)	0	410	(0)	54
Gabriel J	59-66	255	(1)	33	25	(0)	2	5	(0)	0	15	(0)	1	300	(1)	36
Gannon M	1961	3	(0)	0	0	(0)	0	0	(0)	0	0	(0)	0	3	(0)	0
Gerrard P	96-	8	(1)	0	0	(0)	0	2	(0)	0	0	(0)	0	10	(1)	0
Gidman J	79-80	64	(0)	2	11	(0)	0	3	(0)	1	0	(0)	0	78	(0)	3
Glover G	64-65	2	(1)	0	0	(0)	0	0	(0)	0	0	(0)	0	2	(1)	0
Godfrey B	1959	1	(0)	0	0	(0)	0	0	(0)	0	0	(0)	0	1	(0)	0
Goodlass R	75-77	31	(4)	2	7	(0)	0	9	(0)	0	0	(0)	0	47	(4)	2
Grant A	94-	30	(13)	2	1	(3)	0	4	(0)	0	0	(0)	0	35	(16)	2
Gray A	83-84	44	(5)	14	14	(1)	3	0	(1)	0	3	(0)	5	61	(7)	22
Green C	60-61	15	(0)	1	2	(0)	0	1	(0)	0	0	(0)	0	18	(0)	1
Griffiths B	1958	2	(0)	0	0	(0)	0	0	(0)	0	0	(0)	0	2	(0)	0
Hamilton B	75-76	38	(3)	5	2	(2)	0	7	(2)	0	0	(0)	0	47	(7)	5

PLAYERS' STATISTICS

Player	Seas	LEAGUE			FA CUP			L CUP			EUROPE			TOTAL		
		Ap	Sb	Gl	Ap	Sb	Gl	Ap	Sb	Gl	Ap	Sb	Gl	Ap	Sb	Gl
Harburn P	1958	4	(0)	1	0	(0)	0	0	(0)	0	0	(0)	0	4	(0)	1
Harper A	83-87 & 91-92	148	(30)	4	12	(9)	1	22	(3)	0	3	(1)	0	185	(43)	5
Harper J	72-73	40	(3)	12	4	(0)	2	2	(0)	0	0	(0)	0	46	(3)	14
Harris B	55-66	310	(0)	23	31	(0)	4	5	(0)	0	12	(0)	2	358	(0)	29
Harris J	55-60	191	(0)	65	14	(0)	5	2	(0)	2	0	(0)	0	207	(0)	72
Hartford A	79-81	81	(0)	6	11	(0)	1	6	(0)	0	0	(0)	0	98	(0)	7
Harvey C	63-74	317	(3)	18	34	(0)	4	10	(1)	0	19	(0)	2	380	(4)	24
Heard P	78-79	10	(1)	0	0	(0)	0	0	(0)	0	0	(0)	0	10	(1)	0
Heath A	81-88	206	(19)	71	24	(5)	6	33	(2)	11	4	(0)	1	267	(26)	89
Heslop G	62-65	10	(0)	0	1	(0)	0	0	(0)	0	0	(0)	0	11	(0)	0
Hickson D	51-55 & 57-59	225	(0)	95	18	(0)	16	0	(0)	0	0	(0)	0	243	(0)	111
Higgins M	76-83	150	(1)	6	7	(0)	0	19	(0)	0	2	(2)	0	178	(3)	6
Hill J	1963	7	(0)	1	0	(0)	0	0	(0)	0	0	(0)	0	7	(0)	1
Hills J	1996	1	(2)	0	0	(0)	0	0	(0)	0	0	(0)	0	1	(2)	0
Hinchcliffe A	90-97	170	(12)	7	12	(2)	1	21	(2)	1	3	(0)	0	206	(16)	9
Hodge M	79-80	25	(0)	0	6	(0)	0	0	(0)	0	0	(0)	0	31	(0)	0
Holmes P	92-95	21	(0)	0	1	(0)	0	4	(0)	0	0	(2)	0	26	(2)	0
Horne B	92-95	118	(5)	3	11	(1)	0	12	(1)	0	2	(0)	0	143	(7)	3
Hottiger M	95-96	13	(4)	1	0	(0)	0	1	(0)	0	0	(0)	0	14	(4)	1
Hughes D	83-84	3	(0)	0	0	(0)	0	0	(0)	0	0	(0)	0	3	(0)	0
Humphreys G	65-69	12	(0)	2	0	(0)	0	2	(0)	0	0	(0)	0	14	(0)	2
Hunt E	1967	12	(2)	3	1	(0)	0	1	(0)	0	0	(0)	0	14	(2)	3
Hurst J	65-75	336	(11)	29	30	(2)	4	13	(0)	1	6	(1)	0	385	(14)	34
Husband J	64-73	158	(7)	44	22	(0)	10	5	(0)	1	4	(1)	0	189	(8)	55
Hutchison D	97-	11	(0)	1	0	(0)	0	0	(0)	0	0	(0)	0	11	(0)	1
Irvine A	81-83	51	(9)	4	9	(0)	2	10	(1)	0	0	(0)	0	70	(10)	6
Irving D	73-75	4	(2)	0	1	(0)	0	1	(0)	1	0	(0)	0	6	(2)	1
Jack R	1978	1	(0)	1	0	(0)	0	0	(0)	0	0	(0)	0	1	(0)	1
Jackson M	91-95	132	(6)	4	14	(0)	2	9	(0)	0	3	(0)	0	158	(6)	6
Jackson T	67-70	30	(2)	0	3	(1)	0	1	(0)	0	0	(1)	0	34	(4)	0
Jeffers F	97-	0	(1)	0	0	(0)	0	0	(0)	0	0	(0)	0	0	(1)	0
Jenkins I	90-92	3	(2)	0	0	(0)	0	0	(1)	0	0	(0)	0	3	(3)	0
Johnson D	70-72 & 82-83	79	(10)	15	5	(0)	2	7	(0)	2	0	(2)	1	91	(12)	20
Johnston M	91-92	28	(6)	10	1	(0)	0	2	(1)	0	0	(0)	0	31	(7)	10
Jones D	75-78	79	(7)	1	5	(0)	1	11	(1)	1	0	(0)	0	95	(8)	2
Jones G	70-75	76	(6)	12	7	(1)	1	5	(0)	1	2	(0)	0	90	(7)	14
Jones P	1987	0	(1)	0	0	(0)	0	0	(0)	0	0	(0)	0	0	(1)	0
Jones T	50-61	383	(0)	14	25	(0)	0	3	(0)	0	0	(0)	0	411	(0)	14
Kanchelskis A	95-96	52	(0)	20	6	(0)	1	2	(0)	1	0	(0)	0	60	(0)	22
Kavanagh P	1960	6	(0)	0	0	(0)	0	0	(0)	0	0	(0)	0	6	(0)	0
Kay A	62-63	50	(0)	4	5	(0)	0	0	(0)	0	2	(0)	0	57	(0)	4
Kearton J	92-94	3	(3)	0	1	(0)	0	1	(0)	0	0	(0)	0	5	(3)	0
Keeley G	1982	1	(0)	0	0	(0)	0	0	(0)	0	0	(0)	0	1	(0)	0
Kendall H	66-73 & 1981	231	(2)	21	23	(0)	3	12	(0)	3	6	(0)	2	272	(2)	29
Kenny W	70-74	10	(2)	0	0	(0)	0	0	(0)	0	0	(0)	0	10	(2)	0
Kenny W Jnr	1992	16	(1)	1	2	(0)	0	4	(0)	0	0	(0)	0	22	(1)	1
Kenyon R	67-78	254	(13)	6	15	(1)	2	13	(3)	1	7	(0)	0	289	(17)	9
Keown M	89-92	92	(4)	0	12	(1)	0	11	(0)	0	0	(0)	0	115	(5)	0
Kidd B	78-79	40	(0)	12	4	(0)	4	5	(0)	4	2	(0)	0	51	(0)	20
King A	75-79 & 82-83	193	(2)	49	16	(1)	4	29	(1)	11	5	(0)	4	243	(4)	68
King J	57-59	48	(0)	1	1	(0)	0	0	(0)	0	0	(0)	0	49	(0)	1
Labone B	57-71	451	(0)	2	45	(0)	0	15	(0)	0	19	(0)	0	530	(0)	2
Langley K	1986	16	(0)	2	0	(0)	0	4	(0)	1	0	(0)	0	20	(0)	3
Latchford R	73-80	235	(1)	106	17	(1)	10	28	(0)	19	6	(1)	3	286	(3)	138
Laverick R	58-59	22	(0)	6	1	(0)	0	0	(0)	0	0	(0)	0	23	(0)	6
Lawson D	72-76	124	(0)	0	12	(0)	0	13	(0)	0	1	(0)	0	150	(0)	0
Lill M	59-61	31	(0)	11	2	(0)	1	1	(0)	0	0	(0)	0	34	(0)	12
Limpar A	93-96	51	(15)	5	7	(3)	1	2	(0)	0	3	(0)	0	63	(18)	6
Lineker G	1985	41	(0)	30	6	(0)	5	5	(0)	3	0	(0)	0	52	(0)	38
Lodge P	80-81	20	(4)	0	6	(0)	0	5	(0)	0	0	(0)	0	31	(4)	0
Lyons M	70-81	364	(25)	48	29	(1)	6	34	(0)	5	7	(0)	0	434	(26)	59
McBride J	79-81	51	(6)	9	6	(0)	1	6	(0)	1	1	(0)	0	64	(6)	11
McCall S	88-90	99	(4)	6	16	(2)	3	11	(0)	1	0	(0)	0	126	(6)	10
McCann G	97-	5	(6)	0	0	(0)	0	0	(0)	0	0	(0)	0	5	(6)	0
McDonagh J	1980	40	(0)	0	5	(0)	0	3	(0)	0	0	(0)	0	48	(0)	0
McDonald N	88-91	76	(14)	4	17	(0)	0	7	(0)	3	0	(0)	0	100	(14)	7
McKenzie D	76-77	48	(0)	14	7	(1)	5	6	(0)	2	0	(0)	0	61	(1)	21
McLaughlin J	71-75	59	(2)	1	7	(0)	0	2	(0)	0	0	(0)	0	68	(2)	1
McMahon S	80-82	99	(1)	11	9	(0)	0	11	(0)	3	0	(0)	0	119	(1)	14
McNaught K	74-76	64	(2)	3	10	(0)	0	10	(0)	0	0	(0)	0	84	(2)	3
Madar M	97-	15	(2)	6	0	(0)	0	0	(0)	0	0	(0)	0	15	(2)	6
Maher A	1967	1	(0)	0	0	(0)	0	0	(0)	0	0	(0)	0	1	(0)	0
Marshall C	74-75	6	(1)	0	1	(0)	0	0	(0)	0	0	(0)	0	7	(1)	0

PLAYERS' STATISTICS

Player	Seas	LEAGUE			FA CUP			L CUP			EUROPE			TOTAL		
		Ap	Sb	Gl	Ap	Sb	Gl	Ap	Sb	Gl	Ap	Sb	Gl	Ap	Sb	Gl
Marshall I	85-87	9	(6)	1	0	(0)	0	1	(1)	1	0	(0)	0	10	(7)	2
Meagan M	57-63	165	(0)	1	10	(0)	0	0	(0)	0	1	(0)	0	176	(0)	1
Megson G	79-80	20	(2)	2	3	(0)	1	0	(0)	0	0	(0)	0	23	(2)	3
Milligan M	1990	16	(1)	1	1	(0)	0	0	(1)	0	0	(0)	0	17	(2)	1
Mimms R	85-87	29	(0)	0	2	(0)	0	2	(0)	0	0	(0)	0	33	(0)	0
Moore N	92-93	4	(1)	0	0	(0)	0	0	(1)	0	0	(0)	0	4	(2)	0
Morrissey J	62-71	257	(2)	43	29	(0)	3	8	(0)	1	17	(0)	3	311	(2)	50
Morrissey J Jnr	1984	1	(0)	0	0	(0)	0	0	(0)	0	0	(1)	0	1	(1)	0
Mountfield D	82-87	100	(6)	19	17	(0)	2	16	(0)	3	9	(0)	0	142	(6)	24
Myhre T	97-	22	(0)	0	1	(0)	0	0	(0)	0	0	(0)	0	23	(0)	0
Nevin P	88-91	81	(28)	16	12	(6)	2	10	(1)	2	0	(0)	0	103	(35)	20
Newell M	88-91	48	(20)	15	6	(4)	0	8	(3)	4	0	(0)	0	62	(27)	19
Newton H	70-73	76	(0)	5	6	(0)	1	1	(0)	0	0	(0)	0	83	(0)	6
Newton K	69-71	48	(1)	1	2	(0)	0	1	(0)	0	6	(0)	0	57	(1)	1
Nulty G	78-79	22	(5)	2	0	(0)	0	6	(0)	0	4	(1)	0	32	(6)	2
O'Connor J	95-97	3	(2)	0	0	(0)	0	0	(0)	0	0	(0)	0	3	(2)	0
O'Hara E	58-59	29	(0)	2	2	(0)	0	0	(0)	0	0	(0)	0	31	(0)	2
O'Kane J	97-	12	(0)	0	0	(0)	0	0	(0)	0	0	(0)	0	12	(0)	0
O'Keefe E	79-81	26	(14)	6	4	(1)	1	4	(2)	1	0	(0)	0	34	(17)	8
Oldroyd D	1984	0	(1)	0	0	(0)	0	0	(0)	0	0	(0)	0	0	(1)	0
O'Neill J	50-59	201	(0)	0	12	(0)	0	0	(0)	0	0	(0)	0	213	(0)	0
Oster J	97-	16	(14)	1	0	(1)	0	3	(0)	2	0	(0)	0	19	(15)	3
Owen T	1967	2	(0)	0	0	(0)	0	0	(0)	0	0	(0)	0	2	(0)	0
Parker A	58-64	198	(0)	5	12	(0)	0	5	(0)	0	4	(0)	0	219	(0)	5
Parkinson J	94-	88	(2)	3	9	(0)	1	5	(0)	0	2	(0)	0	104	(2)	4
Parnell R	60-63	3	(0)	0	0	(0)	0	0	(0)	0	0	(0)	0	3	(0)	0
Pearson J	74-77	76	(17)	15	9	(0)	2	10	(2)	2	2	(0)	0	97	(19)	19
Pejic M	76-78	76	(0)	2	6	(0)	0	7	(0)	0	4	(0)	0	93	(0)	2
Phelan T	96-	23	(1)	0	1	(0)	0	0	(1)	0	0	(0)	0	24	(2)	0
Pickering F	63-66	97	(0)	56	9	(0)	8	0	(0)	0	9	(0)	6	115	(0)	70
Pointon N	85-89	95	(6)	5	16	(2)	0	6	(2)	0	0	(0)	0	117	(10)	5
Power P	86-87	52	(2)	6	5	(0)	0	6	(0)	0	0	(0)	0	63	(2)	6
Radosavljevic P	92-93	22	(24)	4	1	(0)	0	2	(4)	0	0	(0)	0	25	(28)	4
Rankin A	63-70	85	(0)	0	7	(0)	0	0	(0)	0	11	(1)	0	103	(1)	0
Ratcliffe K	79-91	356	(3)	2	57	(0)	0	47	(0)	0	9	(0)	0	469	(3)	2
Rea K	56-58	46	(0)	0	5	(0)	0	0	(0)	0	0	(0)	0	51	(0)	0
Rees B	63-64	4	(0)	2	0	(0)	0	0	(0)	0	0	(0)	0	4	(0)	2
Rehn S	1989	1	(3)	0	0	(0)	0	1	(1)	0	0	(0)	0	2	(4)	0
Reid P	82-88	155	(4)	8	35	(0)	3	23	(2)	1	9	(0)	1	222	(6)	13
Richardson K	81-86	95	(15)	16	13	(0)	1	10	(3)	3	2	(1)	0	120	(19)	20
Rideout P	92-96	86	(26)	29	9	(1)	3	11	(2)	7	4	(0)	1	110	(29)	40
Rimmer N	1984	0	(1)	0	0	(0)	0	0	(0)	0	0	(0)	0	0	(1)	0
Rimmer S	81-83	3	(0)	0	0	(0)	0	0	(0)	0	0	(0)	0	3	(0)	0
Ring T	59-60	27	(0)	6	0	(0)	0	0	(0)	0	0	(0)	0	27	(0)	6
Rioch B	76-77	30	(0)	3	7	(0)	1	2	(0)	0	0	(0)	0	39	(0)	4
Robinson N	75-78	13	(3)	1	1	(0)	0	3	(1)	0	0	(1)	0	17	(5)	1
Ross T	77-82	120	(4)	16	13	(0)	3	8	(1)	0	5	(0)	1	146	(5)	20
Rowett G	93-94	2	(2)	0	0	(0)	0	0	(0)	0	0	(0)	0	2	(2)	0
Royle J	65-74 2	29	(3)	102	23	(0)	9	14	(0)	4	6	(0)	4	272	(3)	119
Samways V	94-95	17	(6)	2	0	(0)	0	3	(0)	1	1	(0)	0	21	(6)	3
Sanders A	57-59	56	(0)	0	7	(0)	0	0	(0)	0	0	(0)	0	63	(0)	0
Sansom K	1992	6	(1)	1	0	(0)	0	0	(0)	0	0	(0)	0	6	(1)	1
Scott A	62-66	149	(0)	23	17	(0)	2	0	(0)	0	10	(0)	1	176	(0)	26
Scott P	71-74	42	(2)	1	5	(0)	1	1	(0)	0	0	(0)	0	48	(2)	2
Seargeant S	71-77	77	(3)	1	2	(0)	0	5	(1)	0	2	(0)	0	86	(4)	1
Shackleton A	1959	26	(0)	10	1	(0)	0	0	(0)	0	0	(0)	0	27	(0)	10
Sharp G	79-90	306	(16)	111	52	(2)	20	46	(2)	15	8	(0)	4	412	(20)	150
Sharples G	60-63	10	(0)	0	0	(0)	0	1	(0)	0	0	(0)	0	11	(0)	0
Shaw S	64-65	3	(0)	0	0	(0)	0	0	(0)	0	0	(0)	0	3	(0)	0
Sheedy K	82-91	263	(11)	67	38	(0)	15	31	(1)	9	5	(0)	2	337	(12)	93
Short C	95-	67	(9)	4	4	(0)	0	5	(0)	0	3	(0)	0	79	(9)	4
Smallman D	74-76	19	(2)	6	0	(0)	0	3	(1)	1	1	(0)	0	23	(3)	7
Smith D	65-66	3	(1)	0	0	(0)	0	0	(0)	0	0	(0)	0	3	(1)	0
Smith J	1973	2	(0)	0	0	(0)	0	0	(0)	0	0	(0)	0	2	(0)	0
Snodin I	86-94	142	(6)	3	27	(0)	2	19	(4)	2	0	(0)	0	188	(10)	7
Southall N	81-97	578	(0)	0	70	(0)	0	65	(0)	0	13	(0)	0	726	(0)	0
Speed G	96-97	58	(0)	16	2	(0)	1	5	(0)	1	0	(0)	0	65	(0)	18
Spencer J	97-	3	(3)	0	0	(0)	0	0	(0)	0	0	(0)	0	3	(3)	0
Stanley G	79-80	52	(0)	1	2	(1)	0	7	(1)	0	0	(0)	0	61	(2)	1
Steven T	83-88 2	10	(4)	48	33	(0)	4	27	(0)	4	9	(0)	2	279	(4)	58
Stevens D	61-65	120	(0)	20	10	(0)	1	0	(0)	0	12	(0)	1	142	(0)	22
Stevens G	81-87	207	(1)	8	38	(0)	2	30	(0)	2	9	(0)	0	284	(1)	12
Stuart G	93-97	117	(20)	22	10	(3)	5	9	(0)	3	2	(1)	1	138	(24)	31

PLAYERS' STATISTICS

Player	Seas	LEAGUE Ap	Sb	Gl	FA CUP Ap	Sb	Gl	L CUP Ap	Sb	Gl	EUROPE Ap	Sb	Gl	TOTAL Ap	Sb	Gl
Styles A	72-73	22	(1)	0	4	(0)	0	0	(0)	0	0	(0)	0	26	(1)	0
Tansey J	52-59	133	(0)	0	9	(0)	0	0	(0)	0	0	(0)	0	142	(0)	0
Telfer G	73-80	81	(16)	20	4	(4)	1	5	(2)	1	1	(0)	0	91	(22)	22
Temple D	56-67	231	(1)	72	21	(0)	8	4	(0)	0	16	(0)	2	272	(1)	82
Thomas A	97-	6	(1)	0	1	(0)	0	1	(0)	0	0	(0)	0	8	(1)	0
Thomas D	77-78	71	(0)	4	2	(0)	0	7	(0)	1	4	(0)	1	84	(0)	6
Thomas E	56-59	86	(0)	39	7	(0)	2	0	(0)	0	0	(0)	0	93	(0)	41
Thomas M	1981	10	(0)	0	0	(0)	0	1	(0)	0	0	(0)	0	11	(0)	0
Thomsen C	96-97	17	(7)	1	1	(0)	0	0	(0)	0	0	(0)	0	18	(7)	1
Thomson G	60-62	73	(0)	1	1	(0)	0	2	(0)	0	1	(0)	0	77	(0)	1
Tiler C	97-	19	(0)	1	1	(0)	0	0	(0)	0	0	(0)	0	20	(0)	1
Todd C	78-79	32	(0)	1	1	(0)	0	2	(0)	0	0	(0)	0	35	(0)	1
Trebilcock M	65-67	11	(0)	3	2	(0)	2	0	(0)	0	1	(0)	0	14	(0)	5
Turner D	1967	1	(0)	0	0	(0)	0	0	(0)	0	0	(0)	0	1	(0)	0
Tyrer A	59-61	9	(0)	2	1	(0)	0	0	(0)	0	0	(0)	0	10	(0)	2
Unsworth D	91-96	108	(8)	11	7	(0)	0	5	(2)	0	3	(0)	1	123	(10)	12
Van den Hauwe P	84-88	134	(1)	2	30	(0)	1	20	(0)	0	5	(0)	0	189	(1)	3
Varadi I	79-80	22	(4)	6	6	(1)	1	0	(0)	0	0	(1)	0	28	(6)	7
Veall R	1962	11	(0)	1	0	(0)	0	0	(0)	0	0	(0)	0	11	(0)	1
Vernon R	59-64	176	(0)	101	12	(0)	7	4	(0)	1	8	(0)	1	200	(0)	110
Wakenshaw R	83-84	2	(1)	1	0	(0)	0	0	(0)	0	0	(2)	0	2	(3)	1
Walsh D	1984	1	(0)	0	0	(0)	0	0	(0)	0	0	(0)	0	1	(0)	0
Walsh MA	1978	18	(3)	1	1	(0)	0	3	(0)	0	4	(0)	2	26	(3)	3
Walsh MC	81-82	20	(0)	0	0	(0)	0	2	(0)	0	0	(0)	0	22	(0)	0
Ward MD	97-	8	(0)	0	0	(0)	0	0	(0)	0	0	(0)	0	8	(0)	0
Ward MW	91-93	82	(1)	6	4	(0)	0	6	(0)	1	0	(0)	0	92	(1)	7
Warzycha R	90-93	51	(21)	6	1	(3)	0	4	(2)	0	0	(0)	0	56	(26)	6
Watson D	86-	392	(3)	23	44	(0)	5	38	(0)	6	2	(0)	0	476	(3)	34
Webber K	60-61	4	(0)	0	0	(0)	0	2	(0)	1	0	(0)	0	6	(0)	1
West G	61-72	335	(0)	0	40	(0)	0	11	(0)	0	13	(0)	0	399	(0)	0
Whiteside N	89-90	27	(2)	9	6	(0)	3	2	(0)	1	0	(0)	0	35	(2)	13
Whittle A	67-72	72	(2)	21	6	(0)	2	4	(0)	2	4	(1)	1	86	(3)	26
Wignall F	59-62	33	(0)	15	2	(0)	0	3	(0)	7	0	(0)	0	38	(0)	22
Wilkinson P	84-86	19	(11)	6	3	(0)	1	3	(1)	7	0	(0)	0	25	(12)	14
Williams G	55-58	31	(0)	6	2	(0)	0	0	(0)	0	0	(0)	0	33	(0)	6
Williamson D	97-	15	(0)	0	0	(0)	0	2	(0)	0	0	(0)	0	17	(0)	0
Wilson A	71-72	2	(0)	0	0	(0)	0	0	(0)	0	0	(0)	0	2	(0)	0
Wilson I	87-88	24	(10)	1	3	(2)	0	9	(0)	1	0	(0)	0	36	(12)	2
Wilson R	64-68	114	(2)	0	26	(0)	0	0	(1)	0	10	(0)	0	150	(3)	0
Wood G	77-79	103	(0)	0	4	(0)	0	13	(0)	0	6	(0)	0	126	(0)	0
Wright B	71-72	10	(1)	2	0	(0)	0	0	(0)	0	0	(0)	0	10	(1)	2
Wright M	1989	1	(0)	0	0	(0)	0	0	(0)	0	0	(0)	0	1	(0)	0
Wright T	64-72	307	(1)	4	35	(0)	0	11	(0)	0	17	(0)	0	370	(1)	4
Wright W	77-82	164	(2)	10	13	(0)	0	13	(0)	0	6	(0)	0	196	(2)	10
Youds E	90-91	5	(3)	0	0	(0)	0	0	(1)	0	0	(0)	0	5	(4)	0
Young A	60-67	227	(1)	77	25	(2)	4	3	(0)	3	13	(0)	3	268	(3)	87

Dates shown indicate first year of each season. Thus 70-77 means 1970/71 to 1977/78. A single entry means one season only, e.g. 1964 refers to 1964/65.